D0847897

The Anti-Federalists

and

Early

American

Political

Thought

The *Anti-Federalists*

and

Early

American

Political

Thought

CHRISTOPHER M. DUNCAN

Northern Illinois University Press

DeKalb   1995

© 1995 by Northern Illinois University Press

Published by the Northern Illinois University Press, DeKalb, Illinois 60115

Manufactured in the United States using acid-free paper ∞ ⊕

Design by Julia Fauci

Library of Congress Cataloging-in-Publication Data

Duncan, Christopher M.

   The anti-federalists and early American political thought /
Christopher M. Duncan.

      p.   cm.

   Includes bibliographical references and index.

   ISBN 0-87580-189-7

   1. Political science—United States—History—18th century.

2. United States—Politics and government—1775–1783.   3. United
States—Politics and government—1783–1789.   4. United States—
Constitutional history.   I. Title.

JA84.U5D85   1994

320'.01'1—dc20   94-7159
                                CIP

For David L. Duncan

He Shoots!

He Scores!

Contents

Acknowledgments

Although a book often bears the name of a single author, the reality is far different from what that suggests. Most books, especially a first book like this, are possible only with the generosity, friendship, kindness, support, and tolerance of numerous people. In this regard I have been more fortunate than I deserve. I have taken from those who helped me and cared for me far more than I have been, or may ever be, able to give back. This includes my teachers and fellow students both at the University of Michigan—Dearborn and, especially, at Wayne State University, along with my friends, colleagues, and students at Mississippi State University, Eastern Michigan University, and Henry Ford Community College.

My close friend and adviser Phil Abbott read, reread, and read again each word and phrase of this work in all its various forms with a skillful, patient, and quick critical eye. It is to him that I owe my greatest intellectual debt. Susan Fino, who taught me about "snakes," "old-yellers," and many other things not found in a graduate school handbook, also read the complete manuscript and served as a constant source of support and sport during its formative years. Jim Chalmers took the time not only to read this work but also to engage me in a five-year conversation about the themes it contains. Sandra Van Burkleo gave of her always scant time and abundant intellectual energy to the project in its entirety as well. I wish to thank them all, along with Donald Lutz, Michael Gibbons, Garrett Sheldon, and Dan Coran, my editor at Northern Illinois University Press. I also offer a special thanks to my graduate assistant at Mississippi State, N. George Vargis, for his help in the final stages of preparation.

Aside, however, from teachers and colleagues, there are debts even more important and profound that must be acknowledged: those to my family and friends. I was very fortunate early in my life to meet a group of people who have been my biggest fans and most sympathetic critics for the last fifteen years. David Rodriguez, Michael Curry, and Joan Curry are my friends, and I love them dearly. Later I met others who, each in their own way, have made my life better and more interesting than it ever could have been without them, including Sherwood Merrill, Brian Durocher, Rob Sullivan, Jill Cain, Shanon McCormick, Tom Jankowski, Carla Curley, Cheryl Edwards, Pat Abbott, Mary Herring, Otto Feinstein, Charlie Parrish, Charles Elder, Joanna Scott, Arlene Saxonhouse, David Adamany, David and Darlene Breaux, Greg and Debbie Dunaway, and Michael and Hannah Bernard-Donals.

Finally, there are the debts that are ultimately not amenable to questions of justice, insofar as I could never give back what is properly owed. In partial payment I want to acknowledge members of my family, who loved and sustained me emotionally when it was not very easy or even prudent, and whom I love: Mary Kay and Wayne Moilanen, David and Judy Duncan, Craig, Jeff, Ron, Scott, John, Cindy, and Debbie along with their wives, husbands, and children. My wife, Laura, has borne the greatest burden of all by having to live with me day in and day out without reprieve; yet she still manages to remain the kindest and most loving person I have ever known. My appreciation also goes to my beautiful and already wise daughter, Amelia, who every day allows me the honor of seeing the world again in innocence and awe, for at least a moment, and to hang out with her for a little while when she is not too busy. This book is dedicated to my father, because without him around to call and to share my triumphs and failures, the reasons for doing things would suddenly be much less clear.

Part of chapter 5 was presented as a paper at the American Political Science Association annual meeting at Chicago in 1992; I thank Francis Greene for his comments then. A generous Mississippi State University research initiation grant in 1993 helped bring the project to conclusion. Grateful acknowledgment is also made to *Polity* for permission to reprint material used in chapter 5.

As usual, I alone take responsibility for what follows. At the same time, it should be clear that I alone cannot take credit for it all.

Introduction

> *You are not required to complete the work;*
> *but neither are you free to desist from it.*

—Rabbi Tarpon in *Pirke Avot*

SOME ANSWERS FOR LIBERALS

Unwilling to rely on received wisdom about their past and its relationship to the present, scholars who study America have in the twentieth century struggled to make the nation a very complicated place. Fortunately, perhaps, given the current state of many newly self-conscious and complicated nations, the bulk of the Republic's citizens have nodded pleasantly and gone on about their business.

No one in America will die today or tomorrow over whether we as a people are best defined as republican or liberal. However, an alien that came to this nation and read the most recent scholarly literature about our political history and derivative culture would not think such was the case. On the contrary, it would no doubt believe that the nation was engaged in a life-and-death struggle over a matter of extreme magnitude and monumental political import. If at times I lapse into that particular mode of discourse, I hope the reader will forgive me. It is not that the issues are unimportant but, rather, that by making them seem all-important, we run the risk associated with "crying wolf," and thus suffer the fate of the irrelevant.

Since the publication of Bernard Bailyn's book in 1967, of Gordon Wood's in 1969, and especially of J. G. A. Pocock's in 1975, a debate has raged among students of America's founding period.[1] Some of the exchanges have been quite thoughtful and even fraternal. Others, however, have been confrontational and even acrimonious.[2] I have enjoyed it all. These are the best kinds of wars. I want to join the conversation. Such is the extent of my particular martial spirit. And yet it is not simple academic hubris or a desire for glory that prods my entry into such a contentious field. Rather, it is a hope—a hope to get it right and, more important, a hope to play the great Socratic role of gadfly, to reframe old arguments and make them new, and perhaps relevant to the political and social world in which I live.

The American Anti-Federalists and their political theory serve as the thematic glue of this volume. They are presented as competitors of the eventually triumphant Federalists for the "soul" and structure of the American regime. They are also implicitly held out as exemplars of an alternative persuasion for contemporary political theorizing in America. The potential charge of anachronism rests on a political fatalism that ultimately must be rejected unless we are willing to admit that Zeno's arrow really does not fly when shot. In other words, change is possible even when all evidence suggests the permanence of current arrangements. The rationale for anchoring an argument for social and political change in the past is, quite simply, to show that at least at some point in time, in a particular place, certain ideas and people who held them existed. In turn this allows us to overcome at least the initial charges of political alchemy or utopianism. It may indeed be the case that the circumstances that allowed a particular reality have permanently passed away. Or it may be the case that even if it is possible, such a resurrection or unveiling is now undesirable. In any event, the reconstruction of communitarian/republican thought in America seems to me an effective strategy for establishing the dialogic legitimacy and pertinence of the questions: (1) Were there such people? and (2) Why should we study them? To show both their existance and their importance is my response to Don Herzog's query concerning why we should care whether people championed something 200, 300, or 400 years ago.[3] I will briefly address his other concerns, since they question the legitimacy of any project conducted on the terms of this one.

Herzog accuses contemporary republican theorists and communitarians (not necessarily the same thing!) of putting forth a "remarkably hazy doctrine."[4] Later in the essay he asks that those writers currently working in the history of "civic humanism" articulate precisely what sort of connection they have in mind (between that history and current political debates), lest their discussions lapse into the irrelevant. One can easily see the validity of Herzog's first accusation if one views much of what passes for republican theorizing today (as discussed below). But Herzog's point becomes a non sequitur if in fact the doctrine can be linked to actual historical figures who constructed a political order based on their republicanism. Such is the role played in this volume by the American Anti-Federalists.

In terms of Herzog's second point, this is precisely the reason for the sort of historical mapping he questioned earlier. If it can be demonstrated that there is a parallelism, if not a duplication, of past and present historical debates, then the rationale for contemporary theoretical archaeology is self-evident. Admittedly this is the difficult part for any theorist attempting to make the lessons of history meaningful in a contemporary context. Furthermore, such a project assumes an even greater challenge when it asserts the relevance not only of past arguments but also of past solutions. Herzog is right when he suggests that the important questions are how valuable republicanism really is,[5] and how congenial modern political life is to its rebirth.[6] He is, however, wrong when he claims that republicanism is not the solution to the problems of liberalism.[7]

Republicanism rightly understood is exactly the solution to the defects of liberal theory even if it is not a fault-free substitute for liberal political life. The adage that liberal practice seldom lives down to liberal theory is true, but what many liberals must realize is that much of what is best in the liberal state is a by-product of its republican antecedents. Some of my best friends are liberals, but it is not their liberalism that first attracted me to them, nor them to me. Friendship is ultimately a republican virtue, not a liberal one. Hence, if one of liberalism's defects is social atomism or anomie, republicanism provides at least *a* cure, if not *the* cure. But this is too hazy for Herzog, who asks that republicans offer an "account of what commitments should bind us."[8]

Although the demand for a "blueprint" is among the least interesting methods of theoretical criticism, there are abundant examples of the kind of account Herzog demands. Anti-Federalist political theory and the Articles of Confederation it attempts to sustain is one such account; and for a good contemporary, though clearly unselfconscious, practical *republican* apologia Herzog should look at the work done by Vermont successionists Frank Bryan and John Mc-Claughry.[9] If that is not enough, there is the theoretical work done by Students for a Democratic Society[10] and the Southern Agrarians,[11] who, although very different in many ways, share a basic set of republican commitments.

Perhaps the strangest part of Herzog's critique, however, is not his failure to recognize the historical manifestations or assertions of republicanism but his mystical faith that somehow political life is possible without at least a nod in the direction of republican concerns. When he claims that "Employing a host of constitutional, legal, and institutional safeguards against the abusive exercise of political power would give us sensible ways of moderating political conflict—as would keeping such explosive subjects as conceptions of the good off the political agenda in the first place,"[12] he seems to suggest that the "safeguards" are not representative of the very thing he decries: *a* conception of the good life. Despite the work done by liberal theorists like Hobbes, Locke, and Rawls, which presupposes a uniformly bourgeois human nature, the Aristotelian assertion of man's fundamental political nature has yet to be disproven to my satisfaction. The belief that a neutral political sphere—one where "conceptions of the good [are] off the political agenda"—is possible is truly the "city in speech." The only question, it seems to me, is whether the conception of the good is a priori and self-conscious or de facto and unconscious. The former is a republican strategy, while the latter is the exclusive consequence of the liberal prototype. Whereas the former approach begs for political conflict by demanding a persuasive public accounting of citizen goals and intentions, the latter avoids political conflict at the price of legitimacy by allowing citizens to construct a public sphere on the basis of secret and private motivations. Republican theory can still allow us to ask political questions and provide political answers; liberalism as sketched by Herzog, on the other hand, seems to suggest that if we ignore such questions, they will go away.

LAW'S REPUBLICANISM

Early American political history and historiography is a remarkably muddy and contentious field of study. Part of the problem typically is the failure of many "combatants" to correctly differentiate and clarify the scope, rationale, and methodology of their own work and that of others. In other words, too often we seem to assume that the combatants' projects are directly comparable with our own and those of others when in fact they are quite different. Different objectives obviously are going to yield different modes of argumentation, different evidence, and different conclusions. For example, much of the discord between neoliberal theorists like John Diggins and republicans like J. G. A. Pocock really seems to be as much, if not more, over methodology than substance. Pocock's linguistic contextualism is at odds with Diggins's interest/power-based approach. Thus, where the one finds a language of republicanism, the other finds liberal, individualist behavior. The question, perhaps insoluble, then becomes which approach offers the greater insight into the period in question. Both approaches seem useful, but ultimately the "scientific" dilemma seems Kuhnian in its import and without a proper language of reconciliation. Some sensitive thinkers like Joyce Appleby, Gordon Wood, and Lance Banning are able to benefit from both approaches by producing work that, though clearly favoring one orientation over the other, seems to lack animosity. Perhaps both Diggins and Pocock are correct; perhaps early Americans talked like republicans and acted like liberals. Or, more likely, there were both kinds of citizens.

When Herzog accuses contemporary republican theorists of putting forth a "remarkably hazy doctrine," he is not talking, it seems, to those Pocockian historians qua historians. Their "doctrine" in simplified form is clearly that the use of republican languages and categories of political discourse existed at a particular time, which is more or less an empirical question. The subsequent assertion that such a discourse was dominant is, though more difficult to prove or disprove, also an empirical question. Whatever the strengths and weaknesses of linguistic contextualism as a method of historical inquiry, it does not appear that haziness need be one of them. Furthermore, it seems ill-advised to refer to a particular methodological approach as a doctrine. So who or what is Herzog attacking? The answer must be that he is attacking those partisans of republicanism who find republicanism more normatively satisfying than competing modern ideologies, and/or those who seek to bring about a new republican order through political practice. Unfortunately for Herzog, however, this group is less clearly defined, and ultimately more marginal, than the noted academics whom he casts in the republican role.

Given this, however, Herzog's argument does seem appropriate to at least one group of republican scholars engaging in this sometimes heated debate. That group of scholars, which could be called the legal republicans, includes Cass Sunstein, Frank Michelman, Morton Horwitz, and Suzanna Sherry.[13] The work of these scholars, while clearly worthwhile and intriguing, is flawed. It is flawed in such a way that Herzog's critique suddenly seems appropriate, even though Herzog wrote in advance of their respective conversions. Despite critical differences in their approaches, the legal republicans almost unanimously share a grave conceptual fallacy with people like James Madison. That fallacy, simply put, rests on the belief that somehow *republicanism* can be maintained no matter what size or substantive shape the Republic takes on. In other words, these thinkers all seem to believe that the spiritual dimension of republican thought can be maintained while the historical context and physical configurations that nurtured it are deconstructed and transfigured. To see this process at work, one need only look at the way in which the idea or category of "community" is appropriated and used to describe everything from a small town or a tribe to a thousand-mile-wide nation-state. Fundamental linguistic damage is done to a political discourse that attempts to use the same term to describe the Bay Colony of 1630 and the United States of 1993. Yet this is precisely the sort of theoretical error that certain scholars tend to perpetuate.

Sunstein betrays the theoretical underpinnings of his self-proclaimed project when he writes:

> The tasks for the immediate future are two-fold. The first is to spell out, with some particularity, those aspects of republican thought that have the strongest claim to contemporary support. The second is to describe institutional arrangements and doctrinal shifts, inside and outside the courts, that might serve to implement the most attractive features of the republican vision.[14]

He does this by implying that somehow republican commitments can be manufactured and implemented like any other new public policy. The implications, like it or not, of such a formulation are totalitarian. "Community" cannot be manufactured through an act of political will. "Community" must be provided with an appropriate political soil in which to grow and then be allowed to take its course. Sometimes the result will be the kind of republican community Sunstein and other republican proponents envision, and sometimes it will not. But a strong commitment to the underlying values of republicanism requires a degree of risk associated with decentralized authority and power that Madison and his fellow travelers were unwilling to undertake. Sunstein's emphasis on institutional and judicial implementation belies a Madisonian bias. In bringing the discussion of republicanism to the level of a "national" political community, Sunstein and others distort the ideology beyond recognition. The sort of "public-regarding justifications" that Sunstein claims republicanism demands quickly become meaningless when offered to 265 million fellow citizens. Such a group is no longer a public capable of being consulted; it is a mass to be ministered to, preached at, or controlled.

These theoretical errors are magnified in the work of Michelman and Sherry through their unabashed reliance on the Supreme Court and judicial review for accomplishing so-called republican ends. For Michelman judicial review is transformed from the anti-republican device criticized by the Anti-Federalists well before the advent of Fourteenth Amendment jurisprudence into a vital tool of republican communitarianism. Unfortunately, republicanism itself must be transfigured beyond recognition in order for this feat to be accomplished. While Michelman correctly rejects the vision of republicanism as some sort of unbridled majoritarianist doctrine, his reliance on a "jurisgenerative" politics that discloses a "latent, pre-existent, actual societal consensus respecting the right social ordering,"[15] which can best be discerned by the Supreme Court, is riddled with problems too numerous to mention with regard to republican theory. Take, for example, Michelman's clarification of this "jurisgenerative" concept:

> The basal requirement for republican jurisgenerative politics: that both the process and its law-like utterances must be such that everyone subject to those utterances can regard himself or herself as actually agreeing that those utterances, issuing from that process, warrant being promulgated as law.[16]

Leaving aside any discussion of the Kantian overtones here, the reader is left to wonder whether any promulgated "law-like utterances" are going to be able to garner the sort of consent the excerpt seems to imply. Indeed, such an idea, which may make sense in a small, face-to-face political community, becomes almost humorous, if not ridiculous, in the context of the nation as a whole.

Aside from this difficulty, however, Michelman's republicanism suffers from a broader problem: bad faith. If there can be such a thing as honorable or praiseworthy bad faith, then Michelman's work would fill the bill. His republicanism ultimately suffers less from his theoretical confusion than it does from his primary political commitments. Michelman is at heart a liberal. But like many thoughtful contemporary liberals, his work is plagued by self-doubt about the ability of a liberal political community to sustain its participants in their full humanity over time. In his 1988 essay he wants to provide a republican rationale for a more civil-libertarian outcome in *Bowers* v. *Hardwick,* and in his extended essay of 1986 he wants to defend the First Amendment rights of a Jewish soldier in *Goldman* v. *Weinberg.* Both cases seem worthy of his scholarly talents, and in both cases I agree with his ultimate positions; what I cannot agree with is his use of republicanism to get there. In order to make it accomplish what he wants it to, Michelman must transform republicanism beyond recognition in terms of both procedure and substance. In his hands republicanism becomes substantively indistinguishable from the more sophisticated versions of libertarianism.[17] Furthermore, when he writes of the Supreme Court that "counter-counter majoritarian remedies—such as judicial deference to the 'political' branches—only aggravate a problem they cannot fix . . . [and] that it is as much the Court's office to constitute its own *paideia* as to hold the fort of law's empire,"[18] one is left to only wonder how such a political process can lay claim to the republican mantle.

The rationale for clouding Michelman's good liberal arguments with republican symbols and idioms seems almost inexplicable when they are put forth before a national rather than a state court. As for the Supreme Court "constitut[ing] its own *paideia*," I am almost at a loss for words. The kind of mystical reification that must be undertaken in order to claim that the product of a political process, created by various presidents at various times to accomplish often discrete ideological and political ends, is in and of itself a constituted community with its own *paideia* rather than a particular history is simply astounding! According the Court such an honor would seem to dictate similar status for any bureaucratic agency, congressional committee, or subcommittee, and so on, which seems just plain silly. Furthermore, the reader must wonder why Michelman seems unwilling to accord the military or the state of Georgia the same status and protections from extracommunal interference.

Unable to transcend the logic of *Federalist* no. 78 and unwilling to address the anti-republican implications of *Federalist* no. 22, the legal republicans continue to weave back and forth between their liberal commitments and their republican aspirations. This problem is nowhere better exemplified than in the work of Suzanna Sherry. Although fascinating and informative, it is, like that of the others, blind to its anti-republican foundations.

Sherry equates the idea of republican virtue with what she calls the "feminine voice" in constitutional adjudication. After a very lengthy introduction and review of the competing paradigms in legal interpretation and constitutional jurisprudence, she finally gets down to her argument in a section titled "Women's Perspective: Recapturing the Jeffersonian Moment."[19] Drawing on the work of people like Carol Gilligan,[20] Sherry suggests that within constitutional adjudication a distinctive feminine voice can be found that is due to the differences in male and female moral development. Women, for Sherry, are primarily concerned with "intimacy or connection," whereas men are more focused on "separation or autonomy."[21] This insight allows her to speak of a difference in the way in which men and women judges decide cases. Even where outcomes are the same, Sherry suggests that the rationale for reaching a certain outcome is often vastly different. The "feminine voice" for Sherry is similar to the mode of thought associated with what she calls the "classical" or "civic republican voice," which, she claims, tends to be more "other-directed" and "intersubjective" in its essence.[22] She then sets out to test her hypothesis, using the written opinions of Supreme Court Justice Sandra Day O'Connor as her data. She manages to find just such a voice.

In particular Sherry locates the O'Connor "feminine voice" in discrimination cases and Establishment Clause cases, which she claims are used by O'Connor to "safeguard the individual's right to *belong* to the community," as opposed to the typical use of constitutional rights to protect the individual *against* the community.[23] Sherry's analysis of individual cases and opinions then follows. It is for the most part quite sound, even if occasionally it seems she is reaching a bit to make a given case conform to her model. The difficulty rests on Sherry's linkage of the O'Connor jurisprudence with the classical republican tradition. O'Connor may well be some sort of national communitarian (if such a thing is possible), but she is no republican. Like it or not, republican ideology is concerned with the proper conditions for wielding power over others. Such power, according to republican theory, must consist of a closeness in terms of political orientation, physical proximity, and economic equality— for reasons laid out at length by traditional republican theorists like Aristotle, Montesquieu, and the Anti-Federalists.

The idea that a court of nine members, even if they were all gifted with the feminine voice, could somehow weave together opinions and decisions in such a way as to foster community falls into the trap of believing that community is the product of public policy rather than of political activity. Communities cannot be constructed from without. They are the products of members interacting and creating for themselves. A community formed by decree, or a community that must ask leave of an outsider to rule itself, is not a community in the strong sense. Yet the legal scholars with their emphasis on the national government and, most important, on the Supreme Court, never seem to realize this fact. While their intentions are good, the result of their analysis is ultimately the destruction of political community and the possibility of civic virtue and republicanism. There cannot be such a thing as a "national political community" if we want to maintain any meaningful role for that particular term. Like it or not, republicanism, as Madison knew full well, required that we risk allowing people to rule themselves even when they may do it poorly. This is why he and the other founders ultimately came to reject republicanism in favor of something safer and more stable. The legal scholars mentioned here seem to want it both ways—republican citizens and community without republics. They may as well try to change lead into gold; the rate of success is about the same.

REPUBLICS, REPUBLICANS, AND ANTI-FEDERALISTS

Although the existence of a republic is not in and of itself a sufficient condition for the production of republican citizens, it is a necessary one. Outside of a republican community there can be no republican citizens in the strong sense of the term. And yet this is precisely the theoretical hope upon which Publius rests his collective case in the *Federalist Papers*. Unfortunately, it is also the hope that inspires the legal republicans discussed above. The only difference between the two is that Publius knew he was mistaken, whereas the others do not. True republicans can flourish only in true republics. And despite the fancy footwork of Publius, or the basic haziness of certain contemporary scholars in their reconfiguration or sloppy use of the term, a *republic* is a fairly specific thing. If you dramatically change its size and its constitution, then it is almost certain that you will change the thing itself. Perhaps for the better, or perhaps for the worse; but whatever the case, it is now something different. The Anti-Federalists knew this.

The Federalists knew it, too, which was why they took the actions they did. They wanted change from a traditional confederate republic to a significantly more centralized federal system. In chapter 3 I discuss their objectives and rationale for change in some detail. The Anti-Federalists resisted such change vigorously; their reasons and arguments are laid out in detail in chapter 5. It is precisely this resistance that earned them their often dubious place in American history. Countries do not typically celebrate the work of those who opposed them, and for the most part the Anti-Federalists are no exception to that rule.

For thirty years the work of Cecelia Kenyon[24] dominated historical discourse on the Anti-Federalists. Despite valiant attempts by neo-Beardian scholars like Jackson Turner Main[25] and his teacher Merill Jensen to resurrect their status as democratic resisters, Kenyon's label of "men of little faith" stuck. The result was a consensus view of the Anti-Federalists that marked them as liberal paranoids afraid of their own shadow, lest it coerce them. Thus they were robbed not only of historical fame but also of their earlier historical infamy. Neither heroes nor villains, in Kenyon's hands the Anti-Federalists suffered the cruelest of all historical fates—superfluousness. As I note in the prologue, the Anti-Federalists are not even deemed worthy of a spot in Louis Hartz's index.[26]

In 1981 the late Herbert Storing attempted once again to resurrect the Anti-Federalists and place them in a more positive light.[27] By showing "what the Anti-Federalists were for," he did manage to construct a more respectable and thoughtful image of Anti-Federalist political thought. But in his effort to place them alongside the Federalists as junior cofounders, Storing, while vastly more sophisticated and subtle in his argumentation, ultimately fell prey to Kenyonism. That is, he still refused to recognize that the differences between the two competitors for the American political soul were differences of kind rather than of degree. When the Anti-Federalist Rawlins Lowndes claims that he wishes "no other epitaph than to have inscribed on his tomb, here lies the man that opposed the constitution . . . ,"[28] the reader should quickly surmise that such Anti-Federalists would want no part of founding fatherhood.

The attempt to incorporate the Anti-Federalists into the pantheon of founders, while almost certainly an effort by Storing to render historical justice by
giving them their due, is in the end an unwarranted and unwanted distortion.
Placing the Federalists and Anti-Federalists into some kind of progressive dia-
lectic with one another misconstrues the nature of both political/theoretical
projects. Neither group got all that it wanted, and both groups were unhappy
as a result. The simple truth of the matter is that the projects were theoretically
incompatible. The fact that the dissimilar political projects and theories managed to coexist, even though the Federalist vision was clearly the predominant
one, says more about the American political will and its ability to live with
deep inconsistencies than it does about theoretical and political consensus.
Since the advent of the Fourteenth Amendment, industrialization, and New
Deal jurisprudence, I think we have a good idea of what an all-Federalist
United States would have looked like. What we do not have, for obvious
practical reasons, is a good idea of what the United States might have looked
like politically had the Anti-Federalists carried the day in 1789. It is important,
I believe, to try and point out some of those lost possibilities.

The work that most closely parallels the argument here is Joshua Miller's
The Rise and Fall of Democracy in Early America, which was published in 1992.[29]
This volume was nearing its initial completion about the same time. I had
mixed feelings as I read Miller's work. On the one hand, I felt a degree of
vindication for my own argument and understandings, but on the other hand,
I now had some modest insight into the way Leibniz must have felt after he
invented the calculus. Like the present work, Miller links the American political tradition to the early Puritan settlements in New England and traces their
conception of membership and community through the American Revolution
to the Anti-Federalists and their confrontation with the Federalists over ratification. Miller's fundamental concern, however, is democracy and democratic
theory, a conservative democratic theory. The Puritans, revolutionaries, and
Anti-Federalists thus become for him sources of a profound democratic narrative in American political thought. This volume, while agreeing with Miller's
general argument, is expanded in many places to include a broader, more detailed encounter with Anti-Federalist theory.

Like Miller, I begin the body of the volume (chapter 1) with a discussion of
the political significance of Puritan theology. But rather than starting de novo
with the Puritans, I trace the structure of Puritan theological/political organization through its Calvinist antecedents in an attempt to illustrate the interrela-
tionship between religious/doctrinal and theoretical/political transformations
that took place on the American shore. Both works here owe a debt to Andrew
C. McLaughlin, who was the first to suggest an important link between the
Puritan notion of a covenanted community and American constitutionalism.[30]
And both are surpassed to some extent in this particular area by the rich and
detailed work by Ellis Sandoz, *A Government of Laws: Political Theory, Religion,*

and the American Founding.[31] Other scholars—Wilson Carey MacWilliams, Donald Lutz, Robert Bellah, Sanford Kessler, and of course Edmund Morgan—have also contributed greatly to contemporary understandings about the relationship between America's religious past and its revolutionary constitutionalism.[32] It is this body of work, coupled with the contributions of republican scholarship, that has aided the process of Anti-Federalist reconsideration to a significant extent.

That reconsideration has in large part been fueled by the works of Michael Lienesch, Robert Hoffert, Russell Hanson, and Peter Onuf.[33] Some of these works focused primarily on the nature of the confederate period and the economic dimensions of revolutionary thought in America. In chapter 3 I explore the confederate period with a more ideological eye. This leads to a focus less on interests and more on ideas even though the distinction is admittedly tenuous. Robert Hoffert's work also focuses on the confederate period in general, and on the Articles of Confederation in particular; but it differs substantially from that of Onuf in its emphasis on the question of "nature" and its theoretical manifestations during the period in question.

Hoffert argues that early American, as well as contemporary American, political thought is characterized by a tension that results from two competing constructions of "nature." For Hoffert, Hobbes and Rousseau are the real competitors in American politics. The former leads to a politics steeped in the language of contracts that "assumes a heterogeneity of interests among associates," and the latter, to a politics of covenants that "assumes a homogeneity of interests among associates."[34] The Articles of Confederation, Hoffert argues, "resonates more with the assumptions of covenanted communities than with those of self-interested competitors driven to contract for protection and stability."[35] The Anti-Federalists are the exemplary figures of that tradition in American politics. The Federalists, on the other hand, serve as representatives of the Hobbesian conception of nature that Hoffert suggests underlies the events of 1787–1789. Since then, American politics and life have existed in tension that draws its energy from these competing poles:

> The tradition of American political ideas does not express a single pattern of democratic life. There are clearly broad and deep patterns of competing impulses that are as central to the fundamental shape of American political debates today as they were to the American founding more than two centuries ago.[36]

Hoffert's conclusions, however, do not lead him to suggest a resolution but, rather, to promote an understanding of the system as it is. He warns early on in the work that "the price of consistency is likely to be devastating for America."[37]

To an extent Hoffert is correct, but as well argued as his work is at the descriptive level, it seems to miss the point that the very tension he celebrates is in great danger of giving way. Though Rousseau and the Anti-Federalist voice are still alive in American political discourse, they are not well. Though Americans long for community and speak in communal and republican idioms, we have lost the theoretical awareness that would allow us to sustain those very conversations over time. Hoffert's book, while a fine contribution to the literature, sometimes seems to lose sight of the fact that with each new political loss in the form of community disempowerment, the covenanted community and its republican voice become ever fainter. To that end, then, it may not be possible to achieve equilibrium until the scales are to some extent rebalanced. The present volume ultimately, then, chooses a side.

The leading theoretical spokesperson for the Anti-Federalist reconsideration under examination is Michael Lienesch. It is Lienesch who first articulated the contemporary view of a founding underscored by ideological and theoretical tension rather than one of competing interests or consensus. According to Lienesch, America gave birth to a nation neither republican nor liberal; rather, it was a new order that combined both in a tension that persists until this day.[38] Rather than comparing the Federalists and Anti-Federalists against the backdrop of a single standard, he suggests that "it is better and truer to see the Federalist founders not as so astonishingly superior to their Anti-Federalist counter-parts, but as simply different."[39] Those differences are summed up efficiently by Lienesch:

> In sum, though they seemed to be incompetent framers, the Anti-Federalists were in fact only framers of a different kind, who on their own terms were extremely efficient. Like most republicans before them they believed that every generation had the right to legislate for itself. According to the theory, founders provided examples for later citizens to follow, not laws for them to obey.[40]

Unlike the Anti-Federalists, who, Lienesch argues, were "content to forgo fame in order to seek assurance that they would not live in infamy,"[41] the Federalists were audacious.[42] They were attempting to "create a timeless form of politics," which transcended "any need for lessons of the past" and prevented "any possibility of declension in the future."[43] According to Lienesch, "the American Constitution [was to exist] entirely in a theoretically perfect present."[44] Unlike the Anti-Federalists, who saw history as a usable foundation and something to emulate, the Federalists saw failures and "beacons" directing their course between the jagged rocks of political destruction.[45] These contrary views of history, rather than contrary views of nature, become Lienesch's foundation for his earlier contentions about Federalist and Anti-Federalist theoretical differences.

This volume shares in that basic argument of difference in its lengthy treatment of the Anti-Federalist position in chapter 5. Lienesch is absolutely right when he claims that republicans had always thought that future citizens would be active citizens—but that the Federalist founders believed "that the new Constitution put an end to the need for such activism."[46] He is also right when he claims that "by the mid-1780's, what remained of the revolutionary consensus had been shattered, with radicals and conservatives diverging dramatically in their plans for revision."[47] Once again, however, this volume parts company with Lienesch in its resistance to the idea that the best outcome was inevitably achieved.

While Lienesch provides us with one of the most sympathetic accounts of the true Anti-Federalist position(s), he does so from within a progressive framework that suggests it all worked out for the best. The prologue of this volume represents an attempt to illustrate, using some rather broad strokes, why that might not be the case. Throughout the volume the political costs of the Federalist victory, however incomplete it might be, are underscored while the potential gains of an Anti-Federalist victory are repeatedly suggested in various formulations. At the root of the entire discussion is a seemingly simple question: Is private happiness possible without public happiness? For the Federalists the answer was "yes." Their Anti-Federalist competitors, I believe, knew better. And despite their not having managed to carry the day in 1789, they may have managed to win the argument.

The Road Not Taken

It is perhaps understandable, given their less than heroic historical pedigree, to leave the Anti-Federalists out of our political tale, as Hartz did. But to leave them out distorts not only American political history but also contemporary American political thought, by making it seem as though liberal hegemony was our national fate rather than the result of very important choices and struggles made at particular times by particular people who believed particular things about the way the political world works and the way it ought to work. Furthermore, it is equally important to understand that had the other side carried the day, the political world that Americans inhabit today might, for better or worse, have been quite different from what it is. Since it is impossible to know what might have been had they won, the best that we can do is to articulate what those who lost believed their vision could have produced had they succeeded. In other words, we can try as political theorists to understand their particular political faith and to underscore the lasting significance, if any, of that faith for the political thought (and perhaps even history) that followed. It is my argument that the American Anti-Federalists were different from their Federalist counterparts not merely in degree but also in kind, and that each group constructed a political theorization congruent with its political faith. In the course of the volume I hope to map out the political theory or faith of American Anti-Federalism and to offer it as an alternative mode of American political discourse, or as a concrete representative of an American "second political language."

In the prologue I explore the contemporary relevance of Anti-Federalist theory in the context of various conceptions and understandings of American political life. The historical body of the volume begins in chapter 1, where I attempt to link Anti-Federalist thought with that of the earliest English settlers, the Puritans, in whom I find the first sustained attempt at correcting those modern forms of political community suggested by Robert Bellah and associates (see the prologue), which rejected both chaotic openness and strict authoritarianism by linking members to one another and to the community through the process of collective decision making and mutual watchfulness.[48]

In chapter 2, I trace the extension of that thought into the earliest colonial political arrangements and constitutions, and argue that as the more biblical forms of discourse were diluted, what appeared was an Americanized version of civic republicanism with an emphasis on local political associations, collective decision making, and above all civic virtue in the form of participation in public life and the construction of the public good. This line of argument is extended up to and including the American Revolution by suggesting that the Revolution was fought primarily as an effort to prevent British usurpation of what was now traditional local political authority and the republican praxis to which it had given birth and lent legitimacy. This suggests that the Revolution was indeed a republican rather than a liberal event.

In chapter 3 the nature and consequences of the American Revolution are illustrated still further through a discussion of the first American founding under the Articles of Confederation. This first founding, I contend, was the only legitimate attempt to embody the underlying principles of the Revolution in an American constitution. The second part of chapter 3 is concerned with the opposition to that document by those who later wrote and supported a second founding under the Constitution and an exploration of the "critical period" in American history.

In chapter 4, I provide a close reading of Federalist political theory as contained in the *Federalist Papers* and argue that at its most basic level this political project represented an attempt to overcome not only the defects of the Articles of Confederation but also, and more important, to overcome the republican faith they were meant to embody. In its place, I argue, the Federalists sought to insert an aristocratic political order that, although intended to be a new form of republicanism, was in reality the birth of a liberal political order.

In chapter 5, Anti-Federalist thought is examined and interpreted as an alternative to the Federalist political project. There I contend that the Anti-Federalists were indeed the true representatives of the American Revolution and the political arrangements that resulted from that event. They are men of a different faith: a localist, republican faith that sees political participation as an end in itself rather than a means to other things. The Anti-Federalists come to defend the sanctity of political activity as necessary for public happiness.

In the conclusion, I attempt to show the continued relevance of Anti-Federalist thought to contemporary American political conversations. It is my hope that by "going home again," and attempting to understand what is really there, we can construct a more clearly delineated picture of where we have been politically—and perhaps make some important decisions about where we are to go.

The Anti-Federalists

and

Early

American

Political

Thought

A man, says Aesop, coming into a wood, begged the trees to grant him the favor of a handle to his axe. The whole forest consented; upon which he provided himself with a strong handle; which he had no sooner done, than he began to fell the trees without number, then the trees, though too late, repented of their weakness, and a universal groan was heard throughout the forest. At length, when the man came to cut down the tree which had furnished him with the handle, the trunk fell to the ground uttering these words: Fool that I was! I have been the cause of my own destruction.

—*An Old Whig*

Prologue

A Crisis of Faith

I shall be telling this with a sigh
Somewhere ages and ages hence:
Two Roads diverged in a wood, and I,—
I took the one less traveled by,
And that has made all the difference.

—Robert Frost

Do not go gentle into that good night.

—Dylan Thomas

The American Anti-Federalists, those often-forgotten, maligned historical losers, represent the general focus of this volume. But this is not, strictly speaking,
a historical work, although history as an academic discipline certainly contri-
butes a great deal to the project. Instead, this is a work of political theory, and
thus I am less concerned with the Anti-Federalists as historical people, or even
Anti-Federalism as a historical movement, than I am with Anti-Federalism as
a set of political ideas and ideals, as a language of political discourse, as a cultural
system, as a set of symbols, grounded in history as politics must be, and yet
with aspirations and offerings that look to transcend particular circumstances.
This is not, however, a quest for some general theory or Hegelian system, but
an attempt to understand the political conversations of America's founding
period and the implications of those conversations, if any, for our own political
discussions. Furthermore, as part of the genus, and perhaps even the species, of
what it seeks to explain, this volume adds to that long-term conversation
through its own set of interpretations, criticisms, and arguments that can be
judged independently of the body of work from which they are derived.

The context of the original Anti-Federalist work is fairly straightforward and includes, ranging from the general to the particular, the Enlightenment, the early American colonial settlements, the American Revolution, and the two founding periods that followed. The context of this volume on the Anti-Federalists is less clear and more difficult to label. And that difficulty begins with the logical questions (a) why someone (besides a historian interested in narrative completeness) would want to write about these people and their ideas, given the earlier description, and (b) why anyone else should be interested in it. These are both good questions, and I will briefly try to sketch out appropriate answers.

Like any work of any political theorist, no matter how renowned or how obscure, this one must begin in one of two general places: either it is the product of dissatisfaction with the way things are and hopes to provide an alternative course or understanding, or it seeks to defend the current state of affairs against alternatives. This work is marked by the former description, and on a general level it shares in the definition of *the* critical project as defined by Michael Walzer, who writes that if there is one common mark of that project, it is that

> It is founded on hope; it cannot be carried on without some sense of historical possibility. Criticism is oriented toward the future: the critic must believe that the conduct of his fellows can conform more closely to a moral standard than it now does or that their self-understanding can be greater than it now is or that their institutions can be more justly organized than they now are. For all his foretellings of doom, a prophet like Amos must hold open the possibility of repentance and reform, else there would be no reason to prophesy.[1]

On the other hand, the body of work that serves as the eventual focal point of this volume—the Anti-Federalist text—shares in the nature of the latter project, defending an older set of arrangements against emerging alternatives.[2] Thus this current project runs the initial risk of simple anachronistic longing; the only things that can save it from such a charge and keep it within the critical family as defined above are the continued relevance and potential usefulness of that body of thought for addressing modern concerns, and its ability to offer aid in the search for contemporary opportunities for "repentance and reform."

This distinction between the two critical projects and their conflation in this volume is the reason for the two poetic excerpts above. The first, by Robert Frost, suggests that there are moments at which individuals or nations are faced with mutually exclusive choices or historical paths that will, from that point forward, determine future circumstances and possibilities. Frost's own choice was the less conventional one, and he would seem to be recommending it to his readers. The second brief passage, taken from the poet Dylan

Thomas, suggests that things of value and importance—in this case, the life of his father—ought to be fought for and their demise struggled against. Among the tasks of the political theorist as historian, then, is to make explicit the moments in a nation's or individual's history at which the "road" diverged; to explain the nature of the choice that was made, along with its theoretical and practical justifications; and then to explore as much as possible the "other" road.

It is at this point that the historian, or the political theorist as historian, must either stop because the data effectively end, or become the historian as political theorist, or political theorist as political theorist, in order to continue along that other road. This act of exploration represents both the theorist's refusal to "go gentle into that good night" by simply accepting the choices previously made and exploring their content, and the theorist's positive political project of re-creating or creating anew another point at which the road diverges. The latter project reenables political choice. This is both the attraction of political theory and its danger. Not all opportunities for choosing a new or different road will make a positive difference. And yet, even given those dangers, it is a project that is difficult to resist because, as George Steiner puts it, "Opening doors [or choosing roads] is the tragic merit of our identity."[3]

What, then, do we do about Thomas's injunction? In his circumstances the choices were quite simple: life or death, with his clear predisposition to "rage against the dying of the light." But in terms of its application to the world of political theory, I think it should be read as a more general injunction against going gentle into *any* "good night." In other words, it should be read by political theorists as an injunction against any unreflective choice of roads, including, most important, the road that on its face seems the most appealing or reasonable. We must ignore the protestations of those who would dissuade us and pay very close attention to the "man behind the curtain," and thus quite often to "the road less traveled"—in this case the road suggested by the Anti-Federalists.

The important twentieth-century novelist/poet/political activist Milan Kundera has given artistic form to the essence of this approach to political theory in his work *The Unbearable Lightness of Being*. The work deals with, among other things, the political currents running through Czechoslovakia during the eventful year of 1968. There we find Tomas, the story's protagonist, contemplating the actions taken and not taken by his nation when faced with the power and might first of the Germans under Hitler, and then of the Soviets. Should they have stood up to powers that were immeasurably stronger, as they had done in 1618—which had resulted in the Thirty Years War and, incidentally, had brought them to the brink of total destruction—or should caution have been their guide, as it was this time? Such thoughts lead him to posit a universe in which history could be repeated, testing each possibility each time and finally choosing the best solution based on the outcome. But he knows that "We are not granted a second, third, or fourth life in which to compare various decisions."[4]

Although Kundera is right about specific historical moments, there is some room to argue in terms of history in general. While it is true that America can never again, strictly speaking, choose between the ideas of the Federalists and the Anti-Federalists concerning the Constitution, we can choose in our new circumstances to re-create the general underlying theorizations and values of the two (as well as others) and use them as guides when we face the branchings in the road of our own political future. This is where the spirit of Dylan Thomas's injunction becomes important, and it is also where Kundera's poetic warning becomes visible in his construction of kitsch.

According to Kundera, kitsch (a German word born in the middle of the sentimental nineteenth century, says the author) "excludes everything from its purview which is essentially unacceptable in human existence,"[5] whether the unacceptable things exist or not. Thus he describes a central character's revolt against communism not in rationalist/utilitarian terms associated with modern political ideologies, but in the following manner:

> Sabina's initial inner revolt against Communism was aesthetic rather than ethical in character. What repelled her was not nearly so much the ugliness of the Communist world (ruined castles transformed into cow sheds) as the mask of beauty it tried to wear—in other words, Communist kitsch. The model of Communist kitsch is the ceremony called May Day.[6]

To embrace kitsch is to go gently and happily into "that good night." The May Day parade in what was the Soviet Union, the Fourth of July celebrations in the United States, and other such annual events in the ongoing life of a country, though different in terms of their ostensible focus, are indeed of the same political genre: kitsch. They exist to conjure up and parade around an unblemished portrait of a unified national past and a national future that is supposedly all-inclusive and very progressive. Kundera asserts that "kitsch is the aesthetic ideal of all politicians and all political parties and movements."[7] And to some extent he is right. Political life, since it is public and shared, must depend on the construction of some artificial symbols and ideals, or myths, and it is only natural that those constructs are brought forth in idealized form. But we do not have to accept the kitsch as the thing-in-itself, as Kundera notes: "Those of us who live in a society where the various political tendencies exist side by side and competing influences cancel or limit one another can manage more or less to escape the kitsch inquisition."[8] The time to worry is when "a single political movement corners power, [and] we find ourselves in the realm of *totalitarian kitsch*."[9] This phenomenon he describes in the following way:

> When I say "totalitarian," what I mean is that everything that infringes on kitsch must be banished for life: every display of individualism (because deviation from the

collective is a spit in the eye of the smiling brotherhood); every doubt (because anyone who starts doubting details will end by doubting life itself); all irony (because in the realm of kitsch everything must be taken quite seriously). . . . In this light, we can regard the gulag as a septic tank used by totalitarian kitsch to dispose of its refuse.[9]

This volume, then, is a response to what I take to be American kitsch as it is manifested in our understanding of the American founding period: the kitsch that tells us there were political sinners (Anti-Federalists) and saints (Federalists), and that the saints of course won; a kitsch that despite recent scholarly work to the contrary has remained relatively intact.[10] The reality of the period is that there were different groups who wanted different things based on their perceptions, political/theoretical understandings, and even interests. Each group provided a different road, and each group had its own kitsch that it used to beckon people. But both also had real costs and benefits, just as Kundera's gulag had its reality, and thus no one should mistake kitsch for something frivolous or trivial. This having been said, it is important to connect the philosophical apparatus above with the project and circumstances at hand. Kundera's context is easy to see; after all, he was confronting the kitsch of one of the most bloodthirsty, oppressive regimes in history. The kitsch of the Federalists and the America their Constitution helped to foster can in no reasonable way be considered contextually similar to the Soviet Union and the terror that it wrought on its own people and on its neighbors. So the problem becomes that we know why Kundera writes his fiction, but why do I write? What is my context (and perhaps my kitsch)?

AMERICAN POLITICAL LANGUAGES

The political conversations that members of a society hold with each other, and the way they represent themselves when questioned about their concerns, can tell us a great deal about their political culture and political thought. Furthermore, the language used to conduct those conversations, and to frame discussions about both public and private life, can tell us quite a bit about the possibilities and limits of their political worlds.[11] At the most basic level, those who would know a particular world must know at least what the most important or fundamental "unit" of analysis is: the state, the community, the tribe, the family, or the individual. In other words, with what or whom are the people who inhabit a particular place, in a particular time, most willing to promote and protect? To what end are policies enacted, and when there is a conflict, how are benefits and costs distributed?

In a recent popular novel, a writer speaking through a fictional American Supreme Court justice claimed that in deciding cases, he had a simple rule of thumb: the individual over the state, the state over business, the environment over everything, and give the Native Americans anything they want. This is about as blunt as you can get, but it makes the point. Every society either explicitly or implicitly develops a hierarchy along these lines, and that hierarchy in turn sets the boundaries and determines in large measure the available kinds of legitimate choices within which a government can conduct its work and citizens can relate to each other. For example, there are still some tribal-based societies in Asia that have no first-person-singular pronoun, the equivalent of the English "I"; therefore, in connection with these groups it would make precious little sense to talk about individual rights in the strong sense of, say, American politics. Among the questions with which I am concerned in this volume are How Americans converse politically with each other, within their boundaries and hierarchies, and What kind of political life is possible within our mode(s?) of discourse.

Historically the most important work on American political culture comes from the French political theorist Alexis de Tocqueville. In his noted *Democracy in America,* Tocqueville covers the entire range of American political practice and custom in his discussions of our political institutions as well as our political and social mores and beliefs. In his discussions of the latter, he constructs for one of the first times the term "individualism," which he proceeds to use as an important descriptive device for his discussion of American character. Later Tocqueville differentiates his new term from the older "egoism," which he defines as "a passionate and exaggerated love of self which leads a man to think of all things in terms of himself and to prefer himself to all."[12] He claims that individualism "is a calm and considered feeling which disposes each citizen to isolate himself from the mass of his fellows and withdraw into the circle of family and friends; with this little society formed to his taste, he gladly leaves the greater society to look after itself."[13]

This withdrawal and isolation, coupled with the concerns for what is purely private and the total disregard of the public sphere, is a hallmark of classical liberalism that rests on the supposition of multiple visions of the good life, all deserving of equal protection if not respect by the state and other citizens. It represents the rejection in large measure of the classical concerns for the public good as an independent or extrapersonal object to be sought, and substitutes in its place the notion of a de facto public good, one that is the collective product of all the various private or individual goods taken together. In Tocqueville's words, "Individualism . . . dams the spring of public virtues."[14]

The decline in "public" or civic virtue that Tocqueville associates with individualism was not merely the result of a national character defect that caused people to become increasingly self-absorbed; rather, it represented, as do most social inventions, a response to something else. For Tocqueville that something else was the rise of equality associated with democratic states, which causes man's feelings to be "turned in on himself." But it would seem more likely that both equality and individualism are responses to the widespread social and political stagnation and oppression the majority found themselves forced to accept under much of feudal rule. In any case, using what he calls an "aristocratic age" as his model, Tocqueville claims that among the elements leading to greater concern for the public welfare is the fact that

> Each citizen of an aristocratic society has his fixed station, one above another, so that there is always someone above him whose protection he needs and someone below him whose help he may require. So people living in an aristocratic age are almost always closely involved with something outside of themselves, and they are often inclined to forget about themselves.[15]

While there is certainly something to be said for being "involved with something outside" of oneself, there is also the unacknowledged element of coercion and disproportional sacrifice placed upon those whose help is required. Tocqueville's "aristocratic society" is merely a code for a feudal hierarchy that attempted to bring forward the public good at the private expense of the serf, the peasant, and the artisan, who shared extensively in the burdens, but little in the happiness, of public life. Those from the ruling and propertied classes, however, enjoyed an inverse scenario. Thus, as a response to this state of affairs, classical liberalism, with its emphasis on political equality, individualism, and private property, represents an attempt to make sure that the "something outside of themselves" in which individuals participated was also something that served them in rough proportion to their service to it. Liberalism as an ideology asked a very radical and important question of the standing social and political order: What is in it for me? This question, though often in more eloquent form, represents the germ of what eventually became known as social contract theory. It represents a simple plea on the part of the disenfranchised and the subservient for access to the public realm, for a share in its benefits as well as its labors. Thus it is not nearly as vulgar a question as it might appear when couched in a more contemporary context.

Yet if we sidestep Tocqueville's own aristocratic bias with its partially truncated ideological disposition and deal with his more important argument concerning the dangers of American individualism, there is a sage warning to consider, as well as a very prescient set of observations. He claims that as equality increases, and thus as individualism becomes more rampant, there will fast appear a majority of citizens who "owe no man anything and hardly expect anything from anybody. They form the habit of thinking of themselves in isolation and imagine that their whole destiny is in their own hands."[16] Thus, he continues, "Each man is forever thrown back on himself alone, and there is danger that he may be shut up in the solitude of his own heart."[17] Rather than seeking admission to the public realm as an equal participant, the newly constructed "individual" may in fact use that status as a passport to avoid the public realm altogether. The danger then becomes not so much the oppression of an aging feudal order as the nihilism or emptiness of a fully realized liberal one. The world that Tocqueville foreshadows is one where there is no shared public life among citizens engaged in conversations concerning their collective good; there is only the world of isolated individuals or groups of individuals engaging in private life and personal concerns while sharing with their fellow citizens only the desire to be left alone. This "privacy" then becomes the task of the government to ensure. This state of affairs turns problematic if later such a society, with its minimal political life, proves not to be enough to solve the political problems we collectively face, sustain us as full human beings, or allow us to live what we would consider fully realized lives.

We know even at a glance that Tocqueville finds American individualism problematic, since two chapters after his brief disquisition on the American character we find the heading "How Americans Combat the Effects of Individualism by Free Institutions." Thus individualism is rendered something to be combated and, one must imagine, subdued. But for the majority of Americans individualism, and the liberal context from which it emerges, is not explicitly problematic. Quite the contrary—for them it is immutable, unimpeachable, and highly desirable. In fact, it often leaves little or no room for anything else.

Among the most important contemporary works on American political thought and culture is Louis Hartz's *The Liberal Tradition in America* (1955). Drawing heavily on Tocqueville's basic depiction of America as an exceptional land where "men were born equal rather than having to become so," Hartz, in opposition to conflict-minded historians like Charles Beard and his students, takes as his starting point what he sees as a basic consensus among the vast majority of American citizens on core political values. The basic equality among Americans first noted by Tocqueville becomes for Hartz sufficient reason to discard European political/theoretical models, with their class-based language of political discourse and analysis, for one that he finds more appropriate to the unique American circumstances. Those circumstances are the absence of feudalism and the unwavering national attachment to classical liberalism as taken from the teachings of John Locke.[18] The former circumstance accounts for the basic absence of class conflict in America and provides support for the notion of Americans having been born equal rather than having to become so. This historical fact, whereby America skipped the "feudal stage," deprived American political discourse of the conservative language of the propertied, old money, European aristocracy, or ancien régime, and, most important for Hartz, of the socialist discourse that he claims has its roots in the antagonism to feudalism.[19] In other words, without the oppositional relationships of lord and serf, there can be no dialectical transubstantiation into the classes of proletariat and bourgeoisie. Thus, all that is left is what is in the middle—no "Left" and no "Right" play out the Marxist historical drama in America.

The consequence for American political thought of this historical "exception," according to Hartz, is a country naturally disposed to liberalism with its emphasis on individual rights, private property, and political equality. "A society which begins with Locke, and transforms him [remember, Locke is a revolutionary figure where there is a conservative tradition], stays with Locke, by virtue of an absolute and irrational attachment it develops for him."[20] That "irrational" attachment in turn creates an American political discourse that "has within it, as it were, a kind of self-completing mechanism, which insures the universality of the liberal idea."[21] The "irrationality" of the attachment is due to the absence of other modes of ideological discourse, which are marginalized both by the historical circumstances noted above and by the cultural momentum that is made possible by the lack of alternatives. The "self-completing mechanism" is Hartz's way of saying that all other possible forms of political/ideological discourse are either co-opted or ignored, along with their representatives and exemplars. Thus Hartz can claim, in one of his more famous lines, that in America "law has flourished on the corpse of philosophy, for the settlement of the ultimate moral question is the end of speculation upon it."[22] This ideological closure causes political disputes—that in other countries, at other times, would have led to serious discussions and ideological conflicts—to become merely problems of technique.[23]

The next important question that Hartz as a scholar, and more particularly as a political theorist, must answer is the "So what?" question. In other words, although this might be an important phenomenon for political comparativists or historiographers, why should political theorists bother to study America, since it appears to have solved the most important questions with which political theory tends to be concerned? Instead, the question could continue, should we not concern ourselves with the proper education of public administrators, who will keep the system fine-tuned and running smoothly?

It is in response to this sort of question that Hartz's magnification and extension of Tocqueville's rudimentary concerns about American individualism becomes in its own right among the most important contemporary contributions to American political thought. For Tocqueville, America was able to combat the effects of individualism through free institutions and political liberty, using civic associations that "there provide a thousand continual reminders to every citizen that he lives in society [which] . . . at every moment bring his mind back to this idea, that it is the duty as well as the interest of men to be useful to their fellows."[24] For Hartz, however, writing in the 1950s, there were far fewer reasons for optimism. His formative period, intellectually and politically speaking, saw the rise of mass society in the United States, the Great Depression, an unparalleled world war, a vast increase in the size and central authority of the national government, the birth and use of the atomic bomb, and the postwar economic dominance and affluence of the United States.

Though sometimes overlooked, it seems quite important that Hartz's work appeared within the same general historical context as Hannah Arendt's *The Origins of Totalitarianism* (1951) and *The Human Condition* (1958); T. W. Adorno and associates' *The Authoritarian Personality* (1950); David Riesman's *The Lonely Crowd* (1950); and a number of other works confronting the social, political, and economic problems of the modern age in America.[25] Although this is a rather eclectic group, and unusual since it is typically thought more appropriate to place Hartz with the historians and theorists who have dealt with America's founding period and political history (Beard, Jensen, Kenyon, Wood, etc.), it is still, I believe, a legitimate one. Each of these thinkers, like Hartz, was concerned with the rise of mass society and the struggle to remain fully human, or unalienated, in the face of that movement.

Thus, when Hartz says, "I believe that this is the basic ethical problem of liberal society: not the danger of the majority which has been its conscious fear, but the danger of unanimity, which has slumbered unconsciously behind it: the 'tyranny of opinion' that Tocqueville saw unfolding,"[26] he not only is answering the "So what?" question but also is telling us about America's inverted "totalitarian kitsch," a kitsch that, like Kundera's, leaves no room for anything else, but different from his in that what is left is not the solitary state but the solitary individual—not collectivized out of existence but left completely alone in the "solitude of his own heart." Without the mediating institutions that Tocqueville thought could save us, Hartz is forced to present to his readers an America that is fast becoming rootless and alienated because of individualism and not as a result of the lack of it.[27] The real American equivalent of the Soviet May Day parade is not so much the Fourth of July but the Horatio Alger characters Ragged Dick and Matchbook Mark, or Benjamin Franklin's construction of himself in the *Autobiography*. And if the gulag is Kundera's negative exemplar, his "septic tank" for the collective society, then Willy Loman is America's.[28] Thus, rather than celebrating American conformity to the pervasive liberal ideal, as writers like Daniel Boorstin[29] had done, Hartz calls on America to transcend its past, to leave behind what he calls our political adolescence.[30]

This transcendence, however, is no easy social or political option, as Hartz's entire work, spanning the period from the Revolution to the early Cold War, testifies. Hartz notes that "the liberal society analyst is destined in two ways to be a less pleasing scholar than the Progressive: he finds national weaknesses and he can offer no absolute assurance on the basis of the past that they will be remedied, he tends to criticize and then shrug his shoulders, which is no way to become popular, especially in an age like our own."[31] The end result is a critical project that does not offer the "possibility of repentance and reform," or any particular "hope for redemption," because the languages of political discourse that Hartz viewed as offering those possibilities—particularly, one can infer, the discourse of socialism—were unavailable, or were "charmed or terrorized" into conformity or out of existence in America. Yet one must still ask why Hartz bothered to write in the first place. It could be, as he claims, that there is "an integrity to criticism which ought to be kept inviolate at any cost,"[32] but I believe there is more: a call for someone to find or create in American political discourse something that Hartz could not—an alternative political language if you will. That is the premise and the objective of this volume.

The contemporary communitarian theorist (and a student of Hartz's) Benjamin Barber makes the following observation:

> To posit and then theorize the individual as an abstract solitary may be helpful on the way to loosening feudal bonds and demarcating a clear space for rebels attempting to individuate themselves from a hierarchical and oppressive order. But it may appear as an obstructive exercise in nostalgia in an era when the bonds that hold together free communities are growing slack. For centuries, there was a need to stake out a circumscribed private ground in an otherwise statist, mercantilist, all-too-public world. In our own day, the need would seem to be to identify and fence in some small public space in an individualistic, anomic, all-too-privatized world.[33]

Despite my basic agreement with these sentiments, there is an element implicit in them that is more than a little problematic, and it is an element that is implicit in Hartz's work as well. For Hartz the potential solution, his one ray of hope for American transcendence, came in the form of America's "coming of age" through world contact: "America must look to its contact with other nations to provide that spark of philosophy, that grain of relative insight that its own history has denied it."[34] This would lead to "nothing less than a new level of consciousness, a transcending of irrational Lockianism, in which understanding of self and an understanding of others go hand in hand."[35] But this small hope is precisely that, since Hartz's entire book seems to argue against such a possibility. Indeed, after almost three hundred pages of recounting America's unique ability to incorporate, overcome, or alienate all such attempts, a hope of that nature would appear to border on the mystical.

And here is where Hartz and Barber share a problem (and perhaps where all writers interested in change in America must struggle as well): their modernist faith, which is fairly weak in the former but particularly strong in the latter. The implication in the passage from Barber above is that liberalism and its alternatives like communitarianism are similar to products that can bought from some sort of historical/ideological supermarket on the basis of current desires and necessities. Whereas Hartz recognizes the difficulty in such a proposition, although he still alludes to it as perhaps our only hope, Barber seems to imply that an act of will can do the trick, all historical boundaries aside. Both writers, however, share the general problem that can perhaps best be described as trying to build a political house without first pouring the necessary foundation. Hartz tentatively suggests that America look outside of itself to other countries and other traditions to solve its defect, and Barber seems to suggest that we avoid tradition altogether, because it lacks the necessary credentials to speak to the modern world, thus implying that we simply substitute a doctrine of motion for reflection.[36]

I propose in this volume to search for a third alternative that does not involve either the adoption of foreign theoretical models or a radical break with all tradition. It is an alternative that accepts the ideological hegemony of Hartz's liberalism for the most part, as well as Barber's edict for substantive change. Yet it has ties to another uniquely American political language that lies submerged or truncated within our past and present, and can be found and made useful only through a closer reading of the American political tradition.

In their acclaimed work *Habits of the Heart* (1984), Robert Bellah and his associates go back to Tocqueville to help them in their quest to understand American social and political culture. But rather than coming away with a single tradition that must be transcended in order for America to come of age, these authors find a group of political languages, from which Americans have historically drawn, that they feel must be given sufficient conversational space in which to flourish.[37] This recognition, however, does not prevent the authors from realizing the linguistic hegemony of liberal individualism. Indeed, they acknowledge that individualism, in what they call its "utilitarian" and "expressive" forms,[38] is America's first political/cultural language, and contend that it is very difficult for Americans to converse with one another in any other manner. Although differing in their expression of this first language, all of the subjects with whom Bellah and his associates are concerned "assume that there is something arbitrary about the goals of a good life,"[39] that "what is good is what one finds rewarding," and that "if one's preferences change, so does the nature of the good."[40]

As summed up in the earliest discussion of the subject named Brian Palmer, "The ultimate ethical rule is simply that individuals should be able to pursue whatever they find rewarding, constrained only by the requirement that they not interfere with the value systems of others."[41] This philosophy is summed up neatly by Brian himself when he says, "I don't think I would pontificate and say I'm in a position to establish values for humanity in general,"[42] which implies that he does not want to be pontificated to in return for *his* judgmental abstinence. This in turn is suggestive of two of the more dominant aspects of American Lockean individualism: the quest for freedom, defined as freedom *from*, as in "being left alone by others, not having other people's values, ideas, or styles of life forced upon one, being free from arbitrary authority in work, family, and political life,"[43] and the quest for economic progress that enables individuals to achieve more of their wants and desires upon being left alone with their preferences. Even American radicalism, as it is embodied for the authors in their subject Wayne Bauer, eventually succumbs to this paradigm. Through his work with the tenants' association, and the corresponding attempt to achieve what he sees as a more just distribution of societal resources and wealth, Wayne is left with the idea of generating for those tenants "the same opportunities as rich people to exercise their wills individually."[44]

The end result of this is a nation whose basic mode of political discourse is liberalism, with its emphasis on individualism, private property, and opportunity. The problem with such a world for the authors is multidimensional. In the first place, it produces a political context in which there is no provision for a vocabulary through which Americans "can easily address common conceptions of the ends of a good life or ways to coordinate cooperative action with others,"[45] and in which "the person who thinks in terms of the common good is a 'sucker.' "[46] In the second place, and perhaps more important for the authors, there is the problem created for the individual self, which is summed up in the following sentence: "What is at issue is not simply whether self-contained individuals might withdraw from the public sphere to pursue purely private ends, but whether such individuals are capable of sustaining either a public or a private life."[47]

Thus American individualism in its most austere formulation tends to generate at least a twofold problem of a lost public sphere, and hence the loss of a common or shared conception of the good life, and an increasingly shallow private sphere in which the individual is left "suspended in glorious, but terrifying isolation."[48] Once there, "the calculating managerial style [is transported] into intimacy, home, and community, areas of life formerly governed by the norms of a moral ecology."[49] But in the same manner that civic associations represented the way to combat the dangers of individualism for Tocqueville, so the authors of *Habits* suggest that "the tensions of our lives would be even greater if we did not, in fact, engage in practices that constantly limit the effects of an isolating individualism."[50] Those practices, for the authors, come in the form of our participation in what they call "communities of memory."[51] These communities consist of groups of people who share particular histories and hopes for the future on a regular basis through conversation and collective action toward common ends. They are differentiated from what the authors call "lifestyle enclaves," "where history and hope are forgotten and community means only the gathering of the similar."[52]

The authors claim that the transformation from the former to the latter is "endemic in America" because "we live in a society that encourages us to cut free from the past, to define our own selves, to choose the groups with which we wish to identify. No tradition and no community in the United States is above criticism, and the test of the criticism is usually the degree to which the community or tradition helps the individual find fulfillment."[53] And yet, according to the authors, "Even if the language of the self-reliant individual is the first language of American moral life, the languages of tradition and commitment in communities of memory are 'second languages' that most Americans know as well."[54]

It is the existence and history of these second languages, or at least one of

them, as well as the political conditions that allow (allowed?) their manifestation, that must be explored if we are to do battle with the notion of an "irrational Locke" in America and thereby forge a more fulfilling and complete American political discourse. In this way we are still bound by tradition while we
avoid traditionalism, and we do not have to reject an authentically American
political discourse in favor of one imported from elsewhere.

Submerged within the liberal/individualist discourse, Bellah and his associates have located what they call "the languages of tradition and commitment
in communities of memory," upon which they claim most citizens draw
"when the language of the radically separate self does not seem adequate."[55]
The authors name these nonindividualistic traditions or second languages: the
biblical tradition and the civic republican tradition, which they say led to a
theorization of political community that rejected "both chaotic openness and
authoritarian closure."[56] They then draw on exemplars like John Winthrop
and Martin Luther King, Jr., to illustrate their point. But most of their historical
references are rather cursory and anecdotal, which is appropriate, given their
focus on contemporary exemplars and types of American citizens.

In this volume, however, I will attempt to locate and describe the historical
context(s) in which those American second languages emerged, specifically the
language of *republicanism* in its particular democratic/participatory form. It is
my argument that far from being a secondary language, republicanism originally, with its emphasis on the priority of the community and local forms of
public association and participation, was the primary language of American
political discourse throughout the early life of the country. Furthermore, given
the secondary nature of the language today, this volume also seeks to explain
its fall from grace and the corresponding emergence of the language of liberalism.[57] Finally, I hope, by reconstructing both the historical context and the
political theory that accompanied the early period in America, to make clear
the value and potential usefulness of that tradition as an American "community
of memory" that may be drawn upon in current political discussions, so that
our modes of political discourse are not overly impoverished by the lack of
viable political/theoretical languages or alternatives.

Puritan Theology
as Political Liberation

The aim of social transformation, for Christians, is community. But we cannot create community. All we can do is remove—or attack—obstacles to community, such as poverty, illiteracy, sharp class distinctions, and secretive and unaccountable governments. That is, we can only set people free for community. Social reform seeks liberation.

—Glenn Tinder

Drawing on the teachings of Aristotle, Hannah Arendt contends that one of the crucial elements distinguishing the ancient political world from the modern one is the strict separation of the public and private realms.[1] The private realm was devoted to mastering the necessities of life, to the household, and to reproduction. In other words, it was the realm in which persons were concerned solely with their own well-being and that of their family. The public realm, on the other hand, was concerned with what was shared and common. Those who had mastered the necessities of life adequately were by definition free to participate in public affairs. Participation in the public realm, however, was different from participation in the private. In public life one had to abridge one's own desires and look to the good of the community. Hence, for Arendt and for others of a similar mind, the realm of politics became a realm of transformation in which human participants were "saved" from the important yet unfulfilling business of life and mere survival. Public activity provided an opportunity to create and to mold, and also to be partially re-created and molded. It was as if human beings could somehow be made better than they would have been had they remained private, self-interested members of a household.

Obviously the preconditions for such transformations depended upon the construction and/or maintenance of a public sphere that was distinct from the private realm of the household. Participation in that sphere would be contingent upon the ability to transcend purely personal or petty motives and to carry on a conversation about a communal good life. In other words, individuals would have to be transformed from members to citizens, with the qualifying mark of such a change being not the quality of their souls but the quality of their behavior.

It is this recognition of a *res publica* (a public thing), coupled with an emphasis on civic virtue and on the expansion of political participation to a wider variety of societal members, that represents the first real rumblings of the political doctrine of republicanism. It is republicanism as a political ideology—or, as I prefer, a political faith—that will provide the opposition to various historical forms of elitism. Typically, republicanism will lose either as a result of its own inadequacies and failures or, more often, as a result of the superior force brought to bear by its intellectual and political opponents or usurpers. That struggle defines early American history, although it originated much earlier, in sixteenth- and seventeenth-century England and New England. It is there, among groups of rebellious Protestants, that we find the earliest "American" manifestations of Anti-Federalist thought. It is also there that we will see the first explicit links between human redemption and a political order that asks not merely obedience but also participation from its members.

These early American settlers, then, represent the first formulation of modern community—modern in that equality will become an increasingly salient feature of the political world; modern in that both consent and resistance to unlawful authority are legitimized, even to the point of becoming obligatory; modern insofar as ideas and law come to replace the patronage and personal relationships that dominated the feudal political world. The emphasis in this emerging world will be less on the transcendent nature of political and moral knowledge, and more on the experiential knowledge often referred to as "common sense." In it we will find a growing dissatisfaction with the notion of hierarchy and a particular view of nature,[2] and in turn will see more emphasis placed on human creative and constructive abilities. This expansion of participation in public life and the changing nature of what counts as knowledge, coupled with the physical circumstances in which these pilgrims find themselves, subsequently led to a democratization of sorts that eventually resonated throughout history.

WHEN THE SAINTS GO MARCHING IN

If Glenn Tinder is right when he claims that "we cannot create community," and that "all we can do is remove—or attack—obstacles to community,"[3] then the issue for the theorist of political community is discovering exactly what those obstacles are and projecting ways in which they might be removed. As Roberto Unger later claimed, "The progressive diminution of domination makes community possible; the advance of community helps us understand and thereby erase domination."[4] The issue, then, is not utopia building but the creation of an appropriate amount of social and political space to allow community to grow. Although they are more often cast in the role of tyrannical religious utopians, it is in the role of political radicals who seek to remove the obstacles to community that I want to place those sixteenth- and seventeenth-century activists known as Congregationalists or Puritans. The first step in seeing them in that light is for the modern liberal reader to get past the fear that "any new institution which destroys individual autonomy is a pathological form of community that must be restricted"[5] and to move toward the understanding that people sometimes "seek new communities because they have already rejected individual autonomy as the central value in their lives"[6] (or, in the case of the Puritans, because such a value was not part of their social and political vocabulary). Once this is done, it may be possible to recast those early forefathers and foremothers as the precursors to more liberating forms of political association and perhaps even to the expansion of political participation we often refer to as the democratization of American political society, rather than as the forerunners of political repression (as they are often remembered).

At its root Puritanism and the Calvinist theology from which it sprang is a religious doctrine with political implications. But like the doctrines of the early Christians as taught by Christ and his apostles, those political implications are pronounced and radical if taken seriously. Among the most important aspects, politically speaking, are the doctrines of consent and voluntary association, the notion of a fundamental law to which such associations and magistrates must conform in order to remain legitimate, the idea of resistance to unlawful authority, and the emphasis on expanded and even compulsory participation (and thus on the creative aspects of community building). Clearly such ideas were antithetical to the political order of the feudal world, which depended for the most part on the passivity of the vast majority of its members. Obedience and loyalty were owed not to the "higher law" but to the king, in whom absolute sovereignty was located. And even though the king was subject to natural law, it was typically argued that he was its ultimate interpreter; thus the king was, as both John of Salisbury and Thomas Aquinas would contend, not "bound by the laws."[7] To overcome the tyrannical implications of such a position, Ewart Lewis argues that medieval political thinkers insisted, at least where basic private rights were concerned, that "royal authority might be qualified by a characteristically medieval device: the insistence that it be exercised through formal procedures—through due process of law or through consultation and consent."[8] Thus sovereignty remained undivided and absolute while being given a degree of structure and predictability that later would be used to impose limits on its use. This is the first step in clearing away obstacles to political community and toward liberation, and it is as a child of this political context that John Calvin emerges.

Clearly, any attempt to understand the teachings of John Calvin must be tempered with the knowledge of his core assumptions about the history and possibilities of the human race. There is no way to overestimate the role played by the biblical story of the fall of Adam and Eve, their banishment from the Garden of Eden, and the subsequent creation of original sin. For John Calvin, men and women are fallen creatures who are unworthy of redemption and God's grace due to their original disobedience. Yet they are from time to time pitied by their creator, for whatever reason—certainly never because they deserve it—and are granted the gift of salvation. This belief that grace is a gift from God of which we are unworthy, and therefore cannot be earned through works, serves as the foundation for the Calvinist doctrine of predestination or sainthood. Calvin writes of God: "He pays no reward, since he can owe none."[9] The best we can hope for, according to Calvinist teachings, is to create the conditions on earth and within our institutions that God might find pleasing. Such works, however, can never obligate God. The role of the civil government in such a theology is to provide support for the external worship of God, to preserve the pure doctrine of religion, to defend the constitution of the church, to regulate our lives in a manner requisite for a society of men, to form our manners to civil justice, to foster "a public form of religion among Christians so that humanity may be maintained among men."[10] In other words, the political world exists to make sure that there are no unnecessary obstacles to the worship of God, including poor manners, disorder, false doctrines, corrupt churches, and so on. Thus political society could create what may be called the necessary conditions for the infusion of God's grace, but nothing could be considered a sufficient condition, because God does not recognize any quid pro quo. The problem with which Calvin and his followers had to deal was how such a polity could be attained in a world of corruption, heresy, and the like.

Here Michael Walzer provides the definitive word on Calvinist politics in his *The Revolution of the Saints*. He contends that Calvinism as an ideology is "marked by its critical view of the patriarchal and feudal world, its political realism, its bold suggestion for social reconstruction and its extraordinary capacity for organizing men and sending them into battle against Satan and his allies—even when those allies turned out to be kings and noblemen."[11] Calvin's rejection of the feudal world caused him also to reject the notion of the state as a natural or organic entity. In its place Calvin and others like him substituted the notion of a man-made secular state in which "the saint was the militant Christian activist [whose activity] carried him outside the Church [where] he not only participated in congregational government, he also created the holy commonwealth."[12] If society was not the product of nature, then it must be the product of something else, and for Calvinists this something else was a covenant.[13] The civic covenant "was a self-imposed submission to divinely imposed law, but this self-imposition was a social act and subject to enforcement in God's name."[14] Thus individuals must come freely to civil society, but once there, they must be willing to submit to the discipline required within that political community as executed by the magistrates. These magistrates were chosen, according to Calvin, on the basis of their good and holy knowledge of Scripture, their ability to communicate that knowledge effectively, and their personal habits and character.[15]

While the theoretical contributions of Calvin to the organization and foundations of the civic/theocratic polity cannot be overemphasized, it is important to distinguish between the setting in which Calvin worked and the setting in which many of his European, and especially English, followers found themselves. With relative ease Calvin moved to Geneva and established a theocracy with himself at its head (1536–1541). Thus he had a rare opportunity to theorize and create almost simultaneously, thereby significantly blurring the line between theory and practice in an almost unprecedented example of political/religious praxis. English Puritans, however, had to contend with an established, although transitional, political and religious world. This meant that they would have to rely more explicitly on political practice to achieve their theoretical goals.

With the settlement of 1559, exiled Puritans began returning to England and confronting Elizabeth's England. It is this return of what Walzer would call the "rootless intellectuals"—who "despite considerable support from titled families and encouragement from the members of the Privy Council [remained] an isolated group"[16]—that provided the starting point for the radical transformation of traditional political society. These Puritan ministers, who would become "heroes of sixteenth-century Puritanism,"[17] were, according to Walzer, by the 1570s "openly demanding parity, the abolition of the hierarchy and its replacement by a series of clerical conferences headed by no one more majestic than an elected moderator, [with] decisions made by prolonged discussion and mutual criticism, and finally by a show of hands," as the new church discipline.[18]

This line of radical thought clearly represented a break with the older forms of political and religious organization in England. The emphasis was now on participatory, voluntary, and even somewhat democratic forms of association that served to break down the vestiges of the older, more authoritarian, and dramatically more passive feudal order. Puritan ministers not only were involved in basic political and religious reform; they also were in the process of deconstructing an entire social order. In opposition to the arrangements of feudal England, where social and political ties were based on neighborhood and kindred, these ministers were suggesting that "allies be chosen for their virtue and godliness."[19] This transformation made possible the idea of independent, ideologically based forms of political association. The result was a group of people who "had abandoned 'father and fatherland' to enlist in Christ's army," an army that was "capable of making war ruthlessly, because it had nothing but contempt for the world in which it moved."[20] In the place of the old order that depended upon one's personal relationships and the sort of patronage associated with feudalism, they would establish a public realm guided by the Word.

To later liberals, and especially modern liberals, the notion of regulating one's community by the Word or any other religious doctrine seems intolerant and repressive, but to those who had been in the grip of a virtually stagnant and arbitrary feudal order, the idea of a standard that was beyond the reach of one's superiors, which could be used to limit their behavior and redefine legitimacy, was fantastically liberating. The Word at this historical juncture once again took on the promise of human possibility that perhaps had not been seen since the earliest formation of the church 1500 years earlier, and that perhaps would not be seen again until Catholic priests and nuns resurrected this militant tradition in later twentieth-century Central and South America. With this theoretical groundwork laid and those alternative forms of association secretly in place, comprising what Walzer calls the "counterpolity,"[21] the question for our revolutionary-minded saints was how to replace the existing social and political structure with their own.

From within Calvinism three interesting and useful strategies or answers to that question emerge. The first lies in the Calvinist and French Huguenot reconfiguration of the idea of political office. The second is found in Stephen Junius Brutus's Huguenot tract *Vindiciae contra tyrannos* (A Defense of Liberty Against Tyrants, 1579). And the third is manifested in the actions of the Plymouth colonists, and slightly later in the person of John Winthrop and company at Massachusetts Bay.

In the *Institutes*, Calvin lays out his theory of princely and magisterial duty:

> Christian princes and magistrates ought to be ashamed of their indolence if they do not make it [religion] the object of their most serious care. We have already shown that this duty is particularly enjoined upon them by God; for it is reasonable that they should employ their utmost efforts in asserting and defending the honor of Him whose viceregents they are and *by whose favor they govern*. And the principal commendations given in the Scripture to the good kings are for having restored the worship of God when it had been corrupted or abolished. . . . These things envince the folly of those who would wish magistrates to neglect all thoughts of God, and to confine themselves entirely to the administration of justice among men.[22]

The role of the civil servant, be it prince or magistrate, becomes one of reformation and proclamation. The idea was to use the civil polity and the bureaucratic apparatus that served as its context as a tool for reform. The reformed civil polity would be better able to maintain those conditions necessary for the religious work to take place. Calvin linked the obligation to engage in this reconstructive work to the idea that rulers and magistrates served at the request and discretion of God, and thus were bound to serve His vision rather than the utilitarian ends of a secular order. The idea was to transform the identities of rulers, magistrates, and administrators from what we might call "social servants" (those who served a particular social order in a manner designed to maintain it) into "civil servants" (those who served society in a manner designed to perfect it). In other words, in Calvin's theory of office we find the first real rumblings of a constitutional order in which representatives of the governing body were obligated to a set of principles and procedures rather than to certain individuals.

Though he calls their efforts to "transform feudal status into constitutional position"[23] unsuccessful, Walzer does recognize the work of the French Huguenots as an important theoretical attempt to install the Calvinist conception of political office as the foundation for the modern state. He describes the efforts of the French Calvinists as "an attempt to turn the 'valiant knight' into a conscientious officeholder."[24] And although the attempt was limited to the work of a small intellectual element within political society, it did manage to foreshadow, even if it could not yet produce, the emergence of Cromwell. Furthermore, the Huguenots' work raised important theoretical questions within Calvinist thought concerning the nature of political obedience and resistance. For Calvinism, with its reductive theory of predestination, questions of authority were difficult to deal with, in that rulers and magistrates clearly could not have earned a position that God had not authorized. If secular rulers were in fact the product of God's placement, then whatever form their rule took was equally the product of God's will—a will that for Calvin was beyond question or comprehension for most human beings. Calvin wrote that "the authority possessed by kings and governors over all things upon the earth is not a consequence of the perverseness of men, but of providence and holy ordinance of God, who has been pleased to regulate human affairs in this manner."[25]

Calvin postulated that obedience was therefore owed to whatever rulers happened to be in place, no matter how tyrannical or repressive. He even went so far as to suggest that non-Christian rulers were acceptable. As Walzer concludes, "Calvin ignored the medieval distinction between legitimate rulers and usurpers; in fact he condemned any effort to make lawful distinctions."[26] Whether or not this seemingly contradictory position was the product of a duplicitous religion that seemed to demand different things at different times from its followers, of the inability of Calvin to see past the fallen nature of men and women far enough to ascribe to them the capacity to judge such situations correctly, or of his duality as both a reform-minded political/theocratic activist and the conservative head of his own theocratic city, the point remains that "Calvin's point of view must be drawn forth, almost against his will, by examining the possibilities his rhetoric concealed"[27] if we are to understand the revolutionary politics to which his thought eventually leads.

Michael Walzer argues that the work of the great Swiss leader of the Reformation, Huldrych Zwingli, is critical if we are to understand the submerged possibilities contained in the teachings of Calvin.[28] Where Calvin had resorted to the almost Hobbesian position of private judgment with regard to seemingly illegitimate authority, Zwingli, in his notion of internally reserving consent, went so far as to link obedience to the natural law of the Decalogue, and the Christianity of the rulers and magistrates to the question of legitimacy. In other words, Zwingli, to a much greater extent than Calvin, was willing to theorize conditions that might legitimate resistance, and perhaps even disobedience, to secular authority. Yet Zwingli represents only a partial shift, and one that to some extent Calvin later acknowledged as legitimate. The real extension or deconstruction of Calvin's thought with regard to the question of corruption within the political realm came in the teachings of the Huguenot theorist Stephen Junius Brutus.

Written in 1579, just fifteen years after Calvin's death, *Vindiciae contra tyrannos* (A Defense of Liberty Against Tyrants, hereinafter referred to as *Defense*) represents an important turning point in Calvinist political thought while remaining theoretically true to it. Such a feat is accomplished through the working out of those possibilities within Calvin's thought that were submerged, or perhaps repressed, by Calvin himself.

The theory of "predestination" is often decried as an insurmountable barrier to the construction of ethical and moral categories of human agency and responsibility, since it would seem indefensible to hold people accountable for acts that they had no choice in committing. But this configuration ignores the wonderfully liberating, and perhaps even terrifying, possibilities that a strong theory of predestination has to offer. To understand this point, one need only ask the most simple, and yet potentially explosive, question of Calvinism: If rulers and magistrates are appointed by God, then why not rebels as well? Surely Christians believed that from time to time God had found it necessary to intervene in the most violent and revolutionary way in the affairs of the earth, or to send messengers and prophets to act on His behalf. This must be especially true for Protestants like Calvin, who saw no essential differences between the Old and the New Testaments in terms of religious theory. This is the point at which French Calvinism adds an important historical and theoretical *political* voice to the discussion.

The *Defense* basically begins with one simple question: Are subjects bound to obey princes if their orders contradict the law of God? The answer given is quite simple: Obedience to God is implicit, and obedience to men is always conditional.[29] Obedience is conditional on the prince's keeping the faith safe and acting in accord with the dictates of the Word. The community was covenanted with God, who in turn preserved their commonwealth so long as they kept His laws and provided for proper collective worship.[30] The language of the *Defense* is particularly noteworthy for both its communitarian overtones[31] and its contractual orientation.[32] The latter can be seen when Brutus describes the nature of the communal covenant in the terms used to describe a bank loan. Here God is envisioned as a divine loan officer who is dealing with fallen people of dubious credit; He insures the "loan" by obligating several for the same amount, like cosigners. Thus each member of the community becomes responsible for making good the community's part of the covenant.[33] Brutus goes on to argue that it would make no sense to obligate the members of the community without granting them the legitimate power to defend themselves against default in the form of maintaining illegitimate leaders in power. This provides an interesting extension of Calvin's thoughts on obedience and authority; now not only are members obligated to obey legitimate rulers, they are also obligated to reject illegitimate ones—not because individual rights are violated but because the security of the community is at stake.[34] Resistance and obedience as activities are thus linked as part of a larger theoretical whole that confers legitimacy on both, depending on the circumstances. What still remains to be addressed, however, is the practical consideration of judgment: Who can determine when the behavior of the prince is outside the boundaries of natural law?

To this question the *Defense* offers a theory that holds the collective body of legislators or representatives responsible for checking both the prince and the people. Though as individuals these legislators are outranked by the prince, collectively they outrank him.[35] If for some reason, however, the legislators fail to be vigilant enough, a particular town can—indeed must, under penalty of treason against God—take it upon itself to close its gates to the tyrant and resist him with all their strength.[36] Finally, if neither the town nor the legislature resists tyrannical behavior, Brutus takes the very radical step of legitimizing individual resistance. Here, however, he is pragmatic enough to understand the difficulties associated with individual rebellion. Instead of obligating the individual to martyrdom, Brutus, by noting that God did not grant the power of the sword to individuals, suggests the option of exodus. If corruption is so ingrained in a particular community (town) that no attempt is made by magistrates or the collective citizenry to ferret it out, the individual should seek refuge in another town.[37] Finally, if none of these alternatives are available to the individual, he or she is commanded to resist to the point of giving up life before giving up God.[38]

Yet almost as quickly as this radical position is staked out, Brutus feels compelled to defend his position from the dangers associated with such a potentially solipsistic vision of religious and political community through a process that transubstantiates individual rebels like Moses. In other words, to protect the sanctity of the community from the dangers associated with empowering each individual to judge for himself or herself in any case where it is felt appropriate, Brutus transforms historical figures of rebellion into messengers of God and judges the appropriateness of their rebellion by its success or failure. This quasi-deterministic stance completes the Calvinist circle.[39] The completion of this theoretical circle carves out a path for the likes of John Winthrop, Oliver Cromwell, and later their synthetic surrogate John Locke.

Cromwell and Winthrop are two sides of the same modified Calvinist coin. The latter, facing what he believes to be insurmountable historical odds coupled with the knowledge of historical possibility offered by America, chooses purification through relocation. The former, for whatever reason, sees the opportunity to purify through revolution. Both responses were, by 1630 and 1640, respectively, theoretically legitimate within the transformed Calvinist thought. As intriguing as the notion of redemption through tyrannicide is, for the purpose of this volume the actions taken by Winthrop and company are more important.

"FORCED TO BE FREE"

In the *Institutes,* Calvin cautions his followers to avoid the desire to overintellectualize the ways of God. God, for Calvin, reveals only those aspects of His mysteries that He deems it necessary for human beings to know; thus He fills His subjects with wonder and awe.[40] As Walzer claims, "Calvinism was far more importantly a doctrine of discipline and obedience than justification."[41] Calvin may have recognized, a century or so before Thomas Hobbes, that "the fear of things invisible is the natural seed of religion,"[42] and that the preservation of "mysteries" was an essential condition of God's power over the consciences of men and women. Perhaps he realized those possibilities submerged in his thought, and recognized the dangers to the order of the civil (and therefore the religious) polity of proceeding with the Huguenots' theoretical reduction. Whatever the reason, it is clear that Calvin was worried about the potential for disorder to which later theorizations on his original teachings might lead.

It is, then, not unimportant that Calvin (1509–1564) shared a substantial part of his life with Copernicus (1473–1543), or that Galileo (1564–1642) was born in the year of his death, or that the *Vindiciae contra tyrannos* (1579) appeared during this time period.[43] The Reformation had unleashed forces that had little to do with the transformation of religion, powerful new ideas began to flourish, science and mathematics made the world knowable to individuals. One by one mysteries were being stripped away, and with them the epistemological justifications for power. Everything was ripe for theoretical challenge and the process of intellectualization, including theology. The forces unleashed by Luther and Calvin were, like the creation of Dr. Frankenstein, now out of their control—they were still afraid of "fire," and thus from time to time could be subdued by repression or the "bloody sword"; but, as the Catholic Church had learned, such techniques were effective only in the short term. It is perhaps the bane of all revolutionaries that the forces they must conjure up in order to accomplish radical social or political transformation soon overwhelm them and their original intention. Perhaps, as Crane Brinton argues, revolutions have a natural course that they inevitably follow,[44] except that in the case of Luther and Calvin the revolutionary moderates attempted to purge the radicals rather than the other way around. Whatever the case may be, there can be little argument that the movement begun by Calvin was quickly devoured by the historical forces amid which it found itself. This is the point at which the American Puritans enter the historical scene.

In his work "The Marrow of Puritan Divinity," Perry Miller argues that by 1630 Calvinism was in a period of transition as the result of at least two key factors. First, the strictness of the doctrine was too much for most followers to bear: "He [Calvin] [had] demanded that they contemplate, with steady, unblinking resolution, the absolute, incomprehensible, and transcendent sovereignty of God; he required men to stare fixedly and without relief into the very center of the blazing sun of glory."[45] Second, Calvinism with its "mysteries" was no more successful in fending off the early rumblings of the Enlightenment than the Catholic Church was in its attempt to maintain Ptolemy's astronomy, or than Pope Pius X would later be with his "Oath Against Modernism" (1910). To survive, Calvinism would have to change and become susceptible to the very sort of intellectualization that its founder had dreaded. To illustrate the transformation, Miller suggests a comparison between the *Institutes* and the *Medulla* (1632) of Fischer Ames. He writes of the differences between the two works:

> It was no longer a question of blocking in the outlines; it was a question of filling in the chinks and gaps, of intellectualizing the faith, of exonerating it from the charge of despotic dogmatism, of adding demonstration to assertion—of making it capable of being "understood, known, and committed to memory."[46]

Calvin as Moses had brought the people to God, but now it was time to bring God down from the mountain to the people, before their interest lapsed. To accomplish this, the faith would need to be secularized to some extent and forced to answer the questions associated with everyday living. In other words, Calvinism would need a more detailed praxis to sustain itself in the intellectual and political atmosphere of the mid-seventeenth century. And for a religious project that denounced a covenant of works, finding such a praxis would be no mean feat.

From the work of Perry Miller we can derive three basic questions that would need answers for Calvinism as an intellectual object to pass muster under emerging Enlightenment standards. In turn the answers to these questions will provide us with a basic outline of Puritanism as both religious and political project in the New World and, in the context of this volume, illustrate what I take to be the foundations of Anti-Federalist political thought. The questions, simply put, are the following:

1. How was God to be known and yet remain hidden?
2. If election was predestined, why worry about works?
3. How were people to know whether they were elected?[47]

Although each of these questions entailed a theological problem, none could be answered, in a community where questions of secular power and authority were tied to religious positions, without manifesting a particular vision of political community.

The first question basically represented a Puritan refutation of Calvin's emphasis on mysteries and politically should be seen as an attempt to determine the form of political rule that would be installed in the newborn community. In other words, a Scripture-based justification would need to be found for claiming anyone's ability to know God's will (the theological question), and once such a justification was found, the issue would become how and by whom those mysteries were to be revealed (the political question). The answer to the theological question, according to Miller, was to be found in the idea of the covenanted or contractual community. Analytically, the narrative was quite simple: The original contract God had made with Adam, based on a system of works, had proven too difficult; hence the Fall, which limited man's ability to help in his own salvation. The second contract, which God had made with Abraham, was therefore designed to fix the defects of the first contract by linking salvation or grace to faith rather than to works. The existence of the second covenant was taken by Puritan thinkers as a sign indicating God's willingness to reveal Himself to His people to the extent that He thought necessary. As a participant in a contract, it was now incumbent upon God to make known to at least some degree what He desired from the deal, although He was of course at liberty to keep as much of Himself hidden as He wanted.[48] The more difficult question was the political one: who would determine when and what God had chosen to reveal.

In Catholicism the model for determining God's will had been one of hierarchy. The pope would speak to God and relay His message to the people through the church bureaucracy. In this way, organizationally and epistemologically at least, the Catholic Church could be viewed as adopting the elite model associated with Plato. Protestantism had rejected such a model in favor of what Luther called a "priesthood of all believers." But this priesthood was not taken by Luther, Calvin, or any other early Protestant leaders as implying individualism with regard to the interpretation of Scripture. Instead, the political organization of most early Protestant sects, and especially Calvinism as practiced by the Puritans, is better understood as a variation of Aristotle's republicanism. In other words, the early Protestants were certainly not political liberals who embraced individual conceptions of the good; rather, they were republicans, and perhaps even Rousseauean democrats, who believed that a right interpretation or answer had to be worked out among the saints, or the "citizens." Thus the political manifestation of the first question was the expansion of participation in the interpretive, and therefore *political*, decision-making process.

The answer to the second question—if election was predestined, why worry about works at all?—is perhaps the most important question one can ask in the quest to understand the Puritan political model. Just as, in the twentieth century, existentialism would constantly have to defend itself against charges of promoting moral and political nihilism for denying God's existence, so did a religion or philosophy that claimed God's mind was already made up have to worry about the liberation that sometimes comes with resignation. On one hand there was the danger that those who believed they were members of the elect would ignore the demands of earthly life, as some Anabaptists had done.[49] On the other hand, there was the even more disturbing possibility that those who believed God had not chosen them would not feel bound by any social convention whatsoever, and would become either despondent or hostile. Hence the doctrine of preparation[50] was introduced into Puritan theology as a way of solving both potential problems.

Thomas Hooker once warned his audience: "You must not think to go to heaven on a feather-bed; if you will be Christ's disciples, you must take up his cross, and it will make you sweat." His point, as I take it, was that being saved was not an invitation to relax but an invocation to work harder. This invocation would be applied to the nonelect as well through a very interesting theological modification in the doctrine of predestination. To ensure human activity, the Puritans theorized a God who worked within the context of human time and history, a fluid and perhaps even flexible God—a God who at any time could choose to infuse a person with His grace and make him or her one of the elect. Furthermore, since such a God could not be bound by the works of men and women, there was no way to be positive of one's status as part of the elect. This doubt allowed the Puritans to theorize the doctrine of preparation, which suggested that members of the community must remain constantly vigilant and be in a state of readiness *in case* God decided to bless them. Thus, in a theological shift that foreshadows the religious work of Søren Kierkegaard, Puritans more or less claimed that their members needed to act as though they had faith so that grace *might* be given to them.

In place of conditional election (the Arminian heresy)[51] the Puritans had subtly inserted the idea of a conditional covenant that entailed the moral obligations of preparation but did not bind the Lord, thus narrowly avoiding a doctrine of works. The end result of this shift, theologically as well as socially, was to answer the question concerning works and to bind the community together in a common expectation of grace. This reduced the anxiety of those who were not part of the elect[52] while generating enough uncertainty among those who thought they were, to keep them active and on their best behavior.[53] The political result of this change was to reassert and expand on the Calvinist rationale for community and, as we shall see, to significantly break down barriers to participatory membership in the Puritan community.

The theological doctrine of preparation provided the justification for a second covenant, this time between the members of the community rather than with God. This had a partly political object. For Congregationalists, individuals did not covenant with God (Antinomianism)[54]; their communities did. But for there to be a community to covenant with God, there first had to be a covenant between the members, and since the latter was done in order to achieve the former, it only makes sense that even though the choice to join was free, the choices within the community must be kept consonant with their goal.[55] That goal was to maintain the condition of preparation in the hope of receiving God's grace. For Calvin, all that was necessary to accomplish this was a strong civil polity capable of repression,[56] but for John Winthrop this would not be nearly enough.

His teaching on the flagship *Arbella,* in the form of a sermon titled "A Model of Christian Charity" (1630), slightly predates, and certainly anticipates, the doctrine of preparation. As Winthrop wrote:

> Now the only way to avoid this shipwreck and to provide for our posterity is to follow the Counsel of Micah, to do justly, to love mercy, to walk humbly with our God, for this end we must be knit together in this work as one man, we must entertain each other in brotherly affection, we must be willing to abridge ourselves of our superfluities, for the supply of others' necessities, we must uphold a familiar commerce together, in all meekness, gentleness, patience, and liberality, we must delight in each other, make others' conditions our own, rejoyce together, mourne together, labor, and suffer together, always having before our eyes our commission and community in the work.[57]

Here we see that process of "filling in the chinks and gaps" as Winthrop lays out a vision of community that, far from being a simple order of repression, is filled with images of individual responsibilities, duties, and obligations to each other member and to the whole. Everyone must be prevented from doing evil and encouraged to participate actively and to do good. For the religious project of the "city on the hill," people must become better than they were before their entrance into the community. In other words, through the act of joining together and participating, it was hoped that they would be somehow transformed.[58]

The nature of that transformation for Winthrop can be found in another speech of his, "A Little Speech on Liberty" (1645). Here, anticipating the work of Rousseau, Winthrop lays out the nature of the covenant between the magistrates and the members in a way that suggests the existence of some form of democracy among the members, in that magistrates are chosen by the people ("I entreat you to consider that when you choose magistrates, you take them from among yourselves");[59] he asserts the legitimacy of the Huguenot theory of resistance ("But if he [the magistrate] fail in faithfulness, which by his oath he is bound unto, that he must answer for");[60] finally, and most important, he makes clear the distinction between natural and civil liberty:

> There is a two-fold liberty—natural (I mean our nature is now corrupt), and civil or federal. The first is common to man, with beasts and other creatures . . . it is a liberty to evil as well as good. This liberty is inconsistent with authority, and cannot endure the least restraint of the most just authority. . . . The other kind of liberty I call civil or federal; it may also be termed moral, in reference to the covenant between God and man in the moral law, and the political covenants and constitutions among men themselves . . . it is a liberty to that only which is good.[61]

The construction and care of a general will directed at a collective good life becomes the task of the civil polity for Winthrop and company. For the Puritans, political life becomes a mechanism for *possible* redemption through the constant attention to preparation inherent in the political process of sorting out good behavior from bad. In place of a strong Calvinist theory of justification by faith, the Puritans have introduced a system of justification in which works are necessary but not sufficient and in which the nature of those works must be determined through a political praxis that includes both authority and obedience, *and* resistance and liberty.[62] The amalgamation of apparent opposites in Puritan religious/political theory releases the project of community building from the boundaries imposed by strictly logical and reductivist thinking,[63] at the same time avoiding what we might call the postmodern problematic of "all things are permitted."[64] With this idea in place, we can now turn to the third and final question in order to complete the Puritan circle as distinct from Calvinism; it is this circle that completes the Puritan foreshadowing of Anti-Federalist thought.

The third question suggested by Perry Miller that the Puritans had to answer—how are people to know when they are indeed saved?—again is theological in formation and political in implication. Though all members of the community were told to *prepare,* they were not all allowed to participate in the decision-making process concerning the substance of that preparation. In fact, the doctrine of preparation itself was not universally accepted, and eventually caused serious problems within the Bay Colony. Leaving this aside for the moment, it is important to remember that in 1630 English birth was not sufficient to create a right to political participation. So it follows, according to Edmund Morgan, that leaders of the various colonies, whether patented or proprietary, had significant discretionary power over rules and laws that governed their respective communities.[65] Interestingly, among the first steps taken in some colonies, including Massachusetts Bay, was turning over significant amounts of that power to a relatively large part of the community.[66] In part this could be explained by the emphasis the Puritans placed on the idea of the covenanted community and its corollary of voluntary association.[67] Another partial explanation for this initial sharing of power can be deduced from the fact that many of the early settlers had come for financial gain as well as for the chance to establish their own particular religious communities. Donald Lutz writes:

> Those who came over in the ships were generally recognized as being engaged in an enterprise of some personal risk, and often they were stockholders risking their money as well. Under such conditions, it would have been foolish to expect anyone to emigrate if he had little or no control over matters in which he had invested his livelihood.[68]

Yet given even these two factors, there can be no denying that the power and participation within the Puritan communities was limited to a particular group of people. That group of course was the elect, the members of the local church. And it is how this limitation is viewed that often determines the nature of one's normative/historical/political categorization of the Puritans, as well as the sides one chooses in the particular controversies within their communities.

The theological basis for the Puritan theory of membership is drawn from the early teachings of Paul and his chief theoretical spokesman, St. Augustine.[69] It was Augustine who advanced the idea of two churches, one visible and one invisible. In the invisible church were all those living, dead, and yet to be born whom God had chosen for salvation. In the visible church, membership was much less certain, since it was difficult if not impossible to know the mind of God in such matters. But, however imperfect the visible church was, for Augustine, and especially for the Puritans, it was supposed to be brought as closely into line with the invisible church as possible.[70] The reason for the attempted proximity was to avoid the corruption of the church that could result from allowing sinners to participate in the affairs of the community, which in turn could bring the disfavor of God. Thus, who gained access to membership, and therefore power and status, in the community's church became an important political as well as theological question.

The existence of any limitations to membership and participation within the community is enough to reap the condemnation of those who are sympathetic to modern liberal conceptions of membership. But to hold the Puritans to standards developed some three hundred years later is rather anachronistic and difficult to defend. Yet many scholars have done just that by looking more often at the form, as opposed to the substance, of Puritan political organization. Regarding the Puritan experiment conducted under John Winthrop, Edmund Morgan has suggested that Winthrop was armed with a natural authority, a granted authority, a spiritual injunction against mass participation, a belief that civil rulers were cloaked in the armor of the divine, and that these elements led him and his peers to construct an oligarchy within the colony.[71] Vernon Parrington has claimed that in Massachusetts, magistrates had "cast out the spirit of liberalism."[72]

What these esteemed scholars, especially Parrington, fail to grasp is that the Puritan community was never imbued with the "spirit of liberalism" in the first place. On the contrary, the Puritan experiment was never about religious freedom as contemporary thinkers theorize it but, rather, about the desire to be free to practice *their* religion. It is here that the work of Carey MacWilliams and his pupil Joshua Miller becomes quite important. In his book *The Rise and Fall of Democracy in Early America, 1630–1789,* Miller devotes an entire chapter to the Puritan theory of membership; in it he argues that the Puritan political community cannot be understood as liberal, but that it can be understood as democratic.[73] He goes on to argue that those who conflate the terms "liberal" and "democratic" are often led by this misuse of the language to pass judgment on the Puritan political community while in the grip of a serious misunderstanding.[74] Citing Stephen Foster's *Their Solitary Way,* Miller writes, "Though it sounds strange to say it, few societies in Western culture have depended more thoroughly or more self-consciously on the consent of their members than the allegedly repressive 'theocracies' of early New England."[75]

There is no guarantee that empowering people will necessarily result in the sorts of substantive outcomes for which many liberals would hope. Harkening back to Philip Abbott, who warned that people often "seek new communities because they have already rejected individual autonomy as the central value in their lives,"[76] we can theorize democratic communities that reject liberal values even if we as "liberals" cannot necessarily understand them. Thus, when Morgan writes of the Ann Hutchinson affair that "our natural sympathies lie with the banished Mrs. Hutchinson,"[77] he is probably right; but when Carey Mac-Williams writes that she "taught a doctrine whose implications led directly to individualism. Against the positive moral obligations and the negative force of guilt which Winthrop hoped to inculcate as supports for man and fraternity . . . ,"[78] he is also right. The difference is that there are two competing value systems that may not be subject to mediation on the basis of an exterior or independent authority. Therefore, in order to understand, and perhaps even to judge, the Puritans, it is important that we do so from within their value system rather than across value systems.

Joshua Miller argues, and I believe correctly, that the Puritans placed such a large emphasis on requirements for church membership because of the perception that along with membership went responsibility for the success or failure of the entire religious project, and perhaps the possibility of salvation itself. Writing of modern America, Miller claims that "there is no need to be restrictive in admitting members [to towns and cities] . . . so long as ordinary people do not run them."[79] The inference to be drawn from this is that in Puritan communities, those who were members had real power, and so of course there is likely to be a more rigid set of standards than there would be if there were only the form of power rather than its actuality. The important political question thus becomes how membership was to be determined in a theology that used faith rather than works as its basis for justification. The answer is through the creation of an elaborate morphology of conversion that would allow the community to distinguish various stages in a person's journey to faith.[80]

This imposition of "temporal and recognizable signs," including the one that held that while works could not be taken as definitive, they were allowable as evidence of God working through man toward grace,[81] rationalized the process and unveiled the mysteries surrounding the conversion experience. In turn this institutionalization of the morphology made membership available to a significant number of people. Morgan, in fact, argues that within ten years the practice was so standardized that the conversion narratives used to show the existence of grace were becoming almost indistinguishable from each other both within towns and between towns.[82] Not until later, when membership was expanding and problems within the church arose, did restrictions became more cumbersome. This is not to say that the conversion process was becoming liberalized in the sense of being open to all—it still required that persons seeking membership submit themselves to the standards demanded of church members, which was not easy. But once their character was formed, and the goals of the community internalized, they were quite free to participate in the decision-making process. Thus, in answer to the question of who could participate, the Puritans said "those who share our goals and values." Membership was thus democratized without being liberalized.

MORE WEIGHT, PLEASE

Near the close of Arthur Miller's play *The Crucible* (1952), Elizabeth Proctor is describing the death of Giles, a man who was pressed between two enormous stones in an attempt to gain his confession, and who, when asked at the crucial moment whether he would confess to the stated crimes, said to his persecutors, "More weight, please." The typical response of a modern reader is to recoil in horror and to withdraw any legitimacy or sympathy from a community that would commit such atrocities against its members. And in many ways this would seem like the correct response. But what if, for the moment, we were to reframe the picture and ask a different question: What type of community could produce such a man in the first place? We know, using Miller, that Giles is but one of many who chose death rather than confess—including the protagonist John Proctor, who only at the end truly earns the audience's respect.

Thus it was not merely an act of individual conscience at work. Something more is involved, for somehow these people had been able to cling to their commitments even in the face of injustice and torture. It is important to note that John Proctor was not killed because he would not confess, but because he would not betray the others when asked. Even at the price of his own life, he would not forsake the bonds he felt, the loyalty he had learned—even when the formal structure of the community itself was gone and there was little if anything left to save. The question this brief overview is meant to raise is simple: Could a Giles or a Proctor have been created in a culture or community that was radically different from the one in which they lived and died? If the answer is "no," then it may be important to ask whether we should discard such communities or make them impossible—even when they also might create the persecutors. This is one of the questions that I believe is at the heart of American Anti-Federalism later in our political history, and it is this Puritan legacy that provides much of the context for that body of thought.

Political Liberation as American Theology

. . . our ancestors, before their emigration to America, were the free inhabitants of the British dominions in Europe, and possessed a right, which nature has given to all men, of departing from the country in which chance, not choice has placed them, of going in quest of new habitations, and of establishing new societies, under such laws and regulations as to them shall seem most likely to promote public happiness.

—Thomas Jefferson

Ferdinand Tönnies suggested that an important distinction existed between the entities community and society. The former, he claimed, was the product or reflection of man's natural will *(Wesenwille)* and included the family, the friendship group, and religion. The latter was the product of man's rational will *(Kurwille)* and included the university, business, and especially the modern state.[1] This dichotomy is modernized in the contemporary work of Jane Mansbridge when she draws her distinctions between "unitary" and "adversarial" forms of association.[2] I say "modernized" because, unlike Tönnies, Mansbridge recognizes the importance and desirability of equality. Whereas Tönnies believed equality to be a dangerous symptom of a twentieth-century pathos that inevitably aided in the creation of the total state,[3] Mansbridge, though certainly not a leveler, recognizes that without some sort of rough equality between group members in terms of respect and power, true community becomes improbable if not impossible.[4] Perhaps the transitional or mediating theorist here is Hannah Arendt, who shares in Tönnies's legitimate anxiety over the rise of the "social" to the detriment of both the public and the private spheres, while at the same time embracing the ideal of an Aristotelian ethic in which the realm of citizenship is marked by its lack of rulers and ruled.[5] This distinction between community and society, coupled with the role established for equality, is important to this volume and in many ways looms throughout its pages.

In the previous chapter I suggested that Puritanism in America, as both a religious and a political project, represented an effort at clearing away the obstacles to community. This attempt included both the removal of certain barriers, such as the centralized authority of the Anglican Church and the British monarch through exodus or revolution, and the construction of newer forms of community and authority designed to fill in the "chinks and gaps" linked to the creation of the "city upon the hill." I also suggested that within the newly constructed communities, equality was coming to play an increasingly important role in terms of participation in public life. This in turn allowed me to claim that at its core Calvinism, including the important practical adaptations and theoretical extensions of the French Huguenots and the American Puritans, was indeed the forerunner of modern conceptions of political community, where modern political community was earmarked by notions of consent, voluntarism, fundamental law, resistance to unlawful authority, and expanded participation in political life.

In light of the discussion above, the question with regard to emerging political thought in America is whether that thought seeks to reform and extend traditional relationships that would anchor that thought in *gemeinschaft,* or whether those reformations and extensions amount to a transformation of the political project into one of *gesellschaft.* In what follows, I will begin by attempting to make a prima facie defense of the Puritan religious/political project as one of reformation and extension. I will then elaborate what I see as the relationship between those reformations and extensions and the political thought and practice in colonial America, and try to illustrate how those practices and that thought are related to the movement toward American independence and the subsequent revolution. To make that case, I will then explore in some detail the way in which those theoretical and practical changes are embodied in Jefferson's Declaration of Independence.

MODELS OF REVOLUTION

Although Michael Walzer's contribution to our understanding of Calvinist and Puritan radicalism is substantial, the extrapolations he makes from his analysis are flawed in an important way. His argument is that the Calvinist and Puritan saints are best understood as "rootless intellectuals," who appeared at a time of social and political instability and set about forging a new order to replace the old. Hence he refers to the saints as political entrepreneurs waging a violent attack on customary procedures and engaging in a political experimentation with an ethos that he suggests is akin to political free play.[6] Given such a view of the saints and their activities, it is no wonder that Walzer feels comfortable suggesting that they were the forerunners of such revolutionary groups as the Jacobins and the Bolsheviks. But is this really the case? And if it is the case, what, if any, is the relationship between Puritan thought and the developments in colonial America and the American Revolution?

Whether one sees the American Revolution through the conservative eyes of Edmund Burke, or through the liberal eyes of Louis Hartz, there is always some important element that makes it difficult to integrate a particular vision of that revolution with the revolutions that followed it, such as the French and the Russian. Even Crane Brinton, who appears to have no particular ideological ax to grind, cannot make the American Revolution fit neatly into his typology.[7] Despite these difficulties and, more important, despite the proximity of the Puritan ideas and activities to America—which, one would think, would provide the logical historical context for the extension of their thought— Walzer never (at least not that I am aware of) deals with the American revolutionary question. If he did, I am afraid he would have to rethink the inferences he draws and the linkages he suggests between the revolutions of the saints and the revolutions of the Jacobins and Bolsheviks in some very important ways.

This is important, because under Walzer's model the saints are removing the obstacles to society, whereas under the model presented here they are removing the obstacles to community; politically and historically speaking, the differences between those two is enormously significant. The former view places the Puritans at the forefront of a historical movement that sought to destroy older forms of association that had been deemed natural or organic, and allowed to function in the name of a repressive feudal order, in favor of a progressive, rational political order in which institutional arrangements were substituted for human participation. This new arrangement was meant eventually to free the individual from civic responsibility, and thus free the public sphere as much as possible from the potential for human error—or, worse, the irrationality or the tyranny associated with the more personal forms of feudal association.[8]

The latter view, my view, of the Puritans is quite different. Here the Puritans are indeed tearing themselves away from those older forms of community, but they are not doing so under the mistaken belief that all forms of community are somehow pathological and inimical to progress. Instead, they are forging an altogether new, and perhaps modern, form of community, a form constructed or invented from natural elements,[9] rather than strictly organic. Yet this constructed community is not simply the product of unattached individuals banding together for mutual benefit and protection, as in the liberal model of the state or community. Instead, it is a banding together for the sake of an enriched social and political life to fulfill, as one social theorist might say, "desires for cultural participation, social belonging, and personal status [which had] become irresistible and their frustrations galling."[10] This description is a defining characteristic of the notion of "public happiness" developed later in the chapter. This distinction is especially important—indeed, critical—if we are properly to understand America, its revolution, and how that event is theoretically related to the thought and actions of its first English settlers.

Michael Walzer described the nature of his work in the following manner:

> The moral and political arguments I make are mostly accounts of common experi-
> ences, versions of shared worlds—analytic, interpretive, apologetic, and critical. They
> are aimed in the first instance at my fellow inhabitants, then at men and women who
> are sometime fellows, whose worlds overlap with mine. . . . I make no claim like the
> claim of religious or political missionaries to deliver entire and objective truth to
> them, such that once they hear it they will have nothing to do but repeat it. . . . I
> take seriously Isaiah's notion that Jews should be "a light unto nations." But note,
> please, that there is no definite article in that phrase: *a* light, not *the* light.[11]

Those acquainted with Walzer's body of work should find that brief summation of his overall political project familiar and comfortable. It is a project
to which I myself am deeply sympathetic. This is the view of political theory
as conversation and political activity as repair. The best modern philosophical
statement and defense of this position is Michael Oakeshott's essay "Rationalism in Politics," in which he attacks the politics of technique, or public administration, that are representative of what he calls the rationalist project.

> How deeply the rationalist disposition of mind has invaded our political thought and
> practice is illustrated by the extent to which traditions of behavior have given place
> to ideologies, the extent to which the politics of destruction and creation have substi-
> tuted for the politics of repair, the consciously planned and deliberately executed
> being considered (for that reason) better than what has grown up and established
> itself unselfconsciously over a period of time.[12]

In this we can hear an earlier version of Walzer's voice and draw conclusions
similar to those of Gilbert Meilaender when he sums up Walzer's position:
"For Walzer the political radical will almost always seem too committed to
remaking particular people and communities in the name of some universal—
and presumably more rational—ideal."[13] Meilaender goes on to suggest that
for Walzer, that sort of criticism fails "because it does not embody love for
what is given." He sums up that section of the essay by claiming that this is the
"insight of an essentially conservative thinker."[14] Given all of this, however,
the question that remains is whether the Puritans are indeed a proper subject
against which to level that brand of criticism. Here is where Walzer and I part
company.

Certainly there was a degree of ruthlessness and a large measure of contempt
on the part of the Puritan exiles. And certainly they believed they had come
to a more profound set of truths regarding communal organization, but this
alone is not enough to place them historically where Walzer does. Sometimes
clearing the obstacles to community can be a messy and even revolutionary
task, depending on how impervious those obstacles in fact are. To judge acts

of liberation, no matter how ruthless or destructive, we must look at the substantive nature of the acts by probing the intentions of the actors and asking what the liberation is for. If it is to establish the world anew and reconstitute the political order as a utopia spawned only in the minds or speeches of men and women, without any historical grounding, then the project is indeed dangerous and ought to be rejected as far too risky. This, I think, is the deeper meaning of Plato's *Republic,* as well as the lesson of the French, Russian, and Chinese revolutions. But if the object is to create a space where true community is possible—that is, free public space—then the project is legitimate despite the contempt one has for what is given.

In her book *On Revolution,* Hannah Arendt offers an interesting conceptual tool that may help us escape from Walzer's conundrum: her distinction between "intellectuals" and what she calls *hommes de lettres* (men of letters). The former she describes as

> a class of professional scribes and writers whose labors are needed by the ever-expanding bureaucracies of modern government and business administration . . . [who were used] for the building up of a body of specialized knowledge and procedures indispensable for the growing operation of their governments on all levels, a process which stresses the esoteric character of governmental activities.[15]

The men of letters, on the other hand,

> resented nothing more than secrecy in public affairs; they had started their career by refusing this sort of governmental service and withdrawing from society. . . . They educated themselves and cultivated their minds in freely chosen seclusion. . . . the public realm was invisible to them.[16]

What distinguished the men of letters from others denied access to the public realm was that their exclusion was self-chosen (unlike the exclusion of the poor). In Arendt's words, "Their personal distinction lay precisely in the fact that they had refused to settle in 'the land of consideration,' opting instead for the secluded obscurity of privacy where they could at least entertain and nourish their passion for significance and freedom."[17] Perhaps another way to think about this distinction would be to compare a similar discussion in the work of Julien Benda when he distinguishes between his intellectuals as "clerks" before and after the great betrayal.[18] Though Arendt used this distinction in order to help her differentiate the men who made the French Revolution from the men who made the American Revolution, it is useful to our present discussion as well.

If Arendt's intellectuals are attached to the state in order to rationalize its workings while mystifying its nature, then we might ask what such people would do if they were unattached to any particular government. The answer, I think, would be to become what Walzer calls rootless intellectuals who seek to create the conditions that will allow them to flourish as attached intellectuals again, perhaps even as rulers. This project is conceptually very different from the project of Arendt's men of letters, who seek to create space for action but not to erect any particular monument for themselves or to themselves. The question, for the purpose of this volume, is whether Walzer's description fits the English Puritans. The answer, I am afraid, is "no."

Arendt's image of the man of letters seems much more applicable perhaps not to Cromwell but to John Winthrop, and perhaps even to John Calvin, not to mention the generation of American revolutionaries who followed. The goal of the Puritans was not to carry into existence a full-blown, rationalized utopian order but, rather, to create the social and political conditions in which answers to the questions of public life could be worked out through conversation and action among an expanded class of citizen saints. We should note that in Winthrop's sermon there is also the lack of a definite article; they were interested in forming *a* city on the hill, not *the* city on the hill. It is this distinction that, I think, rescues the Puritans in America from the historical company in which Walzer would place them, and perhaps allows us to link them with their true political heirs—the Americans. And though it may seem a little strange at this late date to claim that the American revolutionary experience is different in many important ways from those that preceded it as well as those that followed, perhaps the truth of the matter is that the only category into which Jefferson and company fit neatly is an exclusive one. To clarify this point, it might be helpful to examine an important, though ultimately mistaken, view of the Revolution, and then to cast the American Revolution in its appropriate context.

There is an important school of American historical/political thought represented by Louis Hartz, Richard Hofstadter, and John Diggins that sometimes is called the "consensus" school.[19] These writers, though distinct in many ways, share a basic idea concerning the American Revolution: that the Revolution was liberal in nature. The first two, especially Hartz, argue this against the backdrop of twentieth-century revolutions and thus limit themselves too readily to a liberal/radical dichotomy. In other words, for someone like Louis Hartz, using a quasi-Marxist framework, there were only two kinds of revolution: a liberal or bourgeois revolution that emancipated individuals and property from an oppressive feudal order à la Adam Smith and John Locke (on Hartz's reading of America's reading of Locke and Smith, at least), or an egalitarian or democratic revolution (read socialist revolution) that sought to overthrow the individualist/capitalist order that had been built on the ruins of the feudal order.

Given the lack of a feudal order to overthrow in America, and with no desire to level society, Hartz is left with an event that resists his basic revolutionary dichotomy and thus is forced to introduce his model of American exceptionalism as his explanatory device. What Hartz fails to ponder is the existence of an older conception and tradition of revolution that transcends his dichotomy. That older tradition might be called a republican form of revolution, a revolution that seeks neither to emancipate individuals and property, and set them in opposition to the public sphere, nor to level society and redistribute property and wealth. Instead, it is a revolution that seeks to remove the barriers to public life and political activity, and to create an expanded realm of public freedom, without necessarily dictating the course or direction that those newly admitted citizens must take in the course of their public conversations. While I am willing to grant that this period was short, I do believe that it did exist. Thus, although Hartz's analysis may be significant, especially in terms of the period after 1787, it fails to capture or explain the revolutionary ethos of 1776 with any sort of precision.

Among the difficulties faced by Hartz in sustaining a purely liberal interpretation of the American Revolution is the extraordinary amount of work that must be done by the term "property." For the Revolution to be "conservative of liberalism," it would also have to be conservative of a definition of property as a specifically private thing that adhered to individuals by virtue of their labor or some other such device, and that could be used by them as they saw fit, provided they did no direct harm to other individuals and their property. This is the definition that has been popularly ascribed to John Locke and represents the basis for Hartz's American Locke. It is, however, not necessarily the correct conception of the term for the historical period in question.[20]

Here the more recent work of Forrest McDonald provides an interesting linguistic lesson that is quite useful and allows us to place Locke in a more appropriate context:

> . . . the word *property* had more meanings than one. In its older and more general sense it was related to the word *proper,* derived from the Latin *proprius,* meaning particular to, or appropriate to, an individual person. John Locke usually (though not invariably) used the term in that way. In the more restricted and more common usage, by the late eighteenth century property had come to be related to the idea of dominion, derived from the Latin *dominus,* meaning lordship, and ultimately from *domus,* meaning house. . . . Under English law, every such dominion originated in, was dependent upon, and was held of some superior lord. . . . The broadest set of limitations upon private ownership involved rights that were reserved to the public in its corporate or governmental capacity. These included the power to regulate economic activity in the public interest.[21]

Thus the idea of property would seem to be less a private construct that adhered to individuals in their capacity as private persons and more related to classical notions of public and private, in which property was the source of a citizen's independence and could be used to claim membership in the political or public realm. This is exactly the classical republican definition of property as well as the basis for political protection of those property rights; it is also the only definition that, given the available lines of discourse, makes any real sense. The inference here that most readers should draw, then, is that it would have been difficult to fight a revolution based upon a set of concepts that were at best only beginning to come into existence, and that had not yet been given any real substantive content, politically speaking. The question was not whether property rights were important so much as *why* they were important, since there is obviously a substantive difference between a defense of property against the rights of the community and a defense of property as necessary to sustain community.

This relationship among independence, property, and citizenship is at least as old as Aristotle's *Politics*. In the simplest sense the difference between classical and neoclassical views of property and modern views of property comes down to whether one sees property as a means or an end. In other words, do you own property for the sake of personal wealth and enjoyment, or does property confer a certain social standing and provide you with access to public life? The latter view is the republican view. The former is typically associated with what we call liberalism. The republican view is associated with the notion of public happiness, the right to participate as a citizen, while liberalism is more consonant with what we would call private happiness or personal welfare. Drawing on the work of Caroline Robbins,[22] who traced the teachings of classical republican thinkers like Polybius and Machiavelli to the great English Whigs like John Milton, James Harrington, Algernon Sydney, John Trenchard, and Thomas Gordon, and setting his work against that of C. B. Macphearson[23] and Hugh R. Trevor-Roper,[24] J. G. A. Pocock argues this very point with regard to the work of Harrington and his *Oceana* (1656).[25]

Whereas the other interpretations attempted to place Harrington at the forefront of economic liberalism, Pocock contends that he was in reality concerned with the transmission and progression of a much older political tradition: republicanism as derived from Machiavelli's *Discourses*. Pocock's Harrington is a "country" Whig, and the "country" vision held that

> Society is made up of court and country; government, of court and Parliament; Parliament, of court and country members. The court is the administration. The country consists of the men of independent property; all others are servants. The business of Parliament is to preserve the independence of property, on which is founded all human liberty and all human excellence. The business of administration is to govern, and this is a legitimate activity; but to govern is to wield power, and power has a natural tendency to encroach. It is more important to supervise government than to support it, because the preservation of independence is the ultimate political good. There exists an ancient constitution in England, which consists in a balance or equilibrium between the various organs of government, and within this balance the function of Parliament is to supervise the executive. But the executive possesses means of distracting Parliament from its proper function; it seduces members by the offer of places and pensions, by retaining them to follow ministers and

ministers' rivals, by persuading them to support measures—standing armies, national debts, excise schemes—whereby the activities of administration grow beyond Parliament's control. These means of subversion are known collectively as corruption, and if ever Parliament or those who elect them should be wholly corrupt, then there will be an end of independence and liberty. The remedy for corruption is to expel placemen, to ensure that members of Parliament become in no way entangled in the pursuit of power or the exercise of administration, and to see to it that parliaments are frequently elected by uncorrupted voters.[26]

Property thus became the means by which an individual entered the public realm, since it was the source of independence, which in turn was the source of citizenship. Government, then, was necessary but dangerous, in that power corrupts; and corruption was the act of taking away the foundation of one's citizenship—independence—which could be done by threatening one's property. Hence property was defended not for its own sake but for the sake of what it represented: one's right to participate in the public realm—a right, in other words, to public happiness. While it may be the case that the Whig defense of property embodied in the teachings of Harrington and his interpreter Pocock may have set the stage for the liberal conception of property to emerge at a later date, that was not the intended consequence.[27] Given this, it becomes very difficult to miss the relationship between the thought of Jefferson and others who shared his vision, or were perhaps even more radical (like Thomas Paine), and those country Whigs—and thus the relationship between that opposition ideology and the American Revolution.

The discourse of the American Revolution was a republican discourse of moral corruption and decline with regard to the British, and redemption and regeneration (in the religious sense) with regard to the Americans. The English had shown their propensity toward avarice and luxury, and were threatening to corrupt the Americans. The only way to protect one's soul was to defend the collective soul against this newly revealed devil. The Revolution, according to Gordon Wood, was couched in terms of moral reformation: Americans had been infected by British agents and their corruption—"The Crown actually seemed to be bent on changing the character of American society," which, though naturally suited for virtue, was not necessarily predestined to it.[28] "Everywhere men appeared to be seeking the preferment of royal authority, eager to sell their country for a smile, or some ministerial office."[29] The only way to avoid contamination was to cast out the unregenerate—who in a Puritanical manner had been warned repeatedly by the colonists of the dangers inherent in their actions. The language of conspiracy was everywhere, and the British government, through its colonial representatives, was the source.[30] While it was possible that the various Tea and Stamp acts were simple legislative mistakes, the Wilkes affair, the stationing of troops, the interference with judges and colonial legislatures, and the eventual use of violence made it perfectly clear to the colonists that the corruption was premeditated and that the British were unrepentant.[31] Bernard Bailyn captures the colonial response to British corruption in the following passage:

> It was an elevating, transforming vision: a new, fresh, vigorous, and above all morally regenerate people rising from obscurity to defend the battlements of liberty and then in triumph standing forth, heartening and sustaining the cause of freedom everywhere. . . . Americans stood side by side with the heroes of historic battles for freedom and with the few remaining champions of liberty in the present.[32]

These sentiments are perhaps nowhere more evident than in the work of Thomas Paine, who tells his readers that "the cause of America is in a great measure the cause of all mankind."[33] But it was not an individualist liberty that was being defended; instead, it was the Winthropian civil or federal liberty, the "liberty to that only which is good." Americans were not freeing themselves from government, they were freeing their governments from the oppression and moral bankruptcy of another government. When Thomas Paine exclaimed, "Society is produced by our wants, and government by our wickedness; the former promotes our happiness positively by uniting our affections,"[34] it was a defense of community against tyranny, not a defense of individual license. Those corrupting influences and individuals who were standing in the way of a true political/moral community had to be cleared away to make what had been the case for the last 150 years possible again. Which is exactly what the Revolution was intended to do.

It is perhaps not surprising that the American Revolution has been something like a historiographical/political Rorschach test, something that varies from person to person; or perhaps it is better compared to the Wizard of Oz, who could be all things to all people. It was after all a complex event involving millions of people from two continents, thirteen colonies, and hundreds of local communities, whose elites were often personally confused and interpersonally engaged in serious disagreements with their local and intralocal counterparts. Thus questions and answers concerning the rationale and the meaning of that all-important event are bound to be highly contested and very heterogeneous.[35] After confronting the contemporary scholarly literature surrounding the Revolution, Robert Shalhope, drawing on the work of Clifford Geertz, Kenneth Burke, and Erik Erikson,[36] offered a suggestion for navigating the maze related to the role of "ideas," and thus ideology, in the American revolutionary period, a suggestion that does not discount the work of historians with alternative approaches to that event:

> Just as one needs a map when traveling through strange territory, so, too, one requires a sociopsychological guide at times. Ideology functions in such a way as to make possible a clearly defined political movement by providing "the authoritative concepts that render it meaningful, the suasive images by means of which it can be

sensibly grasped." . . . Thus in the final analysis, ideologies constitute "maps of problematic social reality and matrices for the creation of collective conscience."[37]

Despite whatever intracolonial as well as intercolonial differences there
might have been, and no matter how important some of those finer distinctions
become to micropolitical developments, the macrocontext of the American
Revolution, the ideology (used in a cultural sense here) that provides the map
to the "problematic social reality" of the American revolutionary period and
the "matrices of collective conscience," clearly is "republicanism." And within
that ideology the definitive construct for the purpose of this volume is the idea
of "public happiness."

PUBLIC HAPPINESS

Michael Oakeshott writes, "The heart of the matter is the preoccupation of
the Rationalist with certainty. Technique and certainty are, for him, inseparably joined because certain knowledge is, for him, knowledge which does not
require to look beyond itself for its certainty."[38] There are two enemies of the
rationalist political project—diversity and the public freedom that makes it
possible. Both of these represent disorder and uncertainty, and make life less
and less amenable to bureaucratic organization and its vision of politics by
administration and problem solving. This is the antithesis of the view of politics
as action and of political life as the source of human transformation, and perhaps even secular redemption, presented in chapter 1. That republican vision
required the active participation by citizens in a public conversation about
their shared collective life, not the transfer of power to technicians. In the case
of the former, there would cease to be citizens in any meaningful sense of the
term; and along with their disappearance comes the contraction, if not the
complete destruction, of the public realm. This is what Hannah Arendt be-
moans as the rise of the social and the collapse of both the public realm and
the private. She claims that the most social form of government is bureaucracy,
which she calls the "rule by nobody" and goes on to describe as "not necessarily no-rule," and to contend that "it may indeed, under certain circumstances,
even turn out to be one of the cruelest and most tyrannical" forms of government imaginable.[39] She argues that a defining trait of society is that

> on all its levels [it] excludes the possibility of action. . . . Instead, society expects from
> each of its members a certain kind of behavior, imposing innumerable and various
> rules, all of which tend to "normalize" its members, to make them behave, to ex-
> clude spontaneous action or outstanding achievement.[40]

It is important to keep in mind that even political/social constructions that
acknowledge diversity and do not attempt to erase it but, rather, to control it

either institutionally or ideologically, are no less stagnant in terms of the question of public freedom. Roger Williams could allow religious toleration in Rhode Island only by separating the church from political life, and thereby making it irrelevant in terms of public life; and James Madison's pluralism is really no more than an act of resignation that certainly could never be called an embrace of diversity. As Michael Oakeshott reminds us with his example of Hayek's *Road to Serfdom,* its main significance is not "the cogency of his doctrine, but the fact that it is a doctrine. A plan to resist planning may be better than its opposite, but it belongs to the same style of politics."[41]

It is the emphasis on the social question, or simple well-being, that causes Arendt to lament much of modern political thought.[42] This emphasis flows from the assumptions of political thinkers like Thomas Hobbes who argued that what people wanted was not public power, participatory rights, or glory but security—which subsequently became not simply one aspect of governmental responsibility but almost the whole of it. For most men and women living in the modern liberal world, the term "happiness" refers to one's personal, and therefore private, satisfactions. Governments for many of those people are instituted to protect them in their private pursuits. Revolutions in turn are the result of government failing to protect the rights of the individual or the product of the anxieties and demands of the many to break down class barriers that prevent them from sharing in the wealth and security that would make their individual, and therefore private, happiness possible.

Modern revolutions, starting perhaps with the French, but particularly twentieth-century revolutions, at least until those of the late 1980s and early 1990s in eastern Europe, almost all collapsed into what Arendt might call a "social," or what Oakeshott might call a "rationalist," paradigm. They were "stillborn" because they had surrendered freedom to necessity—"the revolution(s) had changed [their] direction(s); [they] aimed no longer at freedom, the goal of the revolution(s) had become the happiness of the people."[43] And the happiness of the people had come to mean that they were dressed, fed, and taken care of—enslaved, perhaps, but happy.

In countries where this particular brand of revolution did not occur, the problem was no less acute; it was simply different in form. Here liberalism—perverted, perhaps—with its emphasis on individualism, private property, and rights, is the culprit. As Arendt suggests:

> What we called earlier the rise of the social coincided historically with the transformation of private care for private property into a public concern. Society, when it first entered the public realm, assumed the disguise of an organization of property owners who, instead of claiming access to the public realm because of their wealth, demanded protection from it for the accumulation of more wealth.[44]

But this was not always the case. There was a form of happiness that was not linked to one's private welfare and well-being. It was a happiness that was dependent not on what one owned or how secure one felt but a happiness that depended upon having a share in the construction of something larger than a particular individual. The idea of "public happiness" was the idea of something directed at more than personal satisfaction. Public happiness was the feeling one can gain only in conjunction with well-received and respected public activity before one's peers. Whereas private happiness could be gained in the context of the home, family, and work, public happiness could be found only in the political realm of equals engaging in conversation and action about the life of the community, and perhaps the good life itself. Public happiness, compared with private happiness,

> consisted in the citizen's right of access to the public realm, in his share of public power—to be a participator in the government of affairs . . . as distinct from the generally recognized rights of subjects to be protected by the government in the pursuit of private happiness even against public power.[45]

In America prior to the Revolution, and at the base of the Revolution, there was a conception of public happiness that had extended from the first British settlers throughout the colonies, particularly in New England and the Middle Atlantic regions. As Thomas Jefferson contended in a 1774 essay, "A Summary View of the Rights of British America":

> . . . our ancestors, before their emigration to America, were the free inhabitants of the British dominions in Europe, and possessed a right, which nature has given to all men, of departing from the country in which chance, not choice has placed them, of going in quest of new habitations, and of establishing new societies, under such laws and regulations as to them shall seem most likely to promote public happiness.[46]

Although those sentiments are not necessarily democratic, they are republican in that they take as the appropriate end of political community the construction of an order directed at the common good. But if we were to tease out the ideas within the passage a little, as well as to briefly look at other Jeffersonian sentiments, it would be impossible to say that a democratic polity was being ruled out. More likely, we would want to claim that it was, on some important level, being encouraged.

For instance, the rights of people to establish new societies clearly indicates that, at least at the level of foundation or constitution, there is a right to participate. And if that is the case, then it follows that the eventual form chosen could indeed be a democratic one, although certainly other possibilities remain. Yet somehow Jefferson's work suggests that he believes people are capable of governing themselves and that it would be good for them to do so. In various letters he argues on behalf of the people and the importance of their participation in the affairs of public life. He wrote to George Wythe (1786): "No other sure foundation can be devised for the preservation of freedom, and happiness.

If anybody thinks that kings, nobles, or priests are good conservators of the public happiness, send them here. It is the best school in the universe to cure them of that folly."[47] And he wrote to Edward Carrington (1787): "I am persuaded myself that the good sense of the people will always be found to be the best army. They may be led astray for a moment, but will soon correct themselves."[48]

This faith in the people was not blind, however. What was certain was Jefferson's faith in public education, which did not just mean "available to all" but, more important, "required of all citizens"—an education similar to the moral education supported by Aristotle—which would create the proper character and disposition in those charged with making public decisions. This is evidenced by Jefferson's important assertion, "I know of no safe depository of the ultimate power of society but the people themselves, and if we think them not enlightened enough to exercise their control with a wholesome discretion, the remedy is not to take it from them, but to inform their discretion."[49]

Note that the term Jefferson uses is "discretion," which is a far cry from the image that a more modern term like "political education" might evoke. Jefferson's notion of political education was not education in a technique or in administration but an education for what Michael Oakeshott would call an "appropriate connoisseurship."[50] It is the kind of practical knowledge that can "neither be learned nor taught, but only imparted and acquired. It exists only in practice, and the only way to acquire it is by apprenticeship to a master—not because the master can teach it, but because it can be acquired only by continuous contact.[51]

This was an early rejection of the idea that "political machinery can take the place of moral and political education,"[52] or that administrators could replace citizens. It was an assertion that what was necessary for a viable political community was public activity and participation in the public sphere. We can know the value Jefferson placed on that participation in public life by referring to his sentiments a few years before his death in the closing of a letter to John Adams in which he wishes, "May we meet there [heaven] again, in Congress, with our antient Colleagues."[53] What he will miss at his death and all that he appears to hope for in the afterlife is the opportunity to engage his fellows once again in the colosseum of public debate and discourse. It is a wish for a happiness that is not possible in private life, and a wish, Jefferson would say, that any who were allowed to know would never cease to desire. But whether the institutional arrangements of his nation would maintain the conditions necessary for that wish to be enjoyed by others is the question.

THE PURSUIT OF HAPPINESS

We can confirm Jefferson's historical assertions concerning the rights of British settlers by noting the early charters and "constitutions" those people established once they reached the shores of America. Among the earliest of those documents is the Letters Patent to Sir Humfrey Gylbert (1578), which grant Gylbert and his heirs

> free liberty and license from time to time, and at all times for ever hereafter, to discover, find, search out, and view such remote, heathen and barbarous lands, countries, and territories not actually possessed of any Christian prince . . . from then, have full and mere power and authority to correct, punish, pardon, govern and rule by their, and every or any other of their good discretions.[54]

Other documents of the early colonial period share this set of rights to organize and govern as necessary, including the Mayflower Compact (1620), which states in its first substantive paragraph:

> Having undertaken, for the Glory of God and advancement of the Christian faith and Honor of our King and Country, a Voyage to plant the First Colony in the Northern Parts of Virginia, [we] do by these presents solemnly and mutually in the presence of God and one of another, Covenant and Combine ourselves together into a Civil Body Politic, for our better ordering and preservation and furtherance of the ends aforesaid; and by virtue hereof to enact, constitute and frame such just and equal Laws, Ordinances, Acts, Constitutions and Offices, from time to time, as shall be thought most meet and convenient for the general good of the Colony.[55]

Finally, the Fundamental Orders of Connecticut (1639) represents one of the first attempts at an actual written constitution in America. Like the others it claims

> that to maintain the peace and union of such a people there should be an orderly and decent government established according to God, to order and dispose of the affairs of the people at all seasons as occasion shall require; do therefore associate and combine ourselves to be as one Public State or Commonwealth . . . to maintain and preserve the liberty. . . .[56]

The list and citations could include some seventy-six other documents listed by Donald Lutz (which he says is only a partial list).[57] Each of those documents takes for granted the rights of members to organize themselves into a body politic of some kind and to commence the process of policing themselves for their common good. In terms of the ancient English Constitution, and what one writer has called "Tudor Traditionalism," the following was true of the English principles and institutions in general:

> . . . the idea of the organic union of society and the government, the harmony of authorities within government, the subordination of government to fundamental law, the intermingling of the legal and political realms the balance of powers (royal

executive and the legislative embodiment of the people), the complementary representative roles of these two bodies, the reliance on the militia for the defense of the realm and the vitality of local governmental authorities.[58]

Hence the idea of local control and decentralized authority was part and parcel of the English experience, but more important, and to a much greater degree, given the distance between the colonies and England, a crucial part of the early American experience. And if historical precedent is not enough, there is the commonsense argument that, given the dangers and risks of the journey to America, "It would have been foolish to expect anyone to emigrate if he had little or no control over matters in which he had invested his livelihood, indeed his life."[59] Furthermore, although many had come for financial gain, as is evidenced by the corporate nature of their journey, we know that for a good many of those pilgrims the journey had been undertaken to save their souls. That project demanded that they have the power to construct their own social and political worlds.

As alluded to in chapter 1 this religious project led early on to an expansion of the realm of political participation for the saints and other early settlers in the New World. The community depended upon the fundamental agreement between its citizens, and gaining that agreement without force or coercion meant that as many people as possible would have to be brought into the fold. The eventual failure of those early experiments came only after the rights of participation were contracted. Michael Zuckerman has argued along these lines in his work on eighteenth-century New England towns.[60] He suggests that the reason for such an expansion of participation rights was the "absence of any satisfactory means of traditional or institutional coercion," which in turn meant that "the recalcitrant could not be compelled to adhere to a common course of action. Therefore the common course of action had to be shaped [so] as to leave no one recalcitrant—that was the vital function of the New England town meeting."[61] This allows us to mark those early communities as examples of unitary democratic forms of political association that Jane Mansbridge describes in the following way:

> . . . the central assumption of unitary democracy is that, while its members may initially have conflicting preferences about a given issue, goodwill, mutual understanding, and rational discussion can lead to the emergence of a common enlightened preference that is good for everyone.[62]

Given that the role of the crown and Parliament was by and large nonexistent in America for most of its history, the colonists had devised a shadow polity or counterpolity that functionally, though not substantively, mirrored all British political institutions and relationships. Events in England had conspired for much of the seventeenth and eighteenth centuries to leave the colonies and colonists free to invent, construct, and tinker with political relationships appropriate to the setting in which they found themselves. This period of "salutary neglect" saw the rise of politically independent people engaged in governing, and therefore ruling themselves most often at the local level.[63] This opportunity, coupled with the notion of community as voluntary compact, the lack of institutional coercion with the corresponding stress on consensus, the expansion of participation rights,[64] the stated communitarian goals toward which that participation was directed, the emphasis placed on corruption and mutual watchfulness, the relative abundance of property in America (allowing for an independent citizenry), and the relatively small size and face-to-face nature of each community represent virtually every major component of substantive republicanism imaginable. The only thing missing from the equation can be inferred from a statement by James Lovell in 1771: "Free people were not those who were merely spared actual oppression, but those who have a constitutional check upon the power to oppress."[65] And this was a power that events in America eventually conspired to create.

HAPPINESS AND THE REVOLUTION

There are literally thousands of original essays, sermons, broadsides, and books through which one could wade in a quest to understand the nature of the American Revolution,[66] as many fine historians like Gordon Wood have indeed done. But for the purpose of my argument I would like to look to what is perhaps the most general and best-known revolutionary document, the Declaration of Independence, and provide a close reading of that text as a way of tying together the various thematic threads that run through this chapter. Although there are many possible approaches to that text,[67] I will simply attempt to provide a reading in line with the historical context, the political/ cultural orientation, and the views of Jefferson developed in the preceding pages. I take the cue for my reading of the Declaration from Hannah Arendt, who suggests that Jefferson's use of the term "pursuit of happiness" in the Declaration, though perhaps a little ambiguous, was intended to signify not the role of government in protecting people in their private pursuits, nor the idea that government was somehow to make people happy by responding to the "social question," but the idea of citizen participation in public affairs, as discussed earlier.[68] It is a suggestion borne out by the context in which it was written, by its author's predisposition, and, more important, by the text itself.

It is important when approaching political documents from this period in history to keep in mind the specific nature of the language employed. For modern discussants the term "government" is used quite loosely and refers to everything and everyone involved with making, enforcing, and interpreting public laws and regulations. For those speaking the language of eighteenth-century Whiggism, however, the term "government" meant something much more specific.[69] "Society" (community in this volume) was separate from government in that it was represented in government as an entity unto itself by Parliament, which was composed of members from the "country" (independent citizens) and members of the "court" (the administration or government). The role of the country members was to maintain the independence of the various communities of independent citizens, while the role of the court members was to govern, to make sure the community interests did not factionalize or in any other way threaten the safety and well-being of the nation, which would not be in the king's interest or the interest of those other communities or citizens that might be harmed. This was depicted as a balanced regime.

If the government (the administration and the crown) attempted to interfere with the internal workings of a particular community in order to benefit itself in such a way as to harm the independence of that community (acting arbitrarily and without their consent), then the government was in fact corrupt and acting tyrannically. In such a case the government must be reformed or be liable to removal, not because it infringed on the rights of individuals but because it violated the rights of the collective by denying them access to the public realm. Thus either the collective's choices were not being represented in Parliament, or their right to govern at the local level was being usurped. So it was that in theory the government could be removed in a revolution without necessarily changing the fundamental basis of political life. The fact that the basis of political life will always change in a revolution, though important to acknowledge and eventually to understand, is in this case inconsequential to the act itself.

The reader is invited to compare this line of thought with Hutchinson and with John Locke. Thomas Hobbes *(Leviathan)* posited a single-step social contract whereby individuals moved from a violent state of nature to absolute rule of a sovereign in order to ensure their protection. John Locke *(The Second Treatise of Government)* theorized, and I think more realistically, a two-step exodus from the original condition. The first step for Locke was the move from nature to society, and the second step was the invention of a government. The key, for our purpose, is that society (community) was prior to and potentially independent from government, thus implying that the former could be sustained even in the absence of the latter. Locke argues as much when he claims:

> To conclude, the power that every individual gave the society when he entered into it can never revert to the individuals again so long as the society lasts, but will always remain in the community, because without this there can be no community . . . so also when the society has placed the legislative in any assembly of men . . . when by the miscarriages of those in authority it is forfeited . . . it reverts to the society.[70]

Dissolution of the government by whatever means does not return the members of a community as individuals to a state of nature; rather, it returns them to a state of society, with its customs, norms, mores, and even laws, to reinvent government. To return individuals to a state of nature would require that society itself be dissolved, which for Locke is typically possible only through the "sword of the conqueror."[71] Thus, even for Locke it is the case that government can be gotten rid of while community remains intact, thus implicitly suggesting a lexical ordering in terms of importance. It is in line with this sort of reasoning that I want to suggest we read Jefferson's Declaration of Independence.

Jefferson relates the following familiar sentiments in his famous document:

> We hold these truths to be self-evident, that all men are created equal; that they are endowed by their Creator with certain unalienable Rights, that among these are Life, Liberty, and the pursuit of Happiness.—That to secure these rights, Governments are instituted among Men, deriving their just powers from the consent of the governed,—That whenever any Form of Government becomes destructive of these ends, it is the Right of the People to alter or to abolish it, and to institute a new Government.[72]

This is perhaps the most-cited and best-known passage in the Declaration of Independence, and perhaps in the entire historical language of American political culture. Hence it is also among the most-debated passages in terms of its substantive meaning or its author's intentions. Within the passage the greatest source of conflict has arisen over the claim that "all men are created equal," followed closely by discussions concerning the meaning and extent of each of the inalienable rights, with a particular emphasis on the relationship between one's liberty and one's property.

Many of our most important political debates have been fought not simply within the confines of the legal framework of the Constitution but also within the moral framework of the Declaration, a procedure given credence by Lincoln. And yet any praise must be tempered by an understanding of the somewhat ahistorical use of the document by many of its boosters, and the often overtly partisan nature of those debates. Typically the passage cited above is considered the whole of the document in terms of substantive content, while the rest of it is seen simply as illustrative support—a laundry list, if you will—of how King George has deviated from the immutable moral code and why he must now be punished. The problem with such an approach, however, is that while it makes for an interesting and very important normative debate about moral guilt and retribution, it misses the significant and uniquely *political* aspects of the document.

This process of selective use misleadingly transforms what is in many ways an important text on the nature of politics and the proper basis for political life—a text about what is shared and public—into one concerned with what is individual and private. Thus it is transformed into a transcendental manifesto to be used by individuals against both community and government in a manner similar to the Bill of Rights. The historical difficulty with such a conflation, as well as the theoretical/political mistake, is that the Bill of Rights was never intended to apply to the community (state and local forms of political association) but, rather, to the national government.[73] The reasons for this are made clear by referencing the discussion above concerning the way in which the political realm was conceived in the eighteenth century. The theoretical mistake is to turn what is in reality a statement about collective political life into a statement about the rights of individuals. Although such a project is indeed admirable and important, it in many ways mystifies the nature of early American political thought through a process of amalgamation and generalization.

After having finished his introductory remarks, Jefferson moves on in the Declaration to specific claims of wrongdoing to which the king and Parliament have been party. It is here that we can truly begin to glimpse the political nature of the document by asking ourselves who or what has been harmed, and who or what is to benefit by the righting of the wrong. Jefferson writes, "The history of the present King of Great Britain is a history of repeated injuries and usurpations, all having in direct object the establishment of an absolute Tyranny over these States." In clear, straightforward prose Jefferson tells the world that it is the tyranny against the states that has caused this action. The states, which are representative of Locke's society or our community, the realms of republican association, are being treated arbitrarily or perhaps paternally—not, we should notice, *we the people,* though of course such actions affect us as individuals as well.

Jefferson goes on, "He has refused his Assent to Laws the most wholesome and necessary for the public good." The king is not simply ruling in an arbitrary manner, or using his power to legislate in an overbearing manner against the colonists; rather, he is refusing to allow *them* to pass laws within their states and local assemblies that would promote their public good. In other words, he is preventing them from doing what good republican citizens do, which is rule themselves properly.

Next, he writes, "He has forbidden his Governors to pass Laws of immediate and pressing importance, unless suspended in their operation till his Assent should be obtained; and, when so suspended, he has utterly neglected to attend to them." The king is not carrying out the tasks of the government by allowing the members of the court, his administrators, to perform their duties, and he is not performing his duties. The reader should note the idea of positive obligation implied in this brand of criticism; if, for example, a U.S. president vetoes a piece of legislation as "bad policy" or for some such reason, he is playing what many believe to be his adversarial political role. Here, however, there is an implication that, once teased out, suggests that the king's duty is not to sit in judgment of the laws passed by the local assembly but to direct his administrators to facilitate implementation of laws duly passed and deemed necessary.

The list continues: "He has refused to pass other Laws for the accommodation of large districts of people, unless those people would relinquish the right of Representation in the Legislature, a right inestimable to them and formidable to tyrants only." From the earlier discussions concerning the structure of English government, the reader should be able to decode this charge rather easily. Representation in the legislature was necessary, not because one's interests would be represented, as in our contemporary pluralist/adversarial model of political activity, but to ensure that the rights of the community and the independence of its citizens to govern themselves would be protected from usurpation or undue interference from the government. By losing representation, the citizenry was in danger of being reduced to a dependency of the crown, and thus of being placed in a category reserved for idiots and children. The worst-case scenario was enslavement, which meant not so much the reduction of the citizens to chattels, as the colonists had done to African slaves, as the loss of the independent status associated with owning property, which was necessary to participate in public life. Thus, to deny them such protection in their collective capacity was to deny them the traditional English right of local self-government, and thus the necessary access to the public realm that made the republican notion of public happiness possible. Hannah Arendt writes:

> Tyranny, as the revolutions came to understand it, was a form of government in which the ruler, even though he ruled according to the laws of the realm, had monopolized for himself the right of action, banished citizens from the public realm into the privacy of their households, and demanded of them that they mind their own private business. Tyranny, in other words, deprived of public happiness, though not necessarily private well-being, while a republic granted to every citizen the right to become a participator in the government of affairs, the right to be seen in action.[74]

The two sections of the Declaration that follow the passage on representation reinforce this reading of the text: "He has called together legislative bodies at places unusual, uncomfortable, and distant from the depository of their public Records, for the sole purpose of fatiguing them into compliance with his measures.—He has dissolved Representative Houses repeatedly for opposing with manly firmness his invasions on the rights of the people." Both of these sections imply more or less the same thing: that the role of the legislature was indeed to protect and resist the imposition of the king and his will into the collective will of the community as expressed by local assemblies and state governments. The attempt to wear the representatives down was akin to the attempt of the court to overcome the country and to cause the transfer of power to the administration, thereby destroying the necessary balance of the ancient English Constitution.

The next passage is a wonderful example of the Lockean theory of a two-step social contract at work:

> He has refused for a long time, after such dissolutions, to cause others to be elected; whereby the Legislative powers, incapable of Annihilation, have returned to the People at large for their exercise; the State remaining in the mean time exposed to all the dangers of invasion from without, and convulsions within.

Government, or the court, may not be functioning, but that does not mean that society has ceased to exist, nor has anyone been returned to the state of nature. The nonexistence of the crown simply means that what has gone on before—people governing themselves by law—will continue, but now they will have to implement and enforce the laws themselves. Furthermore, they will now have to take on the task of protecting themselves from other nations with whom they exist in a state of nature. The implication here as well is that if the situation is not remedied soon, the colonists will have to create the "court," or its functional equivalent, in order to remain secure in the world at large. A key point to note here is the very limited conception of the role of the court: to protect the communities from without and to enforce laws from within, the actual legislative role being quite minimal within a particular community or state.

After a clause that deals with the restrictions on naturalization and migration to the colonies, Jefferson begins what is perhaps his most republican litany of abuses by touching on universal themes of Whig/republican discourse. He begins with the judiciary, a subject to which he will return in another form. According to Jefferson: "He has obstructed the Administration of Justice, by refusing his Assent to Laws for establishing judiciary powers.—He has made Judges dependent on his Will alone, for the tenure of their offices, and the amount and payment of their salaries."

In 1761 James Otis, a radical, had in his argument against the Writs of Assistance—which had basically allowed the British authorities to search any premises they believed to be related to smuggling, with or without what we would call probable cause—contended that "An act against the Constitution is void," and that "it [was] the business of [the] court to demolish this monster of oppression, and to tear into rags this remnant of Star Chamber tyranny."[75] Although considered outside the mainstream at the time, given British constitutionalism and the lack of a conception of judicial review as outlined in Blackstone's essay on parliamentary omnipotence in his *Commentaries,* Otis's thought within ten years or so became the rule in colonial ideology rather than the exception.[76] However, the reader needs to be aware of a substantial conceptual difference between modern ideas concerning judicial review and this early view as expressed by Otis. The judiciary here is depicted as yet another institution that mediates the relationship between the government and the community, and thus between the government and independent individuals, according to the Constitution. But it is not meant to imply that the judiciary is to mediate in terms of the Constitution in a similar manner *within* a particular community. In other words, the judiciary is supposed to protect the rights of individuals from the will of the court or the crown, but this does not mean that it is allowed to protect us from ourselves.

Given this, when Jefferson speaks of justice as being "obstructed," he means that a significant barrier between the will of the crown and the will of the community and its members has ceased to function, thus leaving them both exposed to usurpation, and thus to tyranny. Furthermore, when he claims that the king has made the judges dependent on his will alone, the argument is not so much with judicial dependency qua dependency, as will be argued later in conjunction with American constitutionalism in order to free judges to render so-called objective opinions, but upon *whom* the judges are dependent. In other words, if the function of the judiciary is to safeguard the constitutional rights of the community and of individuals within the community from unconstitutional interference or usurpation by the crown, then the argument is not that the judiciary ought to be independent but that it ought to be biased (dependent) in favor of the colonists and not the court. Hence, by making the judges dependent on the will of the king alone, the relationship between the judiciary and the Constitution is inverted and the colonists lose yet another safeguard against tyranny. This point will allow us, later on, to rectify what might appear to some as an inconsistency in Jeffersonian thought on the role of an independent judiciary that he here seems to be defending, and that later in American history he so vehemently attacked. It is not that Jefferson changed but that the conceptual understanding of the nature of the judicial branch substantively changed under the Federalists, even while maintaining its form.

The king had also "erected a multitude of New Offices, and sent hither swarms of Officers to harass our people, and eat out their substance." A traditional and very persistent Whig/republican fear is of an ever-increasing bureaucracy, and the expansion of the administrative apparatus and courtly power such an expansion always implies. The multiplication of officers dependent on the king and devoted to the infiltration of the administration into the traditional colonial political domain clearly suggests an expanded rationalization of the political realm. The price paid for increased governmental efficiency will be the contraction of the political realm (the area reserved for public action by independent citizens) and the corresponding reduction of public freedom, and hence of the opportunities for public happiness that had existed before. In turn, the multiplication of offices increased the financial burden on citizens and made it more difficult for them to sustain the level of independence necessary to qualify for such freedom.

As traditional as, and even more frightening than, the expansion of the administration for classical republicans is the fear of a standing army, as evidenced by the next set of clauses in the Declaration:

> He has kept among us, in times of peace, Standing Armies without the Consent of our legislatures.— He has affected to render the Military independent of and superior to the Civil power. . . . —For quartering large bodies of armed troops among us:—For protecting them, by a mock Trial, from punishment for any Murders which they should commit on the Inhabitants of these States.

The delicate nature of such an institution was perhaps best captured by Plato in his discussion of the guardians when he spoke of the need to make the members of the army like dogs who were ferocious toward the enemies of the republic, yet gentle to their "owners."[77] History had suggested that this was a difficult, if not impossible, proposition. Plato himself reinforced this idea with his description of all the various precautions that would need to be in place for this ideal to be made a reality. Given the unlikelihood of those Platonic precautions being practiced, the next best solution for republican thinkers was to do without a standing army during peacetime. The risk a standing army posed was the loss of independence by the colonial citizenry and the further extension of courtly power into the colonial political domain, with the same reductions in the capacity for public freedom and happiness noted above. The fear of a standing army here is magnified still further because it is not only an armed force existing within particular communities but also a force that was not authorized or controlled by those communities. Had its members been drawn, as in Plato's model, from among the citizenry, they could be expected to recognize the civil authorities of those communities and thus, using Plato's logic, could not reasonably be expected to be gentle with the members therein. This particular standing army represented the worst possible scenario for the republican-minded colonists—a standing army during times of peace that was not obedient to the civil authority within the location they were serving, and whose members were typically allowed to avoid the system of justice therein.

Among the battle cries of the American Revolution was the famed "no taxation without representation," which some contemporary libertarians have taken to mean "no taxation." However, the reality was that taxation was a normal aspect of citizenship. What was not normal for the colonists was the idea of taxation imposed by some source other than their locally elected legislatures. This theme was echoed early in the emerging colonial crises when the Stamp Act Congress claimed in 1765: "That only the representatives of the people of these colonies are persons chosen therein by themselves, and that no taxes ever have been, or can be constitutionally imposed on them, but by their respective legislatures . . . all supplies to the Crown being free gifts."[78] The resolutions of that congress go on to explain that only through recognition of the particular circumstances within a particular community can taxes be justly determined and collected without violating the property rights that allow independent citizenship. Thus, when Jefferson contends that the king is in violation of the principles of the Constitution "For cutting off our Trade with all parts of the world:—For imposing Taxes on us without our Consent," what is at stake yet again is not the property rights of individuals qua individuals, claiming a right to be left alone but, rather, the property rights and the right to make a living that entitle one to membership in the political realm. Thus it is not an argument against taxation but an argument for Aristotelian moderation in taxation.

Earlier, James Otis referred to a "Star Chambered tyranny," by which he meant the tyranny of a king acting as something like a puppeteer with regard to the judges serving on his courts, directing verdicts and interpretations while masking them as the decisions of independent judges. The republican solution for such a potential difficulty was the jury trial. Trial by jury was considered to be among the most important rights of all British citizens, because in this way the community could recognize particular local customs and institutions, and deliver a justice consistent not with any universal code but with their shared and agreed-upon sense of justice and communal mores. To strip them of that right, either to impose injustice (the will of the king acting in his own interest rather than in the interest of the realm) or—and this is critical—to impose a rationalized universal code of justice on all people that was thought to apply in all places, at all times, without recognition of particular circumstances was to void the possibility of justice altogether.

Right and wrong in republican thought are the product of conversation and reflection, not transcendent knowledge or revelation. Jefferson holds the king accountable.

> For depriving us in many cases, of the benefit of Trial by Jury:—For transporting us beyond Seas to be tried for pretended offenses:—For abolishing the free System of English Laws in a neighbouring Province, establishing therein an Arbitrary government, and enlarging its Boundaries so as to render it at once an example and fit instrument for introducing the same absolute rule into these Colonies.

He is in effect declaring that increased centralization of the mechanisms of justice, the idea that somehow justice can be detached from particular and local circumstances and mores, and that the process can be professionalized, or made dependent on a single person's will, are indeed illegitimate in theory and unjust in practice.[79]

It is at this point in the Declaration that Jefferson returns to earlier themes and accusations against the king and Parliament concerning their intrusion into the public space of the colonists for the expressed purpose of its contraction and outright destruction. They have lost their right to govern:

For taking away our Charters, abolishing our most valuable Laws, and altering fundamentally the Forms of our Governments [note the use of the plural]:—For suspending our own Legislatures, and declaring themselves invested with power to legislate for us in all cases whatsoever.

And so the list of abuses continues, speaking of failures to protect, inciting domestic turmoil, plundering the seas, burning towns, taking captives, forced conscription, failure to allow for redress, and so on. They all lead to the conclusion of the document, where it is declared:

WE, THEREFORE, the Representatives of the UNITED STATES OF AMERICA ["united" here is used as an adjective, not as part of a noun], in General Congress, Assembled, appealing to the Supreme Judge of the world for rectitude of our intentions, do, in the Name, and by Authority of the good People of these Colonies, solemnly publish and declare, That these United Colonies are, and of Right ought to be FREE AND INDEPENDENT STATES.

Whatever the implications of the Declaration of Independence might be for individual rights and liberties, one thing about the document is clear: it was written to defend a particular set of American political arrangements that could collectively be called republican. The fact that this defense eventually required a revolution in order to legitimize those arrangements illustrates the point that while many of the rights being defended were considered traditional and were time honored, the full realization of the project meant that radical changes had to take place. Those radical changes demanded the recognition of citizen participation in the public sphere, and the corresponding empowerment of that sphere not merely to be "spared actual oppression, but [to have] a constitutional check upon the power to oppress."

The American Revolution was not a Leninist revolution, nor was it a liberal revolution, and the idea of a conservative revolution simply does too much damage to the language to be useful. The American Revolution was a republican revolution, republican because it embraced the tenets of that ideology, a revolution because it involved the creation of new and modern forms of community, and attempted to clear away the obstacles to public freedom and public happiness that allow such communities to form. Political association would no longer be based on the blood ties of the feudal world, nor would it be replaced by economic relationships (at least not yet). What would now be possible would be political as well as social forms of association that were more inclusive and were based on consent, yet still demanded that their members subject themselves to collective authority. In return they would be offered an opportunity to make their part of the world into a place where they would like to live, to experience the fraternity that the state of nature would deny them, to experience the sort of happiness that is possible only among one's fellow citizens, and, if they were fortunate, to become better people than they were before.

Chapter Three

American Political Reformations

In conclusion, then, let those whom the heavens grant such opportunities reflect that two courses are open to them: either so to behave that in life they rest secure and in death become renowned, or so to behave in life that they are in continual straits, and in death leave behind an imperishable record of their infamy.

—Machiavelli

But the game is caught: And I believe it is true, that with the catching, end the pleasures of the chase.

—Abraham Lincoln

*L*ike any definitive event in a nation's history, the American Revolution has become a touchstone through which later generations have come to know the nature and ideals of their society. As is often the case with such an important event, the "meaning" that has come to be attributed to it is often given with one eye on understanding the event on its own terms and the other eye on the current political struggle for which it is being invoked. The latter can sometimes be the cause of partial misrepresentation or even outright distortion as the event in question is used to further some end that its authors could not have anticipated. If there are competing forces that seek to underscore their positions with reference to the key event, its meaning is contested, as is the case with the American Revolution. So it is useful from time to time to try to recapture as much as possible the meaning of the event for the time in which it happened, and subsequently to explore the use made of it in the political conversations and thought that followed it.

In this chapter I will explore some of the political and historical consequences of the American revolutionary experience, both intended and unintended, with regard to American political life and political thought. Then I will proceed to explore the political and theoretical responses to that newly created historical context in terms of both thematic and narrative consistency. In other words, I will be asking and answering the following set of questions:

What did the majority of American revolutionaries hope to achieve after liberation? What, exactly, did they achieve? How were those achievements made manifest in the political realm after liberation? Who opposed either the achievements or the manner in which they manifested themselves politically after liberation? What actions did those who opposed either the achievements or their political manifestations take in response to them? And finally, what was the relationship between the actions and thoughts of those in disagreement, and the intended consequences of the Revolution itself?

In chapter 1, I argued that Puritan theology gave rise to certain *political* problems that had to be resolved within the context of the Puritan faith in order to maintain the bonds of the community. Among those problems was the question of how God was to be known and yet remain hidden. Calvin himself had emphasized mysteries that had made it difficult to in effect know God, and thus had created a potential legitimation crisis for any *political* order, as exemplified by the Anabaptists. The solution to that "crisis of authority" for the Puritans had been to turn to the notion of the covenanted community in which God revealed Himself through Scripture as much or as little as He wanted to, so that his followers could live up to their part of the bargain. What God in fact revealed was determined by the class of citizen-saints in public conversation with one another. Thus the source of authority was still a transcendent God who spoke through Scripture, although, in contrast with Catholics, the nature of that authority was now determined by an expanded class of republican citizens rather than a clerical hierarchy. As time passed, however, and political life in colonial America became more and more secularized, the ties to Scripture became less and less pronounced, and were replaced by something larger and less descript: natural law.

The subsequent distance between the original source of authority and the political life of the community created the necessary conditions for greater diversity between communities and, more important, that distance, coupled with an ever-expanding base of citizen-interpreters, created a political context in which both the *source* of authority and its *nature* began to coalesce around the people at large. In other words, as interpretation of Scripture became more of a private concern to be worked out between members of a congregation and the ministers, political questions were left to the citizenry and their representatives to be worked out within their consensual framework of political life and natural law. Scripture as an intermediary between God and the citizenry was now available only in a secondary capacity as it influenced the private consciences of men and women. In their political lives as citizens, however, they could attempt to go directly to the source as much as possible. The reality of such a shift, however, given the increased distance between God and citizen, was to leave the citizenry with greater and greater responsibilities and discretion. The citizen had in fact replaced Scripture as the intermediary between natural law and human law, thus becoming the source of God's authority on earth. At the same time the citizen retained his or her role of interpreting the nature of that authority. The two roles had become fused beyond our ability to disentangle them.

The argument in chapter 2 illustrated the political/theoretical and historical progression of that development in the American colonial and revolutionary experience. The result was a defense of the American Revolution as a modern republican event that cleared the way for the legitimation not only of government by consent but also of self-government by engaged citizens. Those citizens then constructed social and political communities in free public space, and subsequently authorized agents at the local level to care for those communities while maintaining the space that made the communities possible in the first place. This movement is captured in the work of Fredrick Richardson, who describes the period between 1773 and 1778 in terms of a radical transfer of legitimate political authority from the British government to the colonial legislatures. He writes toward the end of his work:

> One common evolution of political authority can be discerned. Executive power and the classically balanced world came to be discredited in all of the colonies. They were replaced by the power of "the people" expressed mostly in regular legislative assemblies. And this new expression was marked by one vital, central characteristic, popular accountability.[1]

This transfer, not only of power but of authority as well,[2] is significant in that it works against any depiction of the American Revolution as a purely negative event, liberation from England for its own sake. There were specific social and political arrangements being defended that could lay claim to over 150 years of precedent in one form or another. Furthermore, not only were those arrangements made explicit and legitimate by the Revolution, but they were also extended and enhanced by ideological and theoretical developments produced in the context of the event itself. In turn these became part of the political/cultural fabric of the newly legitimated political entity called the United States. Among the more important ideological developments was the advancing of the democratic ideal in terms of an expanded class of citizens who were claiming the right of entrance to the public realm by virtue of their participation, sacrifice, and loyalty during the Revolution. Though the Whig/republican discourse of the Revolution did not necessarily imply the existence of a democratic regime, the nature of the revolutionary struggle—one fought by commoners as well as gentlemen—coupled with the relative abundance of property in America and the outright vilification of any talk of aristocracy, conspired to produce quite fertile historical and political soil for the birth of such a regime—or, more important, regimes—in America.

This argument is made at length in the most recent work by Gordon Wood, *The Radicalism of the American Revolution.* In it, he argues that far from being the "conservative affair, concerned almost exclusively with politics and constitutional rights, and, in comparison with the social radicalism of other great revolutions of history, hardly a revolution at all,"[3] that the American Revolution is often painted to be, it was in fact as radical as any in history.

> . . . if we measure the radicalism by the amount of social change that actually took place—by transformations in the relationships that bound people to each other—then the American Revolution was not conservative at all. . . . In fact, it was one of the greatest revolutions the world has known, a momentous upheaval that not only fundamentally altered the character of American society but decisively affected the course of subsequent history.[4]

The bulk of Wood's argument rests on his depiction of eighteenth-century America as a hierarchically ordered land "composed not of broad and politically hostile layers of classes but of 'various individuals, connected together and related and subservient to each other' . . . connected vertically rather than horizontally."[5] He goes on to claim that "we will never appreciate the radicalism of the eighteenth century revolutionary idea that all men are created equal unless we see it within this age-old tradition of difference."[6] The Revolution, however, did away with such distinctions, which for Wood represents the true magnitude of its radicalism.

> The republican revolution aggravated such anti-intellectual sentiments and rendered suspect all kinds of distinctions, whether naturally derived or not . . . republican equality even threatened to destroy the notion of social hierarchy. . . . The warning was now out against all displays of superiority, whether it was attending exclusive balls and tea parties or flaunting a college degree. . . . Equality became the rallying cry for those seeking to challenge every form of authority and superiority.[7]

This view of America is not particularly new, and much of it can be found in varying degrees in the work of Alexis de Tocqueville, who tells his readers more than once of the American penchant for equality:

> There is indeed a manly and legitimate passion for equality which rouses in all men a desire to be strong and respected. This passion tends to elevate the little man to the rank of the great. But the human heart also nourishes a debased taste for equality, which leads the weak to want to drag the strong down to their level and which induces men to prefer equality in servitude to inequality in freedom.[8]

> I think democratic peoples have a natural taste for liberty; left to themselves, they will seek it, cherish it, and be sad if it is taken from them. But their passion for equality is ardent, insatiable, eternal, and invincible. They want equality in freedom, and if they cannot have that, they still want equality in slavery. They will put up with poverty, servitude, and barbarism, but they will not endure aristocracy.[9]

Wood's observations are borne out still further in the conservative railings of a revolutionary contemporary, Fisher Ames, who in 1805 declared:

> Our materials for a government were all democratic, and whatever the hazard of their combination may be, our Solons and Lycurguses in the convention had no alternative, nothing to consider, but how to combine them, so as to insure the longest duration to the Constitution.[10]

And Ames wrote of democratization:

> Our days are made heavy with the pressure of anxiety, and our nights restless with visions of horror. We listen to the clank of chains, and overhear the whispers of assassins. We mark the barbarous dissonance of mingled rage and triumph in the yell of an infatuated mob; we see the dismal glare of their burnings and scent the loathsome stem of human victims offered in sacrifice.[11]

Wood saw the democratization of America through a vastly different normative lens, and of course much less melodramatically, but his account was similar in terms of analytic content. He concluded his book thus:

> A new generation of democratic Americans was no longer interested in the revolutionaries' dream of building a classical republic of elitist virtue out of the inherited materials of the Old World. America, they said, would find its greatness not by emulating the states of classical antiquity, not by copying the fiscal-military powers of modern Europe, and not by producing a few notable geniuses and great-souled men. Instead it would discover its greatness by creating a prosperous free society belonging to obscure people with their workaday concerns and their pecuniary pursuits of happiness—common people with their common interests in making money and getting ahead. No doubt the cost that America paid for this democracy was high—with its vulgarity, its materialism, its rootlessness, its anti-intellectualism. But there is no denying the hitherto neglected and despised masses of common laboring people.[12]

Unfortunately, this entire discussion leaves out a crucial element of the American political picture while misconstruing the true nature of postrevolutionary American democratic political culture. Despite the sentiments expressed above by Ames and Wood, democratic culture in America was not a Leveler political culture. It was, to be sure, antiaristocratic; and it did indeed seek to destroy the vertical social differences between the "masses" and the "better sorts of people." But it did not do so with the initial intention of rendering the American Revolution a less horrific version of the French Revolution, as Wood's emphasis on the social nature of the event seems to suggest. And this is where the differences between Wood's analysis and Tocqueville's are made quite manifest.

To see the differences, look at the two passages above in which Tocqueville deals with the subject of equality in America and note the following:

> There is indeed a manly and legitimate passion for equality which rouses in all men a desire to be strong and respected . . . which induces men to prefer equality in servitude to inequality in freedom.
>
> . . . .
>
> They want equality in freedom, and if they cannot have that, they still want equality in slavery. They will put up with poverty, servitude, and barbarism, but they will not endure aristocracy.

In fact, Tocqueville could have gone a step further and claimed that Americans would have preferred equality in death to aristocracy, as evidenced by the willingness to fight and die in the Revolution. What Tocqueville knows, as does Arendt, is that the type of social hierarchy that Wood so vividly portrays as existing in America was in fact not a barrier to the sort of "prosperous free society belonging to obscure people with their workaday concerns and their pecuniary pursuits of happiness—common people with their common interests in making money and getting ahead" that represents the private realm with its personal concerns. On the contrary, those differences served as effective barriers to the sort of public freedom and public happiness that allow human beings to transcend "making money and getting ahead." Wood embraces this change despite what he sees as the costs. Fisher Ames rejects this change because of what he sees as the cost. But what neither seems fully to recognize is the political and historical tragedy of it all.

Democracy in America was not so much a theoretical construct as it was a natural outgrowth of community life and the act of revolution itself. Though it may be somewhat banal to say, it is important that we remember that revolutions do not just happen like tornadoes, thunderstorms, or earthquakes—they are not part of some natural or dialectical process weaving its way through history. For all their appearance of spontaneity, revolutions are usually the products of long-term organization and planning coupled with a gradual or incremental period of social incubation. Nowhere is this more evident than in the American Revolution, which evolved through a series of discrete stages beginning with passive resistance (1763–1765) designed to gain parliamentary repeal of what were considered bad (but not conspiratorial) laws; moving on to more active resistance (1770–1771) in the form of boycotts, mock trials of public officials, burning in effigy of those officials, and the rise of organized extrapolitical groups like the Sons of Liberty and the Daughters of Liberty, which were intended to change the British mind but not necessarily to change the form of government; and finally to the stage of revolutionary activity (1774–1776), in which the necessity of independence became the norm and reform became the functional equivalent of Toryism.[13]

Along the way the number of participants in and adherents of the emerging movement and its tenets grew. With each exponential increase in participation came a corresponding increase in political consciousness. Since the cultural matrix of the movement was republican, it only made sense that the political consciousness being developed was republican. But since the Revolution required the participation of greater and greater numbers of people, it also meant that the rights of citizenship, "to be a participator in government," had to be extended. So, procedurally the Revolution was also democratic,[14] but clearly not in the way suggested by Wood.

"LET THERE BE LIGHT . . ." FIRST FOUNDINGS

It is not unusual—indeed, it is likely—that one will find the following kind of institutionalized discourse in contemporary American government textbooks concerning the first American founding under the Articles of Confederation:

The Articles failed for at least four reasons. . . .[15]

The Nation's first constitution failed because. . . .[16]

The Articles had failed at what they were primarily intended to do. . . .[17]

Under the Articles of Confederation, the national government was little more than an aspiration.[18]

In short, the government under the Articles seemed too decentralized to ensure either peace or prosperity.[19]

Although this is not a scientific sample, these are representative of a general historical mood or preoccupation that sees, or wants to see, the first founding as a rough draft. Each of these texts goes on to list the various failings of the Articles of Confederation and to suggest implicitly, when not explicitly, both the necessity of the Constitution and its superiority. I suppose such a thing is natural, first of all because, as the cliché goes, history is written by the winners, and second (perhaps more important) because nations and their people like to believe that their history is somehow one of progress—of rational improvement with occasional setbacks that make them stronger in the long run. Thanks, perhaps, to Hegel, not many people would be willing to embrace the idea that their nation was somehow the product of an historical mistake or, worse yet, chance! The Constitution had to be better than the Articles of Confederation because it came later, and each stage that followed in America's constitutional development was to be equally praised as progressive and necessary. Those who resisted such change or—worse yet—sought to return to some earlier period of American political consensus were labeled anachronistic cranks, or accused of being anti-progress. The truth of the matter, however, is that none of this actually follows as either intellectually necessary or historically certain.

The troubling aspect of such assessments is that they often conceal an important set of normative assumptions about what a government should be, and how a government should be able to act, that remain unargued for, but in fact are critically important if we are to engage in a fair assessment of our political history. The reality of America's founding periods is that they represent two distinct kinds of political regimes with two equally distinct kinds of normative and theoretical foundations.[20] In order to be judged in relationship to one another, if such a thing is possible, they first have to be judged independently. They must be measured in terms of their success in relation to the desires and promises of their *own* political projects. In other words, it is a mistake to claim that the Articles of Confederation failed to do what the Constitution could accomplish.

Much of the confusion and misrepresentation of the Articles of Confederation and the period of the first founding in general are the result of the work of the nineteenth-century historian John Fiske. It was Fiske who coined the term the "critical period" to describe the history of America under the Articles of Confederation. His general argument is revealed in the following excerpt:

> Such was the constitution under which the United States had begun to drift toward anarchy even before the close of the Revolutionary War, but which could only be amended by the unanimous consent of all thirteen states. The historian cannot but regard this difficulty of amendment as a fortunate circumstance; for in the troubles which presently arose it led the distressed people to seek some other method of relief, and thus prepared the way for the convention of 1787, which destroyed the whole vicious scheme, and gave us a form of government under which we have just completed a century unparalleled for peace and prosperity.[21]

This view of the first founding as deeply flawed, if not dangerous or inimical to America's chances for survival, as well as of the founders as the great saviors rescuing America from this "vicious scheme," has by and large been, in either strong or weak form, the dominant ideological foundation for much of political science's foray into early American history. And though such an assumption is often convenient in terms of getting on with the more important issues of the day, it is wrong. As the noted historian Merrill Jensen claimed in the preface to his "response" to the work of Fiske, the latter was "a book of vast influence but of no value as either history or example . . . nothing is to be gained by following a 'chaos and patriots to the rescue' interpretation."[22] Furthermore, such a historical distortion robs Americans of a vital part of their political heritage and history and, even more important, it denies them use of that special "second" heritage or political language in their own political struggles in a manner that was so well argued early on by Tocqueville,[23] and later by Louis Hartz.[24]

This represents cause for concern because of the unique role a nation's past plays in its contemporary political life. Quite often contemporary political discourse must link itself to a past set of achievements or ideas in order to gain legitimacy as a point of view within a particular political tradition.[25] Whenever a group finds itself unable to establish that historical linkage, it, and whatever political project it represents, are automatically suspect. They are marginalized within that society until circumstances conspire, or revolutionary action enables, such a mode of discourse to establish itself within a particular tradition or, in the case of some revolutions, to overcome a particular tradition altogether. In the absence of such radical moments or opportunities, successful counterhegemonic movements must find a way to speak within a particular cultural and political tradition while they attempt to change it.[26] The trouble with such a paradigm, however, is that it rules out possible political projects that may not be expressible within the dominant mode of political discourse. Subsequently, desirable and perhaps even necessary political projects are excluded from consideration.[27] For Louis Hartz this lack of alternatives produced a political culture in America that he could describe only as irrational. The fact that there was, and perhaps still is, another tradition of American political discourse available that remains truncated or concealed, that might help save us from certain political and social dangers, is irrational and may even be tragic.

Aside from the obvious historical problem of reading America's first century as one of peace, in light of the 600,000 Civil War deaths, there is also the question of whether prosperity is the best tool to measure the success or failure of any country, particularly the United States. Given the resources available to the nation, it is difficult to see how Americans could have done anything but prosper, just as certain nations, by virtue of their geographic location—say, in a desert, with no valuable resources hidden beneath the sand—could, with the best constitution and citizenry the world has ever seen, manage *to* prosper.

The more interesting and important question is not whether a particular political project failed some absolute test in which it was measured against a transcendent ideal, but how well it achieved its best version of itself. In other words, each political project or activity as theorized creates an ideal image, toward which it aspires, based upon the values it would like to secure and the outcomes it would like to achieve; judgments of success or failure then become relative to the stated goals and objects of the idealized version. The more a particular project comes to reflect its idealized version, the more successful we can claim such a project is or was; conversely, the less the project resembles its idealized version over time, the less successful we can say the project is or was. If the idealized version changes for some reason—say, a major shift in values or aspirations on the part of a people through reflective choice or conquest—

then the standards by which that political project is to be judged must also change.

This, however, does not necessarily imply that all possible ideal versions are equally legitimate. Rather, whatever the value of any particular political project is, it contains within itself its own discourse for evaluation that cannot be used to judge the success or failure of another political project. Thus the Soviet Union might be judged a failure not because it did not achieve the same sorts of goals the United States was seeking, but because it consistently seemed to fall shorter and shorter of its own ideal version of itself. There is an important difference between failure to achieve in light of a good-faith effort and acting in bad faith.[28] The choice between competing value systems or ideal versions then becomes a prepolitical form of activity dominated by many different sorts of people at many different times, including so-called lawgivers, founding fathers, tyrants, dictators, revolutionaries, prophets, and even philosophers.

The classical image of such an event is provided by Aeschylus in his Orestes trilogy when in the third play, *The Eumenides,* the goddess Athena intercedes on behalf of the young mother-killer Orestes in order to break the cycle of blood and revenge. She does this by establishing a political order that will arbitrate disputes and render a new brand of justice. In that instance a new order, fundamentally different both normatively as well as procedurally, is forged that many will find more satisfying. At the same time, however, we must remember that such an overcoming was not without its costs and detractors. In the case of Aeschylus' tragedy the sense of loss is voiced venomously by the chorus representing the old order as they cry out to Athena:

> Curse on you upstart gods who have ridden
> Down immemorial laws and flinched them
> Clean from my fingers. Abused, disappointed,
> Raging I come—oh, shall come!—
> And drip from my heart
> A hurt on your soil, a contagion,
> A culture, a canker:
> Leafless and childless Revenge
> Rushing like wildfire over the lowlands,
> Smearing its death-pus on mortals and meadows.
>
> Shall I cry—oh, cry for the future?
> Mocked by these burghers!
> Insufferably worsted!
> Bitter Night's daughters, immensely
> Dishonored and saddened.[29]

On one hand, such a tirade could simply be read as the rantings of the losers in a vast historical struggle, but such a reading misses another very important element: a warning about the potential costs, a warning in the best conservative fashion about the unseen dangers of unbridled innovation coupled with a deep sense of loss and fear for the future. Yes, the new order will establish a more rational approach to crime and punishment, but the price of such an establishment will be that a matricide goes unpunished. Perhaps even more important, if we link the events leading up to the conclusion, a father who sacrificed a young girl (Iphigenia) to gain a favorable wind from the gods, so that he could go to rescue his lover in Troy, also is at least partially absolved. When the chorus asks whether they should "cry for the future," it is a good question: the historical path of that world is now altered beyond recognition, the consequences of that alteration are at that point unknown, and whether the alteration will show itself to be an improvement is a question that will have to be answered by history and practice, and not theory. But whatever the final judgment, what is important for our discussion here is that the choice between the old order and the new order is in many ways a dichotomous one. Each order has its positive and negative attributes, both theoretical and practical, that must be accounted for before any sound judgment can be thoughtfully rendered.

As argued earlier, the theoretical defense and the practical basis for the American Revolution grew out of a well-worn set of colonial traditions. The foundings that followed the Declaration of Independence and the Revolution in the states were political extensions of that theory and practice. According to Donald Lutz, "those state constitutions were Whig documents, whether traditional or radical, and thus they assumed the rights of the community to be generally superior to the rights of the individual."[30] But within that framework there was also an emphasis on consent that prodded those states toward democratic participation and majority rule. Furthermore, among the most fundamental rights of the community and its increasingly democratized citizenry was the right to be shielded from outside interference by any central authority in questions of local concern. According to Lutz, that area of concern was quite extensive:

> They regulated the treatment of slaves and servants, built and maintained roads, bridges, streets, and wharfs, regulated navigation on rivers and streams, nominated and oversaw commissioners and surveyors responsible for these duties, collected both local and general taxes, kept standard weights and measures, graded and inspected goods for export, served as local conservation authority, ordered the destruction of pests and the observance of game regulations, provided for the relief of the poor, upheld public morals, took care of orphans, levied troops for the militia and supplied them with provisions ammunition and housing. . . . And yet there were few complaints, not because men in those days did not understand the meaning of freedom, but because local communities were relatively homogeneous, and the laws were, in most cases, made by the majority of local citizens who had common values.[31]

In fact the level of power exerted by the local community was an expression of freedom, public freedom, and not its contrary. While it is true that there were important and sometimes vast differences between the states in terms of internal political organization, constitutions, levels of democracy, and so on, these were only micro differences.[32] On the macro level there was continuity to the extent that each state agreed to leave the others alone to devise and construct their own internal political worlds. This is a distinction that the progressive historians like Charles Beard often fail to acknowledge: that in the country's founding period there was never anything like a national democratic ideology. Instead, there was a series of republican/democratic regimes, each conducting its own political conversations and coming to quite different political conclusions. Whatever importance the differences between the states in passing judgment on their individual constitutions and local political arrangements, they are not important for the discussion here. All that matters is that they were free to choose—even if they chose ways thought ultimately undemocratic in a substantive sense of the term.

This, then, is what marks America as the context in which modern forms of republican community could truly flourish. In the first place, there was a tradition that linked the American colonies to England and its feudal society of interlocking and reciprocal relationships based on social rank and class through the legal presence of the ancient English Constitution and parliamentary rule and the physical presence of the crown's representatives in positions of political authority. But in the second place, there was the development of a political project that transcended those bonds and subsequently replaced them—not with personal or legal precedent nor, strictly speaking, with the more traditional conceptions of civic republicanism associated with Machiavelli or Polybius (because they lacked the emergent sense of equality and democracy found in the American model). Rather, they were replaced with a new political/cultural system that certainly borrowed from all of these "traditions," yet changed them into something new and different, into what we might call a uniquely modern/uniquely American version of republicanism. That modern American theorization of community was one that was neither so completely detached from tradition that it could invent and destroy at will, nor so moored in it that experimentation and substantive reorientation were prohibited. This sense of what American political life had become is partially captured by Arendt:

> American faith was not at all based on a semi-religious trust in human nature, but on the contrary, on the possibility of checking human nature in its singularity by virtue of common bonds and mutual promises. The hope for man in his singularity lay in the fact that not man but men inhabit the earth and form a world between them. It is human worldliness that will save men from the pitfalls of human nature.[33]

What is important to note in the formulation provided by Arendt is what is missing from the equation. Human beings will not be saved by an a priori civically virtuous nature nor, implicitly, will they be protected from themselves by virtuous rulers or Hobbesian sovereigns. What will save human beings is collective activity and political participation (conceived of here as discussions and arguments over what constitutes the public good, as well as the wielding of substantial political power). In other words, human transformation and public sustenance are the products of free public activity by citizens who are both independent and empowered. It was a political project that was at the same time thick with tradition yet bursting with the promise of the new and the untried. The project was both republican and democratic, embraced both political freedom and equality, and created room for rights and responsibilities for the individual and the collective, for the public and the private, and, most important, for meaningful action and thus for meaningful lives. It is against this idealized version of itself that the period of America's first founding has to be measured before any thoughtful judgments can be rendered as to its success or failure.

The institutional context within which this political action was to take place is best captured by Tocqueville in his chapters dealing with post-Revolution political organization in American townships, municipal administrations, and states.[34] Here we find Tocqueville proclaiming the triumph of the democratic ideal as a result of the Revolution:

> The American Revolution broke out. The dogma of the sovereignty of the people came out from the township and took possession of the government; every class enlisted in its cause; the war was fought and victory obtained in its name; it became the law of laws. . . . It was not even permissible to struggle against it any longer. So the upper classes submitted without complaint or resistance . . . their only thought was to gain good will at any price. Consequently the most democratic laws were voted by the men whose interests they impaired.[35]

Tocqueville goes on to document the foundation for this new order that he finds in local political institutions:

> Local institutions are to liberty what primary schools are to science; they put it within the people's reach; they teach people to appreciate its peaceful enjoyment and accustom them to make use of it. Without local institutions a nation may give itself a free government, but it has not got the spirit of liberty.[36]

Here in a sort of modernized Americanization of Aristotelianism we see the process of political education merged inseparably with the act of participating. No longer is one prior to the other, or the domain of philosophers or elites; instead, one becomes inextricably the function of the other. Citizenship now begets *citizenship*. In other words, citizenship is no longer a status that one earns through a system of works; rather, it is earned through faith—faith that by acting as a citizen, one will in fact become a citizen in the fullest and most important sense: one who cares for what is shared and public rather than what is private and personal. This is what I think Joshua Miller means when he says, "Democratic politics in early America was not primarily ideological; it was expressed more in action than in words. The localists lived their ideas: they constituted a political culture and sought to create political and economic institutions compatible with that culture."[37] The price for failing to respect that locus of political power and wellspring of citizenship is grasped quite readily by Tocqueville, who claims, "If you take power and independence from a municipality, you may have docile subjects but you will not have citizens."[38] Here once again we can hear early rumblings or echoes of Michael Oakeshott and those less conservative, but equally perceptive, participatory democrats and communitarians like Benjamin Barber, Jane Mansbridge, Michael Walzer, Carol Pateman, Wilson MacWilliams, Sheldon Wolin, and Roberto Unger. This theoretical and action-oriented shift was the political equivalent of the Puritan doctrine of preparation addressed in chapter 1.

We have seen that the original foundation for this institutional development in America was the product of traditional Tudorism as expressed in the ancient English constitutional protection of local forms of association with regard to their internal police, and that said protection extended to America through the colonial charters. We have, furthermore, seen this tradition modernized through the Revolution, which created (or was intended to create) a "constitutional" "check on the power to oppress." And finally, we have seen that as a result of this change, this removal of obstacles to community, a series of democratic/republican regimes began (or actually continued) to take action and to function as independent political bodies. The final, and inevitable, step in such a process was to solidify and make explicit the nature of the relationship between the soon-to-be-liberated American regimes. In other words, the country that was to be had to invent itself through a founding that formalized the political and cultural transformation that had taken place.

It would be a mistake to think of all political foundings as moments of "absolute novelty," as Arendt wants to suggest in terms of the second American founding.[39] As much as a founding is a beginning of something new, it is also typically the theoretical culmination of something old. The nature of intellectual cause and effect in political life is such that consolidation and constitution (as in the verb form of that term) are in varying degrees formalization, legitimation, and ratification of a body of ideas and/or activities that predated the act of founding. In other words, foundings are always a response to what has gone before, in terms of what has been idealized or of what has been ruthlessly criticized or, more likely, some combination of the two. And although this may be only a rhetorical point, it is one that I think needs to be made, because the closer we get to absolute novelty, the further we get from everyday life and practice. Subsequently we begin to approach the dangerous precipice of "mindless theorizing" that produces the belief in a world that can be re-created at will through speech and then implemented through force. This, however, is a perversion of the modern political project and not its realization.[40] In America, then, the act of founding, of constituting a regime that was consistent with the emergent political culture, fell to the framers of the first American social contract—the Articles of Confederation.

Of all the texts in Whig political theory, none, with the possible exception of Locke's *Second Treatise,* was more influential and important to the American revolutionaries than Montesquieu's *The Spirit of the Laws.*[41] During the founding periods even Locke's work would not contend with that of Montesquieu for comparative prominence. Despite the reach and complexity of that work and its author, we need concern ourselves here only with his teachings on the optimal size of a democratic republic. The Holy Grail of political organization, according to the teachings of Montesquieu, is to construct a constitution that has "all the internal advantages of a republican, together with the external force of a monarchical, government"[42]—in other words, to find a constitution that allows for the use of political power and participation in public life by the citizenry and at the same time is strong enough to defend the nation from external threats or conquerors. His solution to the dilemma is the confederate republic.

Confederate republics were exemplified by ancient Rome and Greece, and later by those who resisted Rome's quest to conquer: the Swiss, the Germans, and the Dutch. Their practical usefulness is evidenced by history, and their theoretical rationale is provided by Montesquieu in the following passage:

> This form of government is a convention by which several petty states agree to become members of a larger one, which they intend to establish. It is a kind of assemblage of societies, that constitute a new one, capable of increasing by means of farther associations, till they arrive to such a degree of power, as to be able to provide for the security of the whole body. The associations of cities were formerly more necessary than in our times. A weak defenseless town was exposed to greater danger. By conquest it was deprived not only of the executive and legislative power, as at present, but moreover all of human property. A republic of this kind, able to do without an external force, may support itself without any internal corruption; the form of this society prevents all manner of inconveniences. If a single member should attempt to usurp the supreme power, he could not be supposed to have an equal authority and credit in all the confederate states. Were he to have too great an influence over one, this would alarm the rest; were he to subdue a part, that which would still remain free, might oppose him with forces independent of those which he had usurped, and overpower before he could be settled in his usurpation. . . . As this government is composed of petty republics, it enjoys the internal happiness of each; and with regard to its external situation, by means of the association, it possess all the advantages of large monarchies.[43]

Among the key points to note in Montesquieu's formulation are the progression he employs and the telos he embraces. First of all, the increasing size of the political association is the product of a bottom-up developmental model in which the important units are the smallest, the cities or local political associations. The larger forms of association, states and nations, are rendered simple utilitarian devices that exist to serve the smaller, sovereign local associations. The second, and related, issue is that of the telos of those larger forms of association—what they were meant to accomplish. The services to be rendered by the larger associations to the smaller were quite limited—according to Montesquieu they were, in good Whig fashion, to provide security such that internal happiness (read public happiness, or the happiness we have associated with political self-determination) would remain possible. Other than a brief allusion to helping each other in instances of popular insurrection, however, Montesquieu is noticeably silent on any "positive" role(s) that those larger forms of association were to play in the internal ordering of any particular state or local community.

Thus we can sketch an outline for judging the success or failure of a particular "national" regime in terms of Whig political theory by asking what a confederate republic—or, more precisely, a confederation of republics—was meant to accomplish, and how well it managed to accomplish it. Such a model would seem to include but one question and answer: Was the confederation capable of defending the smaller forms of association from conquerors? If the answer was "yes," then it was a success; if the answer was "no," then it was a failure. And as simplistic as that might sound, and despite what seem like constant attempts at complication, it is occasionally the case that the world is exactly that simple—or so thought the framers of America's first constitution.

There is no way to read the first American founding under the Articles of Confederation, especially given the prominence of the modern republican ideology before and during the Revolution, outside of the context presented above by Montesquieu. A close reading of the Articles yields perhaps four important themes: the reserved power of the states to control their own political lives; the role of the national government in foreign affairs and defense-related questions; the role of the national government in arbitrating disputes between states; and the embrace of republican/democratic theories of consent, representation, and equality.

Article II of the first constitution makes plain its political theory: "Each state retains its sovereignty, freedom, and independence, and every power, jurisdiction, and right, which is not by this confederation expressly delegated to the United States, in Congress assembled."[44] Compare this with the language of the Tenth Amendment, or the "Necessary and Proper" clause of that same document, and it is almost impossible to mistake the two as documents that differ in degree rather than in kind. Under the Articles of Confederation the state becomes the largest unit of political association that is actually a "rights"-bearing community, one that is protected from external interference in its intraborder political life (though this does not mean it is the only unit

possessing such rights, since quite often each county, city, or town was protected from undue interference from the state through the state constitutions
and the closeness of local representatives to their constituency). They have, in
the words of the Articles, entered

> into a firm league of friendship with each other, for their common defence, the
> security of their Liberties, and their mutual and general welfare, binding themselves
> to assist each other, against all force offered, or attacks made upon them, or any of
> them, on account of religion, sovereignty, trade, or any pretence whatever.

In other words, they have agreed to protect each other from external dangers to their collective—not individual—liberties, and to work together, not
on questions of the general welfare but on questions of *mutual* and general
welfare. If that latter clause is read correctly, it should be clear that there was
no such thing as the general welfare of the country; rather, there was a series
of particular "welfares" that could only be considered general when in fact the
question at issue was one of *mutual* concern as determined by the state itself.
The distinction here is once again of critical importance from a theoretical
perspective, in that under the Articles of Confederation there was no "truth,"
or Platonic form, that transcended the local community and its own particular
determinations about right and wrong, useful or not, other than those basic
natural laws (but these, too, were open to a good deal of "relative" interpretation).

Communal welfare and justice were both the products of local political
conversations, and any attempt to conflate the judgments of those independent
entities had to be agreed to by them and the like associations involved in
order to be legitimate. Thus the mode of operation was consensual rather than
majoritarian or adversarial, which accounts for the nine-vote decision-making
threshold and the provisions for unanimity with regard to amendment that
marked the Articles. The reader should once again notice that the slight linguistic differences between the first and second American constitutions represent very large theoretical and ideological differences. Whereas the Articles
include the term "mutual" before "general," the Constitution uses the term
"general" alone, suggesting that there is indeed a set of interests common
to all the "people" that can be determined by one "universal" government.
Furthermore, the phrase "to insure justice," from the preamble, suggests that
there is a form of "justice" that is not the product of political life but is transcendent, needing to be "insured" rather than practiced or constructed.

What is in fact the most mutual of all needs is the need to be protected from
would-be conquerors. Thus there are quite a few references within the Articles
to the relationship between states and other nations and the United States and
its defensive responsibilities. In Article VI there is an injunction against states
entering into alliances or treaties individually, which is obviously intended to

void any potential conflicts of interest or to prevent potentially hostile foreign interests from gaining influence in the country. In that same article there is also an injunction against accepting any titles from foreign states or princes, which once again goes to the question of foreign influence and divided loyalties. The article further prohibits the granting of titles within the United States by its own Congress, thereby implicitly recognizing the dangers of an overt class system to American republican ideology. Congress is granted the power to determine peace and war in Article IX, as well as many of the powers that correspond to such a power, such as the ability to make treaties and appoint ambassadors. But even within the area of national defense power is not unrestricted. The fact that the states themselves are responsible for the raising and paying of a militia, and that they will be responsible for the appointment of all officers under the rank of colonel, points to a regime that is very suspicious of a standing army, or an army that is in any way too detached from local authority.

One looks in vain in the Articles of Confederation for any hint of political centralization that would deprive states of any but the most rudimentary powers necessary to forge a protective union that would safeguard not the union itself but its critical parts. Thus the question of the success or failure of the Articles becomes a rather simple one. Was the new union of the states able to protect them from conquerors? The answer was "yes," and we know this because the revolution fought under the Articles was quite successful. Was the Articles of Confederation the best devised constitution in terms of economic prosperity? Or, for an expanding "empire," did it provide stability and uniformity within the states themselves? The answer is "no," and it did not do so in large part because it was never intended to do such things. But did it allow each state to determine its own political fate, did it allow for the expanding democratic participation within many of those states to continue, did it allow for local political associations to flourish unencumbered by the larger demands of a more rational, uniform political order or nation-state? Yes, it did.

Historian Merrill Jensen is probably uniquely responsible for the rediscovery of the Articles of Confederation as a legitimate *and* positive part of America's political past. In his work he recognizes that the Articles was not a "failed" constitution, that it in fact represented the manifestation of a far different set of political and social values than did the constitution of the second founding. This is clearly evidenced when he writes:

> Much of the argument against England had been devoted to proving that colonial legislatures were independent of any outside legislative power. Inasmuch as the revolt was in part an effort to maintain that position, it was hardly to be expected that another such power would be set up by the radical party which had brought about the revolt. . . . Speaking broadly, it was democracy they wanted, and they knew full well that the kind of democracy they wanted was incompatible with centralization.[45]

That kind of democracy was local, participatory, and sovereign within its sphere. It was the culmination of 150 years of practical activity and evolving political theory. It represented the republicanism that held that the community was prior to the individual, while at the same time implicitly embracing the emerging democratic political culture that expanded individual participation in the interpretive process within a particular community. The Articles represented a political faith in the ability of political participation and empowerment to make both a better citizenry and a better nation. The strength of the nation would be its plurality, its differences, which would be protected by its constitution. The constitution and the confederation would subsequently be protected not by making them into a unified whole but by acknowledging, as had the Revolution, what people were most willing to fight for and defend—not abstractions or "nations" but local associations and communities, things that were close and known. It was in many ways a perfect, though Americanized, solution to Rousseau's dilemma in the *Social Contract,* of finding "a form of association which will defend the person and goods of each member with the collective force of all, and under which each individual, while uniting himself with the others, obeys no one but himself, and remains as free as before."[46] The Americanization of the solution under the Articles is to define freedom as public freedom, or the freedom to participate in local political life, while at the same time having that right protected with the collective force of the confederation, which helped to ensure both participation and power.

To paraphrase Jensen, the Revolution was above all else a revolt against centralization of political authority.[47] The first founders in the states forged a political theory from practice when they organized to throw off a tyrant and his cohorts, then they enshrined and institutionalized that theory so as to provide the context for further action when they adopted the Articles of Confederation. Whatever its flaws as a constitution might have eventually proven to be in light of its own best version of itself, one of them was not going to be recasting the world as a new and improved version of what had existed before, or would have existed had the Revolution been lost. "The Articles of Confederation were designed to prevent the central government from infringing upon the rights of the states,"[48] for all the political, historical, and theoretical reasons cited and defended above. Viewed in light of this goal, it could never be seen as a "failed" constitution—it did what it was asked to do. Does that mean that the political world was more orderly, prosperous, rational, or able to sustain an empire? No; not because of a flaw, but because of a design. There were options available, and each came with its own set of offerings both positive and negative, and each option represented in its own way a particular political faith. Those options, from the perspective of most who made the Revolution and founded the states and the confederation, were probably expressed as well some years later by Tocqueville as they have been by anyone:

For my part, I cannot conceive that a nation can live, much less prosper, without a high degree of centralization of government. But I think that administrative centralization only serves to enervate the people that submit to it, because it constantly tends to diminish their civic spirit. Administrative centralization succeeds, it is true, in assembling, at a given time and place, all the available resources of the nation, but it militates against the increase of those resources. It brings triumph on the day of battle, but in the long run diminishes a nation's power. So it can contribute to the ephemeral greatness of one man but not to the permanent propriety of a people.[49]

This, then, was part of the vision, part of the faith that supported America's first foundings; but it was not the only faith to emerge in America after the Revolution. There was another group of people, who looked at what we were becoming, with all of its messiness and "irrationality," with all of its democracy and lack of uniformity, and said "Enough is enough." These people then set out to bring order to a disorderly world. The Articles of Confederation, and America's first founding vision, were, despite their appearance of disorder (as in a lack of uniformity), very coherent in terms of their vision and ideology. The vision of their detractors was equally coherent, though vastly different; and it is to them that we turn now.

A NEW WORLD ORDER

There is no shortage of material dealing with the second American founding and the production of the Constitution of the United States of America. There is also no shortage of controversies with regard to that period of American history and how to quantify and qualify it. Furthermore, Americans are lucky in that they are part of a relatively young nation that has been among the most carefully documented in the history of the world. In other words, if people find the prevailing interpretations of our early history unsatisfactory, they have, thanks to the copious scholarship/literary archaeology of American academics like Max Farrand,[50] and the discipline of our forebears who committed so many of their observations to paper, the tools they need to construct their own interpretation of those events and to draw their own conclusions.[51] Thus there is in America an absence of legends and quasi-mythical lawgivers who were "born from the earth" or visited upon us by the gods to create something where there was nothing. This has not stopped us from constructing some myths of our own over time, but it has stopped those myths from prohibitively veiling the past to those who would know it. There are no names that we as a people cannot speak, nor are there any to whom we must give sacrifice. Such is the nature of the modern world.

Nevertheless, there has been, according to Louis Hartz, something of a "Talmudic" reverence for the American Constitution that is so pervasive that he is led to claim "that law has flourished on the corpse of philosophy in America,"[52] in effect denying an American capacity for serious political innovation or political life. In Hartz's words, America is in a state of political "adolescence" that must somehow be "transcended." And though this polemical statement is a rather useful historical device, it is incomplete because we are never told by Hartz exactly *which* Constitution he is talking about.

There are at this writing some twenty-seven different versions of the American Constitution (or perhaps seventeen if the Bill of Rights is taken collectively). Some of the additions (and perhaps the lone subtraction) have been relatively minor procedural changes, but others have represented radical departures from previous versions. And there is the vast body of constitutional law and the subsequent body of commentary on that law that, when taken together, conspire to depict the existence of "multiple" constitutions both consecutively and, in a strange way, concurrently. Thus it is not so much the document itself that Americans "worship" but the *idea* of the document. This is evidenced by the fact that many Americans, including those selected to interpret it officially, "worship" a vastly different substantive Constitution than do their peers or fellow citizens. Yet, however important the questions concerning constitutional interpretation are, they are for the purpose of this volume less important than how the *idea* of the Constitution originated. In other words, before we can turn effectively to questions like what the Constitution means, we would do well to ask why the Constitution is.

The "critical period" discourse given life in the work of John Fiske has now been rebuked by more rigorous scholarship intended to place the American founders in a more realistic and less "Olympian" context. In Merrill Jensen's neoprogressive *The New Nation*, we find a drastic revision of the highly suspect claims of Fiske (and of Publius). Here Jensen argues that the "critical period" was not so critical after all, that many of the problems facing America after the Revolution, such as debt and economic depression, were to be expected and were being dealt with in a way that would have allowed the Confederacy to continue functioning quite well. To Jensen's voice we could also add that of the noted historian Forrest MacDonald, who in many ways is much more sympathetic to the second founding than Jensen:

> Objectively, the first decade of the History of the United States was a whopping success. The greatest achievement, of course, was the winning of independence, but there was more. Despite certain economic dislocations, most Americans were prospering. It was true the country had no national government. . . . The vast majority of the people, however, would probably have agreed that they needed no stronger union.[53]

And yet a stronger union emerged, and it eclipsed the Confederacy in the process. In doing so, it provided American scholars with over a century's worth of historical questions. At least with the Fiske argument in place the Constitution had made nice, neat, historical sense. The story had a beginning, a middle, and end; there was the narrative unity of a popular novel with a precipitating event, a crisis, and a resolution to the crisis, all culminating in a happy ending with only winners. But history is seldom that neat and uncomplicated, and political history far less so than many other subfields. The real tale of the American Constitution is more complex than the one told by Fiske and those who eagerly followed the path of least intellectual resistance, and it is in many ways vastly more interesting. It is a tale about intrigue, conspiracy, money, violence, power, authority, great and not so great men, and even morality. In short, it is a political drama filled with all the rich complexity that human beings bring with them into public life, and as such it militates against any discussion of it within the framework of any single causal model. The best we can do here is, once again, try to find that "cultural matrix," or broad ideological theme, that connected the framers of the Constitution, and then assess the practical and theoretical harvest that results from their collective activities and the impact they had on political life in America.

In the same way that the story of "chaos and patriots to the rescue" is of little help in understanding the political events of the 1780s, a story of "utopia and traitors to the revolution" is not much better. And yet, quite often before some common ground can be reached and a fair assessment rendered, we must begin at the murky fringes of an event and work our way through them. So it is that the work of Fiske and others who would romanticize the framers and the Constitution they produced would have to be challenged in a manner as extreme as the one they themselves had embraced. Thus there is the work of Charles Beard[54] and the "progressive historians."[55]

Beard's now-famous argument was that rather than looking back at America's founding period and constructing our own mythology of great names and olympian figures, we should look at the founding fathers as men endowed with real interests and passions, and ask what motivated them and how those motivations manifested themselves in the political struggles of the day. Beard described his project in the following manner:

> The whole theory of the economic interpretation of history rests upon the concept that social progress in general is the result of contending interests in society—some favorable, others opposed, to change. On this hypothesis, we are required to discover at the very outset of the present study what classes and social groups existed in the United States just previous to the adoption of the Constitution and which of them, from the nature of their property, might have expected to benefit immediately and definitely by the overthrow of the old system and the establishment of the new. On the other hand, it must be discovered which of them might have expected more beneficial immediate results, on the whole, from the maintenance of the existing legal arrangements.[56]

Taken at face value for a moment, this statement of method does not automatically indict one group of founders while championing another—all people are equally "indicted" as Hobbesian interest maximizers, as the product of their economic conditions and desires; and each political system benefits one "class" at the expense of another. The last clause is true; particular political systems do benefit certain people and certain groups more than others. It is equally the case that people do not intentionally act against their own interest. What is not convincing is the narrow conception of interest posited by Beard and others of his ilk, and this is where his work eventually goes astray.

The American founders may have been "aristocratic" in political outlook, but they were not oligarchs. This is an important qualitative distinction that the politics of class often discounts entirely or ignores. It was possible to be for the public good *and* to believe that democracy was dangerous—especially in the eighteenth century. By stressing the monetary aspects of the founder's "interests," Beard undermines his own work and opens it up to the quantitative probes of Robert Brown and Forrest MacDonald[57] that would later diminish the respectability of Beard's approach. The evidence amassed by these scholars and others has shown that the linkage proffered by Beard among fortunes, interests, and political ideology was inconsistent at best and spurious at worst. The contribution Beard did make, however, is not small. He and a few others rescued America's past from the realm of myth and opened the door to important and necessary historical conversations about what America was intended to be and, more important for his own times, what America was and is. As Richard Hofstadter claimed in his often-quoted line, "Beard no longer persuades, but he still sets the terms of debate."[58]

Roughly three kinds of thematic responses to the tenor of Beard's work, as opposed to the more content-based approach of MacDonald, developed over the following five decades in the American academy. I will treat these modes of response with a rather broad brush, since there are many fine literature reviews; then I will sketch what I see as the most viable approach to understanding the second founding in the literature that followed these initial responses and make my own partial case for that synthetic line of thought. Those categories of response, for lack of better labels, could be called consensus, neoprogressive, and Straussian (although I am tempted to refer to this last category as neoromantic). The reader should be forewarned that this approach is at best an exercise in oversimplification, and at worst it is anti-intellectual, in that writers with very different perspectives, projects, sensibilities, and arguments are lumped together in makeshift categories that ultimately deny them the subtle reading many of them deserve.

The consensus school originally included Louis Hartz, Richard Hofstadter, Robert Brown, and Daniel Boorstin. Other authors, such as John Diggins, Isaac Kramnick, and Joyce Appleby, joined later.[59] These writers tend to dismiss the conflict-based approach of the progressives, which suggested that the founding period saw the rise of at least two classes with diametrically opposed interests that each attempted to install at the head of the emerging society. In its place they saw fundamental agreement on the basic political and social issues of the day that centered on a supposed Lockean liberalism of individualism, private property, limited government, liberty, and capitalism. When Hartz's commentary on Daniel Shays and his rebellion ("It is enough to note now that when the Massachusetts radicals frightened the nation they did so in the mood of unhappy kindred spirits, not in the mood of wholesale antagonists. They were inside, rather than outside, the liberal process of American politics.")[60] is read as a metaphor for consensus thought in general, we glimpse a conception of America where the divisions are over technique and not substance. Or if we paraphrase Boorstin, the genius of American political theory is that we do not have any, at least not any in the sense of European class-based political theory associated with modern political ideologies.

Thus, for this group of scholars, conflicts in American politics are not the product of class divisions or their derivative ideologies; rather, they represent intrafamilial disagreements over means but not ends. Those ends were the protection of life, liberty, and property such that private happiness would be possible for those who were willing to earn it. Furthermore, the role of government was to be strictly limited to actions that would facilitate and preserve that particular ideological arrangement without end. As Diggins would later claim, in response to those who would deny the Lockean consensus school's approach, the capacity for political regeneration from man's natural condition, as depicted in the work of Renaissance humanism associated with theorists like Machiavelli, would prove too utopian for the American founders.[61]

Although there is much to be said for this line of argument post 1789, and thus for Diggins's work especially, there is little evidence to suggest anything like hegemony in the period prior to the Constitutional Convention. The liberalism ascribed to Locke and connected to the second American founders was at best a by-product of the convention. It was not for many, especially Madison and others of his general outlook, the rationale for the convention. There is at this point no reason not to take Madison and others at their word when they claim to be searching for republican remedies for republican defects.[62] If the remedies fail to maintain republican virtues (perhaps making the cure worse than the disease), and cause the nation in the long run to enter into a new and different "liberal" cultural matrix, it does not necessarily mean that such a state of affairs was intended by all who sought reform. For all their brilliance, even the American founders were not beyond the reach of the vast contingency of the political world, nor could they escape the limits of time in order to construct a political world based on the *nineteenth-century* liberal theory that would follow in their wake. The *Federalist Papers* were produced as post hoc justifications for work already completed and thus cannot authorize that of which they are a product. This last idea provides an appropriate starting point for the next set of scholars, whom I call the Straussians.

This school includes Harry Jaffa, Thomas Pangle, David Epstein, Thomas West, Christopher Bruell, Robert Webbing, and Walter Berns, but the most important name of all is that of Martin Diamond.[63] Although each of the authors has his contribution to make to a founding discourse, and although many of them diverge from the basic findings proposed by Diamond's work, they all share in some sense a basic fraternity with his (and Strauss's) core political (philosophical?) project.[64] At the center of the general Straussian model there is a seemingly simple proposition: "The classics had taught that justice exists, that it is discoverable by reason, and that it can be a guide for political life. What if the classics were right?"[65] The general argument of these scholars, if I understand it correctly, runs in roughly the following way:

1. There is a form of justice that is prior to man and therefore not created by him, and by which, if at all possible, he should order his political world.

2. The contemplation of that form is the greatest life an individual can live; it is *the* good life.

3. Only a select few in any given time and place have the philosophic nature that allows them to be satisfied with a life of contemplation of the good (justice), and hence they are the ones who in a perfect world ought to rule.

4. The problem that arises is that the majority of people are motivated not by the quest for knowledge (they lack the appropriate natures) but, rather, by the quest for lower-order pleasures and bodily satisfactions. They resent the imposition of a just order with its rigorous demands and esoteric concerns, preferring to live by their will rather than reason.

5. This preference for "opinion" rather than knowledge on the part of the majority makes them hostile toward philosophy in general, and philosophers in particular, because the discipline and its disciples typically stand in opposition to the will of the majority.

6. This opposition, if too pronounced, can lead to the "death" of philosophers, and perhaps of philosophy itself, at the hands of a majority and their demagogic rulers, who have a vested interest in the status quo.

7. Thus philosophers must either avoid public life altogether or, if they choose to participate, must do so in such a way that (a) the majority will not feel threatened or affronted by their opinions, so as to avoid persecution; (b) those in power will be directed toward wise decisions; and (c) those of similar natures will be able to read between the lines and understand the true teachings intended, and thus carry on the tradition without suffering the fate of, say, Socrates.

The threefold task of a good Straussian political philosopher is, then, to discover (a) who these philosophers were; (b) how they went about their philosophic duties, given their particular historical contexts; and (c) what their hidden philosophical teachings were. Given this rough outline, it is clear that the ideas contained in this volume so far are diametrically opposed to any such reading of early American political thought. However, I have spent a little time here because without at least a rudimentary understanding of the overall foundation upon which much of the Straussian-centered work rests, what follows may be denied the reading it deserves.

Martin Diamond's specific argument with regard to the second American founding is quite simple. Succinctly put, Diamond argues that the political/philosophical teachings of the framers are contained in the primary documents of the founding period, including the Declaration of Independence and the *Federalist Papers*. Those teachings are teachings about democracy as a form of political organization. The specific concern of the framers, and more specifically of Publius, was to find a form of political organization that rested upon the doctrine of popular consent while avoiding the defects of majority rule—in other words, to find a system of government that was pleasing to the many while restraining them from doing serious harm to the few. Diamond's reading of the Declaration is consistent with this mode of thought:

> The Declaration of Independence formulates two criteria for judging whether any government is good, or indeed legitimate. Good government must rest, procedurally, upon the consent of the governed. Good government, substantively, must do only certain things, e.g. secure certain rights.[66]

This set of assertions leads, however, to a more important question for Diamond and, according to him, for the framers of the Constitution as well: "whether the procedure will bring about the substance."[67] The answer, in terms of unfettered participatory democracy, was clearly and resoundingly "no." Thus, he argues, there was the Constitution, which was designed to fix the "genuine defects" of democracy while maintaining the democratic character of the regime. This was done through the institutionalization of national representation and the corresponding empowerment of that national regime.[68] Thus he claims that, far from being an antidemocratic "thermidore," the Constitution represented the product of "wise partisans of democracy":

> Unlike modern "value-free" social scientists, the Founding Fathers believed that true knowledge of the good and bad in human conduct was possible, and that they themselves possessed sufficient knowledge to discern the really grave defects of popular government and their proper remedies. . . . The Founding Fathers did seek to prejudice the outcome of democracy; they sought to alter by certain restraints, the likelihood that the majority would decide certain political issues in bad ways.[69]

Thus we can see the rudiments of the more general Straussian political methodology emerging in the course of Diamond's work insofar as the founders are said to have developed a model that is legitimate in the democratic eyes of the many and at the same time is so well designed as to prevent them from doing any harm to the political order. In that the aims of political life in America are fundamentally altered from the quest for justice (the superior classical aim) to the quest for order and peace (the best possible modern aim), the American founders can at best be said to have founded a "second-best" regime, but perhaps it is also the best *possible regime*. In Straussian language this is a regime that preserves the domain of philosophy from the dangers of majority tyranny even though it ultimately fails consistently to empower those who ought to rule.

Madison's discussion of faction in *Federalist* no. 10 and no. 51 is used by Diamond to illustrate the way in which Madison devised a scheme of government that circumvented the ability of the many to tyrannize the few—in other words, he made the city safe for philosophy even though he could not manage to install philosophers at the helm. The founders have in fact created a political world where the "cure" for self-interest or passion is in fact self-interest or passion; people are not made any better, but the political world is not made any worse. The American founding represents, for Diamond, "a rare moment when the 'prejudices of the community' were on the side of wisdom."[70] His only criticism of the founders, in whom he sees at least a "finger of that Almighty hand [of God]" working, is that they may have failed "to make provision for men of their own kind to come after them," apparently thinking that such men would not be needed, and perhaps failing to perceive the "degree of reflection and public-spiritedness" that might be necessary to help the nation solve modern problems.[71]

The major difficulty in offering any sort of critique of the Diamond model is the same difficulty that one discovers with most work done in a similar vein: it rests on a cosmological foundation that is not only foreign but also hostile to any modern political project that attempts to place people and their ideas in the context of their time rather than measuring them against some transcendent standard. It would seem that one either accepts or rejects the realm of the forms, as understood by Plato, as a source of human knowledge and guidance; but it would not seem that any real compromise is possible between the two approaches. As West, an adherent of the methodology, writes in a similar vein: "Either one views man as Hobbes and Locke did, as a being who is himself the source of meaning for life, or one views man, as Aristotle and Plato did, as guided by his nature towards ends that he did not make up for himself."[72] I am not sure what the epistemological value is of declaring that the founding fathers had "*true* knowledge of the good and bad," as opposed to saying that the founding fathers had valuable opinions, or strong arguments concerning right and wrong that deserved to be listened to, and perhaps even heeded. But, for Diamond and others of his ilk, this is a critical and absolute distinction. It is a distinction that I reject.

This is not to say that there are not worthwhile things to be learned in this work. For example, I believe that the general tone of Diamond's interpretation of the second founding is in large part correct, although I disagree with the normative context he constructs. The founders were working within a democratic framework, and they were attempting to safeguard certain possibilities from the quick reach of a majority. However, there is little need to grant them the status of demigods, as Diamond does. They were men—some good, some perhaps great, some wise, and some not—and their intentions were no doubt distributed in much the same manner as the intentions of any group might be. Their teachings should be accepted or rejected on the basis of their usefulness to the goals and values we as a people have acknowledged over time.

This does not, however, mean that we are reduced to the nihilism that claims one opinion is as good as the next, such that all things are permitted. What it means is that there is no good reason to believe that received values are superior in the political world to created values.[73] What we lose, I suppose, in bringing the founders down to earth is the certainty that would remove many of the persistent ambiguities of modern political life, as well as the notion of a natural hierarchy and bastion of authority from which we could learn to order our lives and our political realm "properly." But then we might need to question whether that reverence would not simply compound the problem Diamond himself recognized at the close of his work. In other words, is it just possible that the whole notion of the founders as superior sorts of people who knew the "truth" is the cause of our lack of "reflection and public-spiritedness"? Is it possible that the price we might be forced to pay for such a citizenry is the power to make mistakes?

The final model of the second American founding that I would like to explore, and the one that I find the most useful, is the neoprogressive model; we could also call it the *political* model. Here the founders are depicted as political actors forced to conduct their activities in a certain historical/political context. They are motivated by a particular conception of the political realm and a particular vision of America's future that they feel would best be served by a particular kind of political regime that was not being served under the Articles of Confederation. The list of names attached to this model is rather eclectic and will at first glance strike many readers as perhaps a dubious thematic grouping, but the common thread that I believe exists among them is their willingness to follow Beard's lead and to bring the founders down to earth and see them behaving as men behave, at the same time keeping them within the political/historical context in which they had to work.[74]

To begin with the obvious, no one does something that is harmful to his or her interests—and that includes the American founders. This is something many critics of republicanism, such as Don Herzog, never seem to grasp—

republicans are self-interested, just like liberals. The difference is that they have different conceptions of what sort of regime serves those interests best. There have been, thankfully, few self-chosen political martyrs throughout history, and especially throughout American history. The fact that a certain set of political arrangements fails to harm someone, and perhaps even benefits him or her, does not in itself mean that something is nefarious or ethically suspect. Even Plato, Diamond's great implicit exemplar, places philosophers at the helm of state. Beard's broad project of unmasking the founders as self-interested "politicians" seemed striking only because for so long the nation had been under the spell of the founders as deliverers who had, out of sheer concern for the public weal, forged a new nation.

The most nefarious part of Beard's work, the claim of particular economic benefits accruing to particular founders in some sort of oligarchical coup, was ultimately unsupported by the evidence. We can sustain the broad Beardian critical project—bringing the founders down to earth—as valid even while rejecting the more specific positive claims contained in the work, without doing any intellectual damage to our understanding of the second founding. The important distinction thus is not between self-interest and selflessness, but between good faith and bad faith. In other words, it is possible that the founders were doing what they did because they thought it served their interests *as well as* the interests of the nation as a whole, and thus were acting in good faith. While good and honest people may disagree with their choices, or believe that they may ultimately have been mistaken in their particular judgments, that does not necessarily mean their motives must be ethically suspect.

In his work *E Pluribus Unum,* Forrest MacDonald paints a dark picture of a union at risk from the messy, turbulent, sometimes corrupt, and always, it would seem, self-aggrandizing state governments. He calls the constitutional reformation of 1789 a "miracle":

> That the American Revolution and the American people—of all the world's peoples the most materialistic and most vulgar and least disciplined—should have produced a governmental system adequate to check the very forces they unleashed; this was the miracle of the age, and of the succeeding age, and of all ages to come. The French, the Russians, the Italians, the Germans, all the planet's peoples in their turn, would become so unrestrained as to lose contact with sanity. The Americans might have suffered a similar history, had they followed the lead of those who, in 1787 and 1788, spoke in the name of the people and of popular "rights." But there were giants on the earth in those days, and they spoke in the name of the nation, and the people followed them.[75]

Yet despite this unrestrained praise of 1965, MacDonald twenty years later reassessed the criticalness of the "critical period." It perhaps was a "miracle" that a national government could come into existence, given the aims and ideology of the Revolution, but it was not the result of divine intervention;

rather, its source was the persistence of a well-organized, systematic group of politician-statesmen. The key to MacDonald's formulation above is the last sentence, which tells us there was a concerted effort by a respected group who spoke in a new and, we should add, previously marginal or nonexistent political idiom of nationalism.

In the previous pages I have gone to great lengths to show that the primary locus of political power and authority was in the states and local political communities, and that for most people the Revolution was justified and fought on the basis of protecting that locus from centralization and usurpation. Given this, it is a mistake to believe that for any but a small number, if that, of American patriots the idea of a national regime with significant power, let alone "supremacy," was the object of the Revolution. Given the basic design and history of colonial America, per the British charters and territorial grants, until at least the mid-to-late eighteenth century the concept of "American" nationalism was at best a political non sequitur for any but the most prescient or the most covetous actors. And although the prescient people are a curiosity of some note, the important ones for our purposes are the covetous. And in the revolutionary period, and for some time after, these were the ones who spoke in the language of nationalism.

Pre-Beard and post-Brown/MacDonald conventional wisdom, along with Publius, tells us that the framing of the Constitution was a response to the aftermath of the Revolution and the excess it invoked. Often overlooked by that wisdom is the period between Beard, and Hartz and Brown/MacDonald when some very important work was being done by scholars in the Beardian mode, but without Beard's specific progressive turn-of-the-century political agenda. In an essay titled "The Idea of a National Government During the American Revolution," Merrill Jensen makes what seems to be a very sound case for the existence throughout the revolutionary period, both pre- and post-, of a persistent group of predisposed nationalists. His contention rests on the claim that

> it is difficult to maintain that the Articles of Confederation were the result of ignorance and inexperience or that the Constitution was the result of wisdom and experience. Actually both governments were the results of choice by men, very few of whom changed their minds between 1776 and 1787. Differing conceptions of government, not ignorance, lay at the bottom of the political conflicts and changes of the American Revolution.[76]

The argument, simply put, is that the Revolution was fought and led by two groups, one of which envisioned increasing democratization and the preservation of local political associations, and one that favored, if not continued ties with England, at least the replication of a strong central government. The main figure in the latter group is Alexander Hamilton, but there were others as well; and some of them, like Washington, were quite prominent and well respected at the close of the war. The turning point, according to Jensen, for the nationalists was the Newburgh conspiracy, during which some nationalists flirted dangerously with a military solution to their ideological quest for a national, centralized, post-Revolution government.[77] Washington's well-known refusal, and the subsequent disbanding of the troops, forced the nationalists to achieve their goals by more reasonable political paths.

There is a danger in using Hamilton as the exemplar for the nationalist political project rather than, say, Washington or Madison. Reasonable men could still believe that a strong central government was necessary without being potential tyrants. This is the "conspiratorial" influence of Beard that Jensen cannot completely escape—nor, perhaps would he want to. In the first place, the idea of a conspiracy is too suggestive of a well-orchestrated plot with very particularized goals, such as achieving power through a military coup. The movement by the constitutionalists was much more complex and the goals of the movement much less particularized, in that they sought to create a government and not simply to usurp power and authority for themselves. If this had been what they wanted, there is a good chance they could have succeeded with Washington's help.

This leads me to my second point, which is that the context in which the framers chose to operate—persuasion—forces us to expand the notion of conspiracy beyond useful linguistic limits. In other words, leaving aside the secrecy of the convention itself for now, if the word "conspiracy" can be used to describe both private and secretive acts designed to achieve some selfish end, and basically public acts designed to convince and persuade people to behave in certain ways, then it would seem to be a word without much substantive content. Finally, there is an assumption built into this framework that is mistaken: the assumption of a Godlike omnipotence that conspiracy theorists, as well as those who argue along similar lines (such as Diamond), seem to ascribe to the framers, which holds out the idea that somehow they knew explicitly what the outcome of their experiments would be—which they most assuredly did not!

The useful contribution that Jensen makes to a discussion of the second founding is the depiction of the "nationalists" as something like a political party with all of the attributes we ascribe to such things: an ideology, an agenda, particular members, internal divisions, and so on. Given this, it makes no more sense to accuse them of being conspiratorial that it does to accuse the Democrats of conspiracy when a Republican is in the White House or vice versa. This is not to say, however, that the struggle between these two "parties" was not dramatically more important, as well as more normatively substantive, in that the winner would in many ways determine the political future of the nation. Rather, the point here is that the struggle took place between groups who, even though they had widely divergent visions for the country and its future, ultimately accepted, with a few notable exceptions, the common political framework in which the battle was to take place. And this is the point where the work of people like Stanley Elkins and Eric McKitrick, Douglass Adair, and John Roche becomes somewhat controlling.

In their essay Elkins and McKitrick differentiate between two groups of partisans in a manner that reflects the work of Jensen, but without the conspiratorial overtones. They argue that what distinguishes the first founders from the second is the process of political socialization that each group underwent. Those who defended the first founding—Sam Adams, Patrick Henry, Richard Henry Lee, George Clinton—came of age mainly in the period before the Revolution and had made their careers in the muddy political world of state politics. The second founders, the "young men of the Revolution"—Hamilton, Madison, Washington, Henry Knox, James Wilson, Robert Morris—"quite literally saw their careers launched in the Revolution"[78] itself. Although some of them had participated in public affairs somewhat earlier, they

> became nationally known after 1776 and the wide recognition which they subsequently achieved came first and foremost through their identification with the continental war effort. All of them had been united in an experience, and had formed commitments, which dissolved provincial boundaries; and they had come to full public maturity in a setting which enabled ambition, public service, leadership, and self-fulfillment to be conceived, for each in his way, with a grandeur of scope unknown to any previous generation.[79]

Thus we have two groups of politicians, one socialized by a political world that envisioned the Revolution as both a defense of an older cultural matrix and an opportunity to create the conditions for formal legitimacy and fine-tuning, and another who came of age in a political context that demanded that, for at least a certain time, the old matrix be transcended. For the latter, that period of transcendence pointed toward a new and vastly different political matrix whereby the Revolution became an opportunity for a new beginning. Thus the emphasis of Elkins and McKitrick on "inertia" and "energy" comes to make perfect sense in light of these two different readings of what had now become a contested historical event. This theme is also evident in a slightly different context in the work on the American military establishment by Richard Kohn, who argues in his opening chapter that the Continental Army was the first truly national *political* organization. He says of those who held places of great responsibility—Washington, Hamilton, Knox, et al.:

> Young at the beginning of the war, for many of these men service in the Continental Army provided the first real taste of public life. Significantly enough, the experience was at the national level fighting for the whole country, serving in the first large organization which threw citizens from different states together. . . . At the formative stage in their lives they were exposed to military values; they learned the strength of

executive leadership in contrast to the weakness of Congress under the Articles of Confederation.[80]

Theoretically this interpretation is quite strong, once again owing its intellectual origin to the work of Plato in his *Republic*. It was there that Western readers first encountered a sustained argument concerning the expected causal relationship between the guardians and their loyalty to the whole, and the corresponding reduction of all forms of particularistic association like the family, the tribe, and the guild. The guardians must be taught (even though it was unnatural) to love the *general* rather than the *particular* if the unitary society was to flourish without the disrupting affects of multiple loyalties. But the framers were not fully socialized Platonic guardians, reared from childhood to perform the tasks of state. They were also men, men who were interested in their place in the world and in the annals of history. It is here that Douglass Adair makes his important contribution to an understanding of the framers and their political project by showing how they as individuals reacted to their nationalist facticity both as patriots or self-appointed guardians, and also as self-interested individuals seeking a proper remembrance. One of the leading fallacies undergirding many accounts of the framers was the idea that interpretation meant an either/or choice: Either the framers were self-interested "possessive individuals," or they were disinterested patriots. It is entirely possible, and even likely, that most of them were both—concerned about themselves and concerned about their country. The second leading fallacy—and here Adair is exactly right—is that self-interest is strictly reserved to economic self-interest, when in fact there are many different ways in which self-interest can be expressed and carried out.

According to Adair, the framers were first of all transformed by their Revolutionary experiences insofar as their personal goals changed dramatically as a result of their participation in the event, as noted in the discussion above.[81] The most important aspect of that transformation was the increased desire for what he calls fame. Adair describes "fame" very politically, in strict historical/linguistic terms:

> *Fame,* in contrast to honor, is more public, more inclusive, and looks to the largest possible human audience. . . . it is the action or behavior of a "great man," who stands out, who towers above his fellows in some spectacular way. To be famous or renowned means to be widely spoken of by a man's contemporaries and also to act in such a way that posterity also remembers his name and actions. . . . The love of fame encourages a man to make history, to leave the mark of his deeds and his ideals on the world; it incites a man to refuse to be the victim of events and to become an "event-making" personality.[82]

Adair perceptively goes on to claim that "the love of fame is a noble passion because it can transform ambition and self-interest into dedicated effort for the community."[83] Thus he paints a picture of self-interested men transformed through public service into better individuals despite what may have been somewhat suspect initial motivations on their part. Furthermore, self-interest and patriotism are hereby merged so as to become mutually inextricable sorts of behavior, much to the chagrin of any strict Beardian. Perhaps this was Madison's ultimate hope for the majority of the population. Clearly it was his intention with regard to the representatives in the national government as per *Federalist* no. 51, with its emphasis on supplying "the defect of better motives." The question, however, that is raised by such an interpretation is what price the average citizen paid for the fame of the framers. I will turn to this question in the next chapter. But first, to finish this line of interpretation, we need to turn to a procedural question concerning how this fame was gained.

The picture painted so far of the second founders is one that sees them not as inspired by the hand or finger of God, but as politicians with a particular political vision who are acting in the sort of well-organized, concerted effort over time that is associated with the behavior of a political party. It depicts them both as the products of their circumstances, in that they came of age in the midst of the nation's first "national" moment, and as the authors of new circumstances designed to remain consistent with their received values and to further those values as well as, at the same time, to provide the opportunity for personal distinction or fame. There are two questions, however, that remain to be answered in terms of this process: (1) how they managed to execute their plan, given the general predisposition in the country against a national regime and the existing republican/democratic cultural matrix of the Revolution (which in itself is quite telling in terms of assessing the second founding), and (2) what theoretical justifications were used to legitimize that particular political project.

The history of the events leading to the Philadelphia Convention is well documented, but it also is highly contested historical ground. Events like Shays's Rebellion are subject to widely varying interpretations, as was the status of the country during the "critical period." Here, however, I am more interested in establishing the general nature of the process itself.

After the failure of Hamilton and his cronies to incite a military solution at Newburgh in 1783, the nationalists were forced to regroup and direct their energies into more civilized channels of "constitutional" reform (note that this event predates Shays's Rebellion by three years). Those channels took the form of a series of meetings in which nationalists managed, a little at a time, to manufacture momentum and consent for a Constitutional Convention.[84] In March 1785, James Madison, who had been unable to convince the Virginia Assembly that the Articles of Confederation needed revision, helped arrange a meeting of commissioners from Virginia and Maryland at Mount Vernon, ostensibly to discuss the friction over Chesapeake Bay and the Potomac River. The meeting was unsuccessful in resolving the existing problems, but it did result in an agreement between the two states on the need for some interstate cooperation. This led Madison to call for a general convention in September 1786 of all the states, to discuss general commercial problems. The result was the Annapolis Convention of 1786, which commissioners from New York, New Jersey, Pennsylvania, Delaware, and Virginia attended. Even though fewer than half of the existing states had been present, the convention, led by Alexander Hamilton, managed to issue a report calling for a Constitutional Convention in the summer of 1787. And despite the hubristic nature of the report, the Convention did ultimately become a reality due to the persistence and organizational skills of the nationalists.

In the most realistic depiction and assessment of the Constitution's framers and the Convention itself, John Roche argues that the framers were demo-cratic politicians engaged in behavior befitting a reform caucus. While that likeness is a bit too understated, given the sheer magnitude of the event, his essay does manage to underscore the *political* nature of the nationalist project, and thus captures the *political* nature and intentions of the individual members of that movement. Roche tells us that the representatives at the Convention "were, with their colleagues, *political men*—not metaphysicians, disembodied conservatives, or Agents of History . . . they were committed (perhaps willy-nilly) to working within the democratic framework, within a universe of pub-lic approval . . . the Philadelphia Convention was not a College of Cardinals or a council of Platonic guardians . . . it was a *nationalist* reform caucus."[85]

Yet despite what Roche discounts as proper descriptions of the framers, the reader should not be complacent about how radical and even subversive a "nationalist" reform caucus actually was at this period in the country's history. As Roche writes: "Effectively, the Constitutionalists had to induce the states, by democratic techniques of coercion, to emasculate themselves."[86] This would clearly be no easy task, especially if they chose to be explicit about it. Roche here also provides support for the "socialization thesis" suggested above, though his national institution, or frame of reference, is not the Conti-nental Army but the Continental Congress. He tells us accurately that thirty-nine delegates to the convention had served at one time or another in Con-gress, and that having done so, they possessed "a universe of discourse which provided them with a conceptual common denominator."[87] Once again, the idea that participation in a national regime could supply the "defect of better motives," or at least less parochial motives, is adopted.

Leaving this point aside, however, it is necessary to note Roche's largest contribution to the discourse on the second founding: the step-by-step map-ping out of the nationalist strategy and Convention maneuvering. The first stage in the process was to convince the majority of people that fundamental change was necessary. To do this, the nationalists began with the seemingly innocuous question of how anyone could be against reform. By all accounts, most average people, as well as political elites, both Federalist and Anti-Federalist alike, were in favor of some reform in the status quo. Thus, to resist the Convention would be the functional equivalent of attempting to thwart progress or improvement—something that was not done lightly in the Age of Enlightenment. And yet the call for change required action and commitment on the part of delegates who had to leave home for an extended period of time, and thus it is not surprising that those who went for the most part were the most committed to change. Roche points this out as well when he contends that there was "a lack of clear-cut ideological divisions in the Convention."[88]

The fact that the Convention was a "remarkably homogeneous body on the ideological level" was due more to the lack of interest on the part of those who felt that fundamental change was unnecessary, and unlikely, than to nationwide agreement or consensus. Roche perceptively writes, "It takes an iron will to spend a hot summer as an ideological *agent provocateur*,"[89] and this was a will that few had at the time. Thus, among those who remained, the differences of opinion "were not ideological; they were *structural*," according to Roche. The nationalists had thus completed two of the most difficult tasks: convincing people of the need for reform and successfully stacking the meeting with like-minded men. Their next move would all but seal their success in accomplishing at least a large measure of their program.

That next move was to introduce the Virginia Plan, which "envisioned a unitary national government effectively freed from and dominant over the states,"[90] as "just a model" from which to work. That model, however, clearly set the agenda for the weeks and months that followed; and although compromises were made along the way, the basic ideology underlying the Convention from that point forward was nationalist in character. What followed, then, was the series of additions and subtractions that was to be expected in a group of important, intelligent, and egotistic men. The specifics of the document and the nature of the compromises are well known, but there is still contention over the intent and theory of the document as produced. This is not necessarily the fault of contemporary readers, since, as Roche tells it:

> The Convention was not a seminar in analytic philosophy or linguistic analysis. . . . There was a good deal of definitional pluralism with respect to the problems the delegates did discuss, but when we move to the question of extrapolated intentions, we enter the realm of spiritualism. . . . Probably our greatest difficulty is that we know so much more about what the Framers *should have meant* than they themselves did.[91]

All that we have to work with in terms of figuring out what they intended or did not intend are the post-Convention defenses of Publius and the sentiments expressed by the participants over the course of their lives and through their political work. That work will be the focus of chapter 4, as we return to the theoretical underpinnings of the Constitution and the ideological/cultural/political ramifications of the *Federalist Papers*. What we can be certain of at this time, however, is that the basic intention of the Convention and the nationalists who by and large attended it was to establish a new constitutional order that would in large measure unify the states under a central authority and sovereign in order to solve perceived problems with the current union and to put in place a more ideologically acceptable form of government. The change was neither necessary (whatever that means) nor ordained by God; it was not the product of history operating as some detached, extrahuman force but of self-interested, educated, political men who knew what they wanted, and who strategically went about getting it. They did all of this while operating within the broad democratic context in which they lived, and whether they liked it or not is of no real concern for us here and now.

So it is that thinkers like Forrest MacDonald, who claims that the framers were "mainly young and practical-minded men, idealistic, but non-ideological,"[92] are partly right and partly wrong. They were not "born from the earth" but from the Revolution itself, which they saw as an opportunity for greatness for the nation and themselves. They were filled with a national "ideology" that drove their thinking and their actions. They were politicians of the first order and first-rate radicals as well. They were better organized and more forceful than their opposition for the most part, because the idea of a "decentralist party" is rather odd. But their success, organization, and intelligence do not guarantee their ultimate rightness, just as the fact that they were "politicians" does not condemn them to being wrong. To make these determinations requires that we assess their arguments and the historical realities that flow from their praxis in light of other possibilities and arguments. The answer, perhaps as banal as it is correct, as to why we have the Constitution is on the face of it quite simple—we have the Constitution because a group of well-organized and highly motivated men managed to forge a consensus for change, to take the lead in determining the direction in which that change would occur, and to convince enough people that that direction was the right one. Whether they got what they wanted, we can never be sure; but whether we as a nation got what was best for us, we can, and people did, argue about.

The Faith of the Federalists

. . . we were under a necessity of either returning to the house, and by our presence enabling them to call a convention before our constituents could have the means of information, or time to deliberate on the subject, or by absenting ourselves from the house, prevent the measure taking place. . . . Thus circumstanced and thus influenced, we determined the next morning, again to absent ourselves from the house, when James M'Calmount, esquire, a member from Franklin, and Jacob Miley, esquire, a member from Dauphin, were seized by a number of citizens of Philadelphia, who had collected together for that purpose, their lodgings were violently broken open, their clothes torn, and after much abuse and insult, they were forcibly dragged through the streets of Philadelphia to the State house, and there detained by force, and in the presence of the majority, who had the day before, voted for the first of the proposed resolutions, treated with the most insulting language; while the house so formed proceeded to finish their resolutions, which they meant to offer you as the doings of the legislature of Pennsylvania.

—The Subscribers Members

The remembrance above[1] paints a slightly different picture of the ratification of the Constitution than accounts emphasizing a collective, consensual, cathartic experience on the part of Americans during the second founding. There were people who disagreed and did so on the basis of principles and tradition, not caprice and fear. As Sheldon Wolin reminds us, the second founding was "revolutionary in the precise sense that it broke with the established direction of political development and available political experience."[2] It was also a "metaideological" revolution in the sense that a "new science of politics" was substituted for more traditional experiential conceptions of political life and political change. In other words, as much as the shift from the Articles of Confederation to the Constitution was the result of a political/ideological movement that we have called "nationalism," it was also representative of a critical shift in the way in which *politics,* and ultimately constitution making, were conceived teleologically. No longer was political theory in America going to flow from political life itself; rather, political life was now to be the product of political theory. This distinction for Wolin becomes the difference between "tending" and "intending" a Constitution, where the former "inclines toward a democratic conception of political life . . . it implies active care of things close at hand, not mere solicitude. Active care is not, however, a synonym for expert knowledge."[3] "Intending" is defined as "an authoritarian conception as the nineteenth century understood that term: one who loves the principle of authority, that is, the right to command and enforce obedience . . . to seek deliberately to bring about some desired effect or purpose . . . to stretch, strain, make tense, intensify, to direct (the mind) toward some objective . . . [it is] less concerned with taking care of things than with acting effectively, not in the future, but toward it . . . unlike the tending mode, intending will subordinate collective identity to the needs of power."[4]

Along with the substantive political changes wrought by the Constitution, then, there are also crucial "metapolitical" changes that must be understood if we are to grasp the full impact and importance of the second founding on American political life as well as on American political theory. Those changes, like all political changes that are driven by theory rather than understood *through* theory, must by their nature make an appeal based on an intended future. This means that they must by definition rest not on past experience so much as on a promise of what could be. And to understand the promise of the nationalists, as well as to judge correctly whether that promise was indeed kept, we must turn briefly to their most prominent statement of that promise, *The Federalist Papers*.

The Federalist begins: "After an unequivocal experience of the inefficacy of the subsisting federal government, you are called upon to deliberate on a new Constitution for the United States of America."[5] Publius then presents twenty-one essays constructing a ruthless critique of the existing Confederation and the constitution under which they are organized, thereby providing ample historical fodder for the "critical period" thesis that arose in the century following ratification. The bulk of that criticism is by now well known, but any overview, however brief, should include the threat to the union from foreign force and influence;[6] from wars betweeen the states;[7] from faction, domestic convulsions, or internal wars within the states or toward the union;[8] from the inadequate organization of commerce and the economy;[9] from the kinds of popular (read moblike) legislation passed within the states;[10] and ending with Madison's polemical summation in *Federalist* no. 20, the last in a series beginning with *Federalist* no. 17, collectively titled "The Tendency of Federal Governments Rather to Anarchy Among the Members Than Tyranny in the Head":

> This unhappy people seem to be now suffering from popular convulsions, from dissensions among the states, and from the actual invasion of foreign arms, the crisis of their destiny. All nations have their eyes fixed on the awful spectacle. The first wish

prompted by humanity is that this severe trial may issue in such a revolution of their government as will establish their union and render it the parent of tranquility, freedom, and happiness. The next, that the asylum under which, we trust, the enjoyment of these blessings will be speedily secured in this country may receive and console them for the catastrophe of their own. I make no apology for having dwelt so long on the contemplation of these federal precedents. Experience is the oracle of truth; and where its responses are unequivocal, they ought to be conclusive and sacred. The important truth, which it unequivocally pronounces in the present case, is that a sovereignty over sovereigns, a government over governments, a legislation for communities, as counter-distinguished from individuals, as it is a solecism in theory, so in practice it is subversive of the order and ends of civil polity, by substituting *violence* in place of the mild and salutary *coercion* of the *magistracy*.[11]

No radical deconstructive reading is necessary to decode the subtext of the above passage or to understand the direction that the author's "positive" political project will take. The entire core of the Federalist political vision is readily laid out and acknowledged by Madison. He concedes that theirs is a "revolutionary" undertaking, and since the revolution resulting in the separation from England had already been accomplished, this can only mean that the new revolution was to be "fought" against the Articles of Confederation. This new revolution was to secure the lexically ordered values—tranquillity (order), freedom (private, as opposed to public), and happiness (also private, as opposed to public)—as expediently as possible. And the way to secure these goals is by avoiding the "solecism" (improper construction) of the national government. Aside from the practical defects outlined in the twenty or so previous essays, Madison here underscores the dominant theoretical problem with the current national construction, which he construes to be the primacy of the community over the individual, and the primacy of the community over the national government:

> The important truth, which it [experience] unequivocally pronounces in the present case, is that a sovereignty over sovereigns, a government over governments, a legislation for communities, as counter-distinguished from individuals . . . is subversive of the order and ends of civil polity.[12]

To correct the current defects, then, the authority of the states and local political associations must be replaced by the authority, "the mild and salutary *coercion* of the *magistracy*" (read national government). The "ends of civil polity"—the trilogy of tranquillity, freedom, and happiness noted above—will now be aspired to as preexisting "forms," rather than constructed through public/political activity by the citizenry participating as active members in local/democratic political conversations. The nature of political life will also be dramatically reoriented in terms of average persons as they are replaced by experts, or guardians who will take over the task of construction under the guise of truth and knowledge. These arguments are then summarized and fleshed out by Hamilton speaking as Publius in the critical essays *Federalist* no. 21 and no. 22.

In *Federalist* no. 21 Alexander Hamilton, sounding like Athena, who warned that she alone of the gods was privy to the keys of chambers where the thunder was locked up, claims:

> The peace of society and the stability of government depended on the efficacy of precautions adopted on this head. Where the whole power of the government is in the hands of the people, there is less pretense for the use of violent remedies in partial or occasional distempers of the state.[13]

The veiled threat here is plain to see: either adopt the Constitution and empower the national government, or face anarchy and violence within the state that you may not be able to control. The larger context of this particular essay is the danger to other states from the violence within particular states, as noted by the question Hamilton asks: "Who can predict what effect a despotism established in Massachusetts [by, say, Daniel Shays acting as Cromwell] would have upon the liberties of New Hampshire or Rhode Island, of Connecticut or New York?"[14] Hence the implied danger here is the threat of diversity and difference between the states. Only when there is a uniform government with the power and energy necessary to impose universalist principles when needed, can order and tranquillity be guaranteed. Yet while this set of sentiments is a rather straightforward statement of nationalist beliefs, the theoretical apparatus Publius utilizes here, and in the preceding essay, is something of a Trojan Horse.

In *Federalist* no. 20 Madison portrayed any government that did not operate on individuals qua individuals as solecistic (improperly constructed), thereby implying that a proper construction would be a government that *did* act on individuals as individuals rather than as a mediating body between sovereign political communities. In *Federalist* no. 21 we see Hamilton arguing the same point as he suggests that the nation will be safe only when "the whole power of the government is in the hands of the people, [in that] there is less pretense for the use of violent remedies in partial or occasional distempers of the state." But what does this really mean? Is Publius arguing for a national participatory democratic union? We know that the answer to this question is "absolutely not." What, then, does this emphasis on the people mean? It means that by dismantling the sovereignty of the states, and in turn any local political associations protected therein, and turning the power of government over to the people at large—who are, of course, too numerous to take any meaningful political action as a group—the real power will come to rest with the representative institutions of the national government like Congress, the president, and, most important, the Supreme Court. Thus what on the surface appear to be an argument for greater democracy in reality becomes a mechanism for ensuring elite rule on the basis of a Burkean "trusteeship."

Edmund Morgan has described this process as discovering "a new and more effective way of bending the sovereignty of the people to overcome the deficiencies of locally oriented representation,"[15] and Joshua Miller has called it the construction of "the ghostly body politic."[16] The end result of this was, then, a vast reduction in the actual political power of the average person through the process of amalgamation, with the corresponding reduction in the possibility of public happiness, and the proportional increase of political disinterest and apathy that results when political life is made more distant and more abstract through centralization. To harken back to the discussion of Tocqueville, the subjects will be made more docile, but the price we pay is that there are no longer citizens. The end result of this is probably best described by Tocqueville when he tells of Americans withdrawing into the small, exclusive circles of private life: "As the extent of political society expands, one must expect the sphere of private life to contract. Far from supposing that the members of our new societies will come to live in public, I am more afraid that they will in the end only form very small coteries."[17]

The end result of such a movement away from public life into private is twofold. First, the political playing field is left open only to the most serious players or supposed experts. Second, the withdrawal of former citizens from a public life/private life dichotomous existence (or their defeat) and their movement to one preoccupied almost exclusively with private life simply magnifies their possessive, individual concerns to such a great extent that there is no longer concern with, or perhaps even knowledge of, anything else—especially of what is shared and public. Whether this was Publius's explicit intention is ultimately unimportant from a theoretical perspective, since by all indications this is what indeed occurred in American politics. It is entirely possible that this particular historical progression was unavoidable, but that does not negate the fact that Publius's constitution authorized such a progression even if it could not entirely author it. There is, however, an important indication, in an earlier essay by Madison, that he thought such behavior in a republic was inevitable, if not already in place at the writing of the *Papers*. That essay, *Federalist* no. 10, is now rightfully among the most famous.

In *Federalist* no. 10 we see Madison's familiar argument concerning the nature, dangers, and possible solutions to the problem of faction in a republic, in his "republican remedies for republican defects" argument. The emphasis we now place on this essay is due primarily to the work of Charles Beard, who thought he had discovered within it the key to the entire Federalist project of usurpation and self-interested protection of class privileges in the form of property rights.[18] But this early attempt at historical deconstruction seems a little misplaced, in that the essay itself is fairly straightforward about its author's political intentions and requires very little exploration in terms of any Machiavellian subtext. After all, the Revolution was fought in part to defend the rights of property owners who by virtue of that property had made the strong republican claim to participate in public affairs. The theoretical arguments contained in the essay are at least as interesting and substantial when taken as acts of good faith as they could ever be when discounted as acts of bad faith. Even if this is not true, good faith on our part requires that we begin with such assumptions. The interpretive trope that will undergird my discussion of this essay is best described as "overcoming contingency." In other words, what I see Madison as doing on the whole in *Federalist* no. 10 is not providing some defense of his class position but, rather, attempting in good Enlightenment/rationalist fashion to rid political life of the diverse and the contingent in a manner consistent with the political culture in which he must maneuver, while at the same time overcoming the parts of that culture that resist such "refinement" (a term with which I think Madison would feel comfortable, and with which I myself do not).

Among the core assumptions made by republican political theorists was that of communal homogeneity, a likeness of interests, mores, and beliefs among the particular citizenry. Among the most serious threats to republican community was the absence of this likeness, because where there was fundamental division and disagreement between citizens over how to constitute the public square, there was the potential for strife and civic unrest. This phenomenon was more dangerous in a republic than it would be in some more hierarchically ordered political community because in the latter the government, in its separateness from the people, could impose the degree of uniformity necessary to maintain the society over time. In a republic, however, the people themselves were charged with this task. If they became corrupt (seeking the interest of the part as opposed to the good of the whole), then there was no recourse and civil war would often be the only possible outcome. Since, as Madison notes, the most durable source of faction was inequality or differences in wealth and property, aristocracy or monarchy had typically been thought to be superior to republican political society because the propertied class, by virtue of their *lack* of want for material goods (they already had them) would be free to seek the public good in a significantly more disinterested manner. Thus republics can flourish only where there is at least a minimal level of economic equality between citizens, thus enabling them to act in a similarly disinterested manner with regard to the public sphere.

This, as Plato noted at the start of Book II of his *Republic,* is possible to sustain without massive social and political engineering only in relatively poor or subsistence-based agrarian economies like his "city of pigs." Once we enter "the feverish city," or the city with "relishes" or luxuries (in contemporary terms, "commercial society"), we encounter the need for "doctors," those who can fix the defects produced by the expansion of society and the introduction of those things that are likely to cause divisions and differences to emerge (factions). Those factions bring with them increasing levels of what we could call contingencies, which at every turn create difficulties for maintaining the degree of homogeneity perceived as necessary by traditional republican theory. The greatest source of contingency is the increasing levels of inequality that accompany "commercial society." The role of the "doctors" in the "feverish" or complex city is to find ways of minimizing the number of contingencies, which Plato does through the restriction of freedom, manipulation of the socialization and educational process, and eventually outright coercion and violence when necessary. Given his cultural matrix, as well as his own predispositions, Plato's particular solutions are not available to Madison; but Plato's problem is Madison's problem as well, and in *Federalist* no. 10 he seeks to find a way of reducing the possibility of the political contingency that he feels endangers the life of his particular republican community.

Madison claims that there are two methods of removing the causes of faction: "the one by destroying the liberty which is essential to its existence; the other, by giving to every citizen the same opinions, the same passions, and the same interests."[19] Both of these solutions were embraced in part by Plato, but Madison claims to reject both, contending that the first option is "worse than the disease" and that the second is impossible.[20] Madisonian empiricism works in fruitful opposition here to a strict Platonic rationalism. Thus Madison is left with his conclusion that, rather than removing the causes of faction, we should busy ourselves with "controlling its effects."[21] But what does this mean? How do you control the effects of something described as a disease without attempting to cure it?

A brief exploration of the metaphor might be helpful here. Suppose that the disease "factions" is like the disease "cancer," and assume that the first set of solutions, "removing the causes," is analogous to amputation or organ removal in cancer treatment. And, finally, assume that such surgery is not an option for some reason, so we, as the doctors, have decided to "control the effects of the disease." The question becomes how we go about doing this. Would such a thing even make sense, given a disease with a massive proclivity to spread when left unchecked? The answer, I suppose, is to isolate the other parts of the "body" somehow, so that they might avoid infection, or to give those parts of the body some kind of preventive medicine that would make them immune. If we were able to do that, then the riddle might be solved—we would have controlled the effects of the disease without removing it from the "body." We know that this is not yet possible with actual cancer, but Madisonian political theory believes that it is possible with the body politic. This, too, however, is a Platonic strategy. Madison, despite his empiricism, thinks much as Plato did: that yet another way of controlling the disease of faction (contingency) is to isolate a class of people within the body politic who would either be uninfected by the disease or, as we will see both here and in *Federalist* no. 51, unable to infect the body any more than the other limbs were able to.

Plato's strategy for controlling the effects of faction, as opposed to his strategy for getting rid of it altogether, was to select his class of guardians and then structure their lives so that they were free from the impulses that other people naturally had. Without getting into a detailed discussion of the *Republic*, suffice it to say that his general way of doing this in terms of the guardians was to make them completely public people, people who cared only for the general (the state) and nothing for the particular (themselves as individuals or institutions like the family). He did this through rigorous education, through isolation, through the destruction of the family, through equalization of wealth, and finally through making them dependent upon the state and the goodwill of the citizenry for their survival. In turn, the citizenry was dependent upon the guardians (political doctors) for their continued good health in the "feverish city." Little attention is paid to the vast majority of other people who live and work in the *Republic*. The reason for this inattention is that so long as the guardians as a class were intact and properly "isolated," it mattered relatively little what everyone else did. The guardians were now fully public people, and everyone else was more or less wholly private (because if they were also somehow "public" in any significant way, they might infect the rest of the body politic with the disease that was "natural" to them: faction).

Despite their epistemological and methodological differences, Madison's strategy in *Federalist* no. 10 is quite similar in many ways to Plato's *Republic*. To begin with, he claims that faction is the natural condition of a free people around whom wealth (luxury) and subsequent inequality combine to produce a situation where "those who hold and those who are without property have ever formed distinct interests in society."[22] If left to judge for themselves, either party or faction would surely judge in its own favor with no regard for the public good, since, according to Madison, "a body of men are unfit to be both judges and parties at the same time."[23] Thus the act of judging must be taken from the hands of those who have particular interests in the outcome and given to those who, like Plato's guardians, love only the general. This leads Madison quickly to reject "pure democracy," since in such a system "there is nothing to check the inducements to sacrifice the weaker party or an obnoxious individual . . . [and the systems] have ever been found incompatible with personal security or the rights of property; and have been as short in their lives as they have been violent in their deaths."[24] Thus we are left with a scheme of government based on representative institutions rather than participatory ones. It is important to note that at this point Madisonian theory briefly diverges from Platonic theory insofar as Madison's "guardians" are to be elected, thus completing his task of securing "the public good and the private rights of other citizens . . . and at the same time preserv[ing] the spirit and the form of popular government."[25] The ultimate theoretical hope of this transfer of authority (though not necessarily power) for Madison serves to

> refine and enlarge the public views by passing them through the medium of a chosen
> body of citizens, whose wisdom may best discern the true interest of their country
> and whose patriotism and love of justice will be least likely to sacrifice it to temporary
> or partial considerations.[26]

It is important to note that here, as well as at other points in the essay, Madison has made two very important intellectual moves. First, he has continued his project of praising the general good and denigrating as the work of small minds and "diseased" thinkers the promotion of the local over the national interest; intimately related to that move is the subtle, yet all-important, introduction of the idea of a "national interest." This language had typically been reserved for speaking about states and local political associations whose interests and rights were to be protected by the government à la traditional Whig theory, but here Madison has, in good nationalist fashion, transformed that mode of discourse and co-opted it for the government itself. The end result is to force the political dialogue into what are at best uncharted theoretical waters, and at worst illegitimate and violently acultural linguistic modes of political discourse. This theoretical maneuver rivals Plato's attempt to replace the traditional/particular family with the state for his guardians.

Once we are pushed to talk about the "good" of the nation, as if it were a local community or even an individual, then predicates that were hitherto thought to be gibberish suddenly begin to make sense, and we see sentences that begin The nation needs . . . ; The country wants . . . ; The United States feels . . . ; and so on. These types of sentences that for the first 150 years (including the revolutionary period) would have made sense only in the broadest and more ephemeral of contexts are now spoken as if they are commonplace parts of legitimate political speech. Just as Plato moved his dialogue from the individual to the city in what he claimed was an effort to see the thing more clearly, so does Madison. In so doing, he has managed to set the agenda and structure the discourse in such as way that, rather than arguing about what is good for particular people and particular communities, we are forced to argue in terms of what is good in general. This leads, as even the most casual reader of the *Republic* knows, to a far different thing than what is good in particular. An important by-product of this shift is that as we move further from what we know on an experiential level to what we can only conceive of in increasingly abstract terms, the more the rationalist, technocratic model of political theory and regime organization addressed in chapter 2 comes to dominate, and the less room there eventually is for citizens as opposed to administrators. Thus, while Madison may have been an empiricist, his emergent theory authorizes a rationalist political order.

Yet, as we know, representative institutions are not necessarily free from defects or disease. There is still the chance that "men of factious tempers, of local prejudices, or sinister designs, may, by intrigue, by corruption, or by other means, first obtain the suffrages, and then betray the interests of the people."[27] Madison's structural solution to this dilemma is his most famous theoretical contribution to political science, the extended republic. While it is true that Madison owes much on this point to David Hume, who had argued in his *Essays, Moral, Political, and Literary,* that "though it was more difficult to form a republican government in an extensive country than in a city; there is more facility, when once it is formed, of preserving it steady and uniform, without tumult and faction,"[28] it is Madison who popularized and made commonplace what had been considered not only unconventional but also illegitimate political thought, given the prominence of Montesquieu.

By extending the size of the republic, and thus implicitly changing the entire cultural/theoretical foundation upon which the country had been formed, Madison hopes to accomplish three tasks in his quest against faction. First, the expansion of the political arena will make it "more difficult for unworthy candidates to practice with success the vicious arts by which elections are too often carried . . . [and] the suffrages of the people being more free, will be more likely to center on men who possess the most attractive merit and the most diffuse and established characters."[29] Second, by expanding the domain, the chances of a representative being unduly bound to local issues or parochial concerns diminishes, thus allowing him to "pursue great and national objects."[30] Finally, even if these two theoretical hopes did not pan out, the expansion of the domain would prevent the "easy concert and execution of any plans of oppression." Madison argues:

> Extend the sphere and you take in a greater variety of parties and interests; you make it less probable that a majority of the whole will have a common motive to invade the rights of other citizens; or if such a common motive exists, it will be more difficult for all who feel it to discover their own strength and to act in unison with each other.[31]

In the passage above the echo of Rousseau suddenly becomes audible in the work of Madison as we see the implicit distinction between what the former would refer to as the "general will" and the "particular will" making itself known. The Madisonian framework of representation and territorial extension clearly is intended to make the "general will," if not the Platonic "form," of the regime a more pronounced possibility. By increasing the number of "particular wills," Madison hopes to make them inaudible in the public sphere, thereby ensuring to the extent possible that the only voice heard is that of the general will or the public (national) good.[32] Embodying this will and speaking on its behalf will then become the task of the representatives in the national government, who, under this theory, will be those with "enlightened views and virtuous sentiments [that] render them superior to local prejudices and to schemes of injustice."[33] And if some members of the regime were to fall victim to the "disease" of particularism, they would be less able to "spread a general conflagration through the other states."[34]

The important theoretical contribution that Madison wants to make can now partially be seen: the creation of a republic without need of republican citizens. What the reader should notice upon close investigation of *Federalist* no. 10 is the lack of attention to the character and behavior of the average citizen, an attitude shared by Plato. What Madison is concerned with here is the creation of structural mechanisms for ensuring, if at all possible, virtue among the representatives (guardians) or, failing that, the erection of barriers to thwart the spread of any corruption that may make its way to the head of the regime. What is expected of the average citizens is that they will withdraw for the most part into their private (particularized) affairs (which Madison and others of this period believed to be the natural condition for human beings), and, upon discovering their inability to carry their private concerns into personally beneficial public policy, will cease to participate in public life other than through casting an occasional vote.

Thus the majority of people are rendered almost purely private beings. The active conception of citizenship, associated with both traditional republicanism and its new American counterpart, which saw the citizen as participating in the construction of the public good, along with the necessity of civic virtue among the masses, is done away with as utopian. Also rejected by Madison and others is the possibility of transformation by any but the most select few (national representatives, who for Madison are seemingly predisposed to such behavior), such as those who in this volume have been associated with citizenship. The end result of this theoretical set of remedies, once coupled with the advent of national political parties and the transformation of the conception of representation from some form of delegation to trusteeship, is the creation of both a theoretical basis for, and the subsequent reality of, a new cultural matrix that can best be understood as liberalism. But that unanticipated consequence was clearly not Publius's intention in general, and especially not Madison's in particular.

The matrix shift desired by Publius was one that could best be described as a shift from democratic confederate republicanism to elitist unitary republicanism. The way to accomplish this shift was to take authority away from the people and give it to the virtuous representatives, while leaving the people in ultimate possession of political power (not much of a concession if we acknowledge that ultimately, whether stated or not, this is where power presides anyway[35]). Once that transfer was accomplished, the enlightened representatives, with their enlarged and refined views, were to set about the crucial task of political reformation through proper administration. (This approach illustrates the central differences between the classical republicanism of Aristotle, who would have described the central task of the elite as educating the majority for citizenship, and this newer modern elitist brand of republicanism that denied the possibility of such an enterprise and opted instead for control and the rule by virtuous expertise; both of these approaches are vastly different from the modern American democratic republicanism that existed in pre-Constitution America and that is defended as another alternative throughout this volume.)

Before that proper administration could begin, however, the new government had to be imbued with the degree of energy necessary to its tasks. The defense of that energy is the subject of *Federalist* no. 23–no. 36, which, interestingly, include not only lengthy defenses of energetic government in general but also important discussions about standing armies and taxation in particular (perhaps two possible means for accomplishing similar ends in different historical contexts). In any case, a reader who wants to understand more precisely the nature of the new and dramatically more energetic regime needs simply to look at two of the most expansive provisions of the Constitution and Publius's defense of them: the Supremacy Clause (Article VI, sec. 2) and the Necessary and Proper Clause (Article I, sec. 8).[36] However, there are more important substantive questions that must be discussed before we can truly understand and assess the Federalist project: what the precise nature of the reformation will actually be, and how Publius intends to guarantee that reformation once the new energy is unleashed.

Alexander Hamilton provides us with a glimpse into the heart of the Federalist political project in *Federalist* no. 22 as he defends the supremacy of national judicial decisions over those of the state courts. This defense takes place in the context of a much more general argument put forth by Hamilton concerning the dangers of diversity and the benefits of uniformity—uniformity in commercial policy, uniformity in military affairs, and so on. Hamilton, no great defender of democracy, goes so far as to defend the principle of majority rule as opposed to the existing principle of unanimity with regard to the states, claiming that the latter principle "contradicts that fundamental maxim of republican government, which requires that the sense of the majority should prevail."[37] This is a defense of democracy in its most adversarial form, where the emphasis is on what we now call minimum winning coalitions. This is democracy as a weapon for erasing difference and forging an agreement by sheer numbers and power (which, Hannah Arendt tells us, in its purest form is all against one[38]). At this point we can see quite clearly the dangers, and perhaps even theoretical perversions, that can result from Publius's adoption of an extended republic.

Hamilton's assertion about the "sense of the majority" prevailing in a republic is correct, but that principle was based upon the existence of a small, relatively homogeneous, and typically face-to-face democratic community like the New England town, where the phrase was not the "sense of the majority," but the "sense of the meeting." In other words, to use Jane Mansbridge's terminology, Hamilton has here, either nefariously or just wrongly, used a principle that was theoretically attached to "unitary democracy" as support for an argument in defense of "adversarial democracy." In the hands of Publius a principle that was intended to illustrate agreement and the existence of general will among members of a particular community is used as a method of subjugating that will and those members to a majority of particular wills or one large particular will. It is as if we have kept the form and gutted the substance that made the form sensible in the first place. Here a passage from Rousseau might help to clarify this line of criticism. He writes in chapter 3 of *The Social Contract* on "Whether the General Will Can Err":

> Finally, when one of those groups becomes so large that it can dominate the rest, the result is no longer the sum of many small differences, but one great divisive difference; then there ceases to be a general will, and the opinion which prevails is no more than private opinion.[39]

It is difficult, perhaps even impossible, to reconcile Publius's fear of majority tyranny in *Federalist* no. 10 with his defense of adversarial majoritarianism here. What becomes obvious is that Publius either is ready and willing to use whatever rhetorical arguments he thinks necessary in order to sustain his overall political project, or he is engaged in a theorization that lacks the most basic internal consistency. Rather than assume the former, as those who would simply like to "unmask" the framers would have us do, I would assume the latter. First, there is little gain from the "good guy/bad guy" approach embodied in the first. Second, and far more important, whether it is internally consistent or not, Publius's theorization concerning the relative strengths and weaknesses of unity and diversity, and the extended republic became the dominant mode of political discourse, as well as the basis on which American practical politics came rather quickly to be practiced.

Hamilton quite plainly tells us in *Federalist* no. 22 what Publius sees as the single greatest problem facing the existing form of political association under the Articles of Confederation. While Hamilton presents the argument under the guise of a foreign affairs problem, we should have no compunction, given the general tone of the essay, about reading it in a far more expansive manner than might at first glance appear justified:

> A circumstance which crowns the defects of the Confederation remains yet to be mentioned—the want of judiciary power. Laws are a dead letter without courts to expound and define their true meaning and operation. . . . To produce uniformity in these determinations, they ought to be submitted, in the last resort, to one SUPREME TRIBUNAL. . . . There are endless diversities in the opinions of men. We

often see not only different courts but judges of the same court differing from each other. To avoid the confusion which would unavoidably result from the contradictory decisions of a number of independent judiciaries, all nations have found it necessary to establish one court paramount to the rest, possessing a general superintendence and authorized to settle and declare in the last resort a uniform rule of civil justice.[40]

Although I do not want to belabor the point, the reader should note yet again a strange duplicitousness in the teachings of Publius, who throughout *Federalist* no. 17–no. 20 stressed in a number of different ways the unique nature of the American experiment, and the failures of older theoretical models (like Montesquieu's small republic theory) to accomplish their goals. Then, when searching for a justification here, he has no trouble using a simple argument from authority like the one denoted in "All nations have found it necessary. . . ." To return to the point at hand, the assertions made by Hamilton above go a long way toward capturing the essence of Federalist republicanism.[41] The Federalist reformation of American political theory and traditional American republicanism involves a very intricate theoretical maneuver along the same lines as the early shift concerning the "virtuous representatives."

Although *Federalist* no. 10 on one level seems to accept, and even embrace, human diversity, it is not a warm embrace between friends; rather, it is an embrace best represented by the cliché about keeping one's friends close and one's enemies closer. Publius does not like diversity, nor does he invent a political system steeped in mutual toleration for difference; what in fact he does in *Federalist* no. 10 is to acknowledge a reality or a "fact," human difference—a fact that, unlike Plato, he realizes he cannot change wholesale because his is not just a city in speech but an actual regime where "facts" cannot simply be argued away. So in *Federalist* no. 10 Publius sets about creating a system that "accept[s] men the way they [are]" (or at least how he thinks they are), takes political authority away from them because of that perception (and gives it to the virtuous), provides the new leaders with the desired energy in the form of things like the expansive Necessary and Proper Clause and the Supremacy Clause to remake the political world as they see fit, and finally directs them to render the political world as uniform and homogeneous as necessary to sustain the nation over time.

Thus diversity was accepted on its face because it was either that or slavery, but it was accepted only as a short-term, necessary evil. Rather than thinking this was a strength, it was considered a weakness that had to be overcome, perhaps incrementally at first. Since Publius had already rejected the classical role of a republican elite as "civic educator" because he believed human nature to be more or less constant and unchangeable, the question then is viewed from a theoretical perspective: What type of uniformity was possible, given what appeared to be intractable diversity in opinions and desires? The answer was "individual self-interest." Since Publius found himself unable to count on the possibility of human transformation or education, he decided to foster a system (or at least provide it with a relatively superficial, culturally acceptable, theoretical matrix) that would emphasize what he could count on. But this shift, like so many theoretical adaptations, brought with it other potential consequences and problems that Publius now had to solve within the confines of his increasingly trenchant theoretical model.

Publius was no fool. Once he had rejected the notion of civic virtue as an organizing principle for the political life of *ordinary* people, he was faced with the dilemma that *all* people were *ordinary* people in America. This is not to say that the Federalists did not believe in a natural aristocracy or in the categories of the "worthy and the licentious,"[42] because they did. But just like finding Plato's "men of gold," Publius knew that there was no way to guarantee that "enlightened statesmen will be at the helm." Even with the extension of the republic and the other "cures" of *Federalist* no. 10, Publius still had to deal with his own root proposition, which was that men were by nature "more disposed to vex and oppress each other than to co-operate for their common good." And even if we were to bypass this overtly negative posture, the best we could hope for from most people would be mutual indifference. Thus we come to the second stage of the Federalist newfangled republican theorization, which is made explicit by Madison when he claims in *Federalist* no. 51 that "You must first enable the government to control the governed; and in the next place oblige it to control itself."[43]

Madison's construction for ensuring this control is his model of separation of powers. Although the model bears more than a superficial resemblance to the older model of a balanced or mixed constitution in which various social orders were represented by the Senate, the Commons, and the crown in a taut and structurally tensioned relationship that recognized that different orders or social classes had fundamentally different interests that, if they were not offset by another power of equal strength, might run roughshod over the others, Madison's model was in reality a radical, and very American, departure from it. As Tocqueville later noted, in America people are "born equal rather than having to become so." This exceptional attribute of American political culture meant that the idea of specific economic classes or social orders that served as the foundation for "balanced constitutionalism" was not available for American political theorists and political actors.[44] The categories that were available centered on virtue, character, and effort broadly defined, which were, at least in theory, open to all people of all classes. Thus the only categories with which Madisonian theory can truly be thought to be concerned are those of the "worthy" and the "licentious," or the deserving and the undeserving. The "fact" that many of the "worthy" people came from advantaged backgrounds was to be treated as simply coincidence. The "fact" that the "worthy" might not always prevail in the democratic electoral arena, or that they might indeed become the "licentious," became the justification for separation of powers in America since, as Madison acknowledges, "men are not angels."

Federalist no. 51 is perhaps the most recognizable essay within the *Federalist* collection, and it is perhaps because of this historical familiarity, which tends to make even the most exceptional things appear mundane or even conservative, that we often fail to see the absolute theoretical radicalism embodied within this brief work. It is here that what we have referred to as the Federalist "faith" is given its doctrinal content, and that content is represented in the following passage penned by Madison:

> A dependence on the people is, no doubt, the primary control on the government; but experience has taught mankind the necessity of auxiliary precautions. This policy of supplying, by opposite and rival interests, the defect of better motives, might be traced through the whole system of human affairs, private as well as public. We see it particularly displayed in all the subordinate distributions of power, where the constant aim is to divide and arrange the several offices in such a manner as each may be a check on the other—that the private interest of every individual may be sentinel over public rights.[45]

In our earlier discussion of the Puritans we came across the idea of "mutual watchfulness," which was a direct extension of the Puritan belief in a communal collective soul that required each member of the community to undertake the positive obligation of checking not only his own behavior but also that of his neighbors. The idea was that by obligating each member to watch over the others, the community would be able to fulfill its "contract" with God. This behavior, however, was not merely one of "moral policeman"; instead, it included that host of requirements outlined broadly by John Winthrop in his "Modell of Christian Charity" sermon: "making each other's burdens our own," "walking with each other in brotherly affection," and so on.

At first glance Madison's model appears to share certain attributes of that earlier one, but only at first glance. Upon further investigation we see how complete the transformation of that older model actually is. Here people are still charged with watching each other, and with watching their government, but it is not the watchfulness of a family member who has your best interest at heart, nor is it the watchfulness of a fellow citizen who worries about the public world you both share; instead, it is the watchfulness of the jealous man, the watchfulness of the covetous or possessive man, who is worried and fearful at every turn that you may infringe upon what is his, or that he may be asked to shoulder more than his share of a particular burden. It is not the fraternal watch of one who shares in your successes and your failures, and thus applauds you in victory and consoles you in defeat like a brother or a sister, but the distrustful watch of one who sees in your every move a potential theft, and in every kindness an ulterior motive. It is the qualitative difference between the idea that you should not steal because it is wrong, and the notion that you should not steal because you might get caught; both social approaches may in fact reduce theft, but each conception carries with it a particular view of the world and its people. In the former world, utopian or not, we are asked to be better people, to live up to the laws that we ourselves have made; and if we succeed, both we and our communities are better off—transformed, if you will. The latter world creates a community of pessimists and sneaks, one ever fearful of being taken and the other always watchful for an opportunity to take.

What Madison is in effect telling his readers here, whether he likes it or not, is the following: Guard your property and your rights with a vengeance and let others do the same, and peace and tranquillity will follow; within that peace and tranquillity you will be able to achieve personal happiness while others do the same, unencumbered by either your fellow citizens, who are now only asked to mind their own business, or by the government, whose tasks will soon be limited to maintaining the necessary circumstances for the pursuit of private happiness. The end result will be the appearance of a virtuous republic, well ordered without licentiousness, that can maintain itself over time by counting on people to do what they would naturally do—which is watch out for themselves. It is the "invisible hand" republic come to life. *Federalist* no. 51 then can be read reductively as the application of this broad social theory to the micro level of national government. Each separate branch will be endowed with certain powers that are unique to that branch, and others that overlap. In turn, the branches will engage in the new "watchfulness" over the people and over each other, and the people will engage in the same over them and over each other. I will not bother to make a list of all the checks and balances this mutual watchfulness and suspicion generates, for they are well known to even the most casual reader.

In the end, only those initiatives with enough general support from the population, or those with a focus specific enough to generate massive indifference, will become the law of the land in what could by an uncareful reader be seen as the embodiment of Rousseau's "general will" theory. But the reality is that there can be no such thing as a positive "general will" once the size of the territory is expanded to include many varied and diverse communities, except in the case of the most basic human needs like survival. Usually there can be only the gradual imposition of a particular will, large though it may be, that renders public life and the public good merely an extension of those baser and more universal private concerns. This leads to greater and greater centralization of authority and power as the nation and the citizenry begin to speak with one consonant voice that may from time to time sound different as the result of particular or individual circumstances, but that in the end can be characterized as of the same genus as private property, individual rights, and the negative state associated with liberalism. Adam Smith in his *Wealth of Nations* believed that the free-market or "invisible hand" approach to things economic would make that realm *more* rational than the mercantile system of government interference that he was criticizing in his work. Thus Hartz's irrational Locke is not born from the American earth as the only possible staple crop so much as the soil in which any competing social or political theory, like early American republicanism, could grow is made too contaminated for any other use. Publius had not necessarily found a new way to achieve the common good so much as he had changed the definition of that good by lowering not only the expectations of political life but also the possibilities. And like Plato in his *Republic,* who needed just one more thing to make his city *possible,* so does Publius.

"ONLY WHEN PHILOSOPHERS BECOME RULERS . . ."

For Plato the divisions within his society did not end with guardians and others. There is, midway through the text, one more division that he felt was necessary in order for the republic in speech to be carried into existence, or at least made possible. This was his proposition in Book V that philosophers must become kings. Publius, too, needs something else to make his republican city possible: some republicans. In broad language, the faith of the *Federalist* examined so far has consisted of the following sort of narrative: The nation is chaotic and bordering on anarchy, and thus something must be done to save it. The root of that anarchy is democratic excess and its corresponding diversity. Thus the solution to the problem lies in forging a uniform republic in which diverse forms of associations are made uniform to the degree necessary to regain order and stability. Since the overt suppression of differences is contrary to republican principles, some other method of erasure must be found that is consistent with the principles of free government. The classical solution of educating the citizenry for virtue is not a realistic option because, on the whole, the majority of people are not capable of transcending their own self-interest, resulting in anti-republican factions within society.

Thus, since neither suppression nor education is an option, the next best thing to do is disempower the factioned masses through a three-step process. First, we expand the size of the republic, and therefore the number of factions, such that the power of any one group will always be offset by other groups. Second, we transfer power and authority through this expansion to the nation as a whole. And finally, we transfer power and authority to the representatives in the national government, who are now so distant and detached from their individual local circumstances that they can render more disinterested decisions, and thereby look to the good of the whole rather than the good of the parts. But this new enclave of republicans still might become corrupted because of their own perversions, or because they are still too close to local situations in the form of elections, and so we must check and balance power within the regime once again to fracture the possibility of faction, thereby disempowering even the empowered to some extent.

But once this is done, once the negative barriers have been put in place, and the people and their representatives have been prevented from doing harm, there still remains the issue of the positive political project of the Federalists. Much to their chagrin, to carry their newly purified republic into existence and make it work, they can no longer avoid empowering someone or *something* to act in the traditional capacity of a citizen who actively constructs the newly, and massively, enlarged realm of the public good. And this task, this final voice, is given to the most democratically distant branch within the entire national regime—the Supreme Court.

Human beings and the scientists among them in the modern era have searched unceasingly and in vain for some kind of machine that would produce more energy than it consumed—a way, if you will, of creating something from nothing or, in the language of some contemporary political discussants, "a machine that would go of itself." In political history this search has often been viewed as the quest for the perfect constitution, a perfect form of political organization where human contingency is made negligible through systematic task distribution and administration. In one of the most vivid, as well as narratively misogynistic, passages in modern Western thought, Machiavelli, *the* most important transitional political philosopher, describes this process in the following manner:

> I am not unaware that many have held and hold the opinion that events are controlled by fortune and by God in such a way that the prudence of men cannot modify them, indeed that men have no influence whatsoever. Because of this, they would conclude that there is no point in sweating over things, but that one should submit to the rulings of chance. . . . I compare fortune to one of those wild rivers which, when they are enraged, flood the plains, tear down trees and buildings, wash soil from one place and deposit it in another. Everyone flees before them, everybody yields to their impetus, there is no possibility of resistance. Yet it does not follow that when they [are] flowing quietly one cannot take precautions, constructing dykes and embankments so that when the river is in flood they would keep to one channel or their impetus be less wild and dangerous. So it is with fortune. She shows her potency where there is no well regulated power to resist her, and her impetus is felt where she knows there are no embankments and dykes built to restrain her. . . . I hold strongly to this: that it is better to be impetuous than circumspect; because fortune is a woman and if she is to be submissive it is necessary to beat and coerce her.[46]

Since Machiavelli's book was addressed to the "Prince," Lorenzo de'Medici, we can assume that the task of building embankments and dykes, of controlling the effects of fortune, fell to the prince and his advisers. But if we attempt to sift through the metaphor in the context of the newly constructed American regime, we must ask to whom such power would fall, given the argued-for similarities of the two projects. The answer is quite complex. To begin with, the metaphor's constituent parts need to be marked off in their American contexts. First, there is the "river," which in the Federalist model represents the people and democratic politics in general; next, there are the "embankments and dykes" that contain the river, which are the national representatives (including both the Congress and the president); and finally, there are those who build the "embankments and dykes," the "founders" who engage in the "beating and coercing" of fortune. But just as Machiavelli acknowledged that "fortune is the arbiter of half the things we do," so the American founders realized that they could not plan their building pattern so well that it could account for all the storms to come, nor could they guarantee that the embankments and dikes would always hold or be made with superior materials, and so they planned still more. For some, like Jefferson, a good embankment-transcending, dike-breaking "storm" every twenty years or so would be a good thing, but for others this was not the case. They had to find an institutional way to maintain a "perpetual founding" without sustaining a "permanent revolution"—a way, in other words, to keep their "worthy" spirit alive. They found that institution in their construction of the Supreme Court and thereby achieved Machiavellian ends with Platonic means.

In *Federalist* no. 78 we find the sustained defense of the Court presented, appropriately enough, by Alexander Hamilton. While it is not completely fair to use past political positions as either confirmation or negation of current political arguments, the reader should keep in mind Hamilton's conspiratorial intentions at Newburgh when he tells them just five years later not to worry, since the Court is the "least dangerous" branch. The primary task of the Court, according to Hamilton (sounding a bit like Machiavelli), is to provide a "barrier to the encroachments and oppressions of the representative body."[47] Yet going back to *Federalist* no. 22, the phrasing he really should have used is "representative bod*ies,*" since the task of the Court was to make general the things that before were particular. And yet he seems quite concerned in the early part of the essay with convincing his readers that the Court is there to protect them from their elected officials: "It is far more rational to suppose that the courts were designed to be an intermediate body between the people and the legislature in order, among other things, to keep the latter within the limits assigned to their authority."[48]

This assertion is followed first by a brief continuation of the argument that says the Constitution is "fundamental law" and therefore superior in all instances to "non-fundamental law," and then by a quick, and logically misleading, disclaimer: "nor does this conclusion by any means suppose a superiority of the judicial to the legislative power, it only supposes that the power of the people is superior to both."[49] It would now appear that even the "enlarged republic" with its "virtuous representatives" is not sufficient safeguard against the particularization of the national will. It, too, must submit its "will" for purification to a yet higher authority that somehow, even though unelected, has become the guardian of the general will of the people. It is difficult, however, to see how, if the people are indeed the locus of power, and those who ultimately speak in the name of the people are the members of the Court, they cannot be said to have power superior to the legislative branch.

Publius attempts to finesse this difficulty with a very telling conceptual distinction between what he calls WILL and JUDGEMENT. The former consists of the "pleasures" of the legislative branch, and presumably of the people, and as such are questions of preference that either have no "right" or "wrong" answer or are open to strictly utilitarian considerations. The latter consists of interpretation and adjudication of the law against the backdrop of the Constitution, which allows only for deontological determinations in which "preferences" are irrelevant in the determination of right and wrong. Thus Publius manages to create not so much a system of separation of powers as a system of "dual sovereignty" within the government. The legislative branch will be responsible for declaring and refining democratic preferences, while the judiciary will be charged with determining which of those preferences are permissible and which are not. The former is to be sovereign over what the people and the nation want and need, and the latter sovereign over the questions concerning whether those declared wants and needs are "right" or "wrong" when measured against the standards provided in the Constitution. Yet the fact that the judiciary has the final say ensures the existence of a hierarchy of sovereignties, which in an interesting manner parallels Plato's distinction between "opinion" and "knowledge" in his theory of the divided line in Book VI of the *Republic*. This hierarchy, I assume, is what leads Hannah Arendt to make her comparison between the American Supreme Court and the Roman Office of Censorship, from which she concludes that "the true seat of authority in the American Republic is the Supreme Court," which, she says along with Woodrow Wilson, acts as "a kind of Constitutional Assembly in continuous session."[50]

Hamilton concludes this section by claiming that if such a distinction (between will and judgment) was not possible, and the Court was "disposed to exercise will instead of judgement, the consequence would equally be the substitution of their pleasure for that of the legislative body . . . [and] would prove that there ought to be no judges distinct from that body."[51] And then, without pausing to recognize the controversial nature of the assertion he has just made, Hamilton quickly assumes into evidence "facts" he has not even argued for concerning the distinction between will and judgment (not necessarily an illegitimate pre-Enlightenment strategy, but clearly a problematic intellectual move in the Age of Reason) as he begins his next section with the following: "If, then, the courts of justice are to be considered as the bulwarks of a limited Constitution against legislative encroachments. . . ."[52] The rest of his argument follows quite easily once his readers have accepted the legitimacy of such a distinction, just as Plato's philosopher-kings made sense to readers who accepted the premises of the myth of the cave, or Hobbes's absolute sovereign made similar sense to those who accepted his vision of the state of nature and his pronouncements on human nature. But just as with the discussion in chapter 3 concerning the Straussian model of political knowledge, I am not sure what we gain, other than polemical effect, from a distinction between willing what is "right" and judging what is "right" (one hopes the good citizen does both simultaneously). And I am not sure how someone could distinguish between the two types of activity to begin with. Yet it is precisely this weak distinction (at least weak in the political realm[53]) that allows Publius to forge and sustain his political hierarchy.

After his self-styled metaphysical coup Publius quickly moves on to less esoteric and phenomenological discussions of the political/theoretical matters at hand. Assume, he seems to say, that there is a knowable and realizable distinction between knowledge and opinion about things political that is not, we must suppose, self-evident. Furthermore, assume that there are at least some people capable of both knowing and doing on the basis of the former rather than the latter. Finally, assume that we can find them. Then, Publius asks, what are the structural conditions that would make such activity possible, given the propensity of human nature to "factionalize"? The answer is independence— which "is equally requisite to guard the Constitution and the rights of individuals from the effects of those ill humors which the arts of designing men, or the influence of particular conjectures, sometimes disseminate among the people themselves, and which, though they speedily give place to better information, and more deliberate reflection, have a tendency, in the meantime, to occasion dangerous innovations in government and serious oppressions of the minority party in the community."[54] By remaining free from elections, monetary punishment,[55] and the demands of a strict patronage position, the members of the Court can render impartial decisions reflecting the needs of the whole rather than of some part, in accord with the fundamental principles embodied in the Constitution.

In other words, the members of the Court must have the characteristics used earlier to describe good republican citizens. The way to ensure that they maintain the necessary degree of integrity is by allowing them to participate in the most important political questions of the day, unhindered by any overwhelming externalities like particular circumstances. In fact, if we extended our view of *The Federalist,* as partially discussed in this chapter, to a more general view, then what we should see is the increasing restriction and narrowing of the category of citizen (at least of republican citizen) even while it in many ways appears to be getting larger, until we reach the point where the only true republican citizens left are the members of the Supreme Court. This suggestion is borne out as we look at Publius's concluding remarks in *Federalist* no. 78:

Hence it is that there can be but a few men in the society who will have sufficient skill in the laws to qualify them for the stations of judges. And making the proper deductions for the ordinary depravity of human nature, the number must be still smaller of those who unite the requisite integrity with the requisite knowledge.[56]

There is another way of looking at the role of the Court that, though just as elevated in terms of its importance in the new regime, is less reductive in its implications for citizenship in America. That view is represented in the work of Ralph Lerner and his essay "The Supreme Court as Republican Schoolmaster."[57] Lerner's essay attempts to rescue the founders from my earlier categorization of them as modern elitist republicans (those who think that the "natural aristocracy" can solve the nation's political problems through proper administration and technique) and to place them, and the Supreme Court, in an older quasi-classical elite republican model that prides itself on education. Lerner, speaking in the voice of Tocqueville, writes of the members of the Court as having "quasi-aristocratic habits of mind [that] fit them to serve as needed politically acceptable counterweights to popular impatience and injustice."[58] He goes on to claim that "the consequence of so regarding the judge is to thrust him (and the whole machinery of justice) into the role of an educator, molder, or guardian of those manners, morals, and beliefs that sustain republican government."[59] This is a role of which Lerner approves, and one in which he finds no contradiction in terms of republican theory.

Embracing the "enlarged and refined" adaptation, Lerner writes glowingly of the original circuit-riding Supreme Court as something like a group of evangelical missionaries bringing the Federalist "word" to the pagan localists through their acutely political charges to the local grand juries.[60] The justices themselves, Lerner suggests, saw their work not as the narrow professionalism of the lawyer, and they viewed themselves as "revolutionary patriots and statesmen whose involvement in the founding and ratification controversies made it natural for them to think politically and to feel some proprietary relationship to the new order."[61] Yet even though *all* the members of the federal court system were Federalists, Lerner refuses to treat this activity as overtly partisan, claiming that "when he did his work with finesse, the teaching judge was more than a scrupulous craftsman, if less than a philosopher-king, and quite other than the partisan."[62] What they were doing, according to Lerner, was making "carefully composed, self-conscious appeals to that portion of the population which was then politically influential—appeals to be good republicans coupled with some rules for being good republicans."[63] What is missing from Lerner's pronouncement is the phrase "good Federalist republicans."

In the end, we must ask what being a good Federalist republican citizen meant. The answer is provided in the earlier essays of Publius and, greatly simplified, comes down to one basic idea: Take care of yourself and guard your rights, let those who know better (and who will, one hopes, be more virtuous) run things, and the public sphere will take care of itself. What remains unclear, however, is how this could be called educating for republicanism in any recognizable sense of the term. It is this question that lies at the root of the Anti-Federalist critique that is the subject of the next chapter.

Sheldon Wolin states that the Philadelphia Constitution deserves to be called "revolutionary in the precise sense that it broke with the established direction of political development and available political experience." Therefore, he claims, it was "a constitution without a political culture distinctive to it," and as such it represented a revolt "against an existing political constitution and its political culture."[64] He is right. Under the claim of finding "republican remedies for republican defects," the Federalists and The Federalist seriously, purposefully, and drastically reconfigured American political culture and theory. They took what they saw as a diverse, potentially dangerous political way of life and attempted to introduce order and unity. And they succeeded. Whatever their intentions, the result was a political culture that was now highly constricted in terms of participatory possibilities and, therefore, of opportunities for public happiness or personal transformation, and even more so in terms of the political efficacy itself; both had been the political lifeblood of American republicanism prior to 1787.

Their faith rested upon the power of good administration and sufficient institutional restrictions rather than on the ability of the people to construct viable political communities and selves. The result of that faith was more or less the banishment of the vast majority of citizens to private life, and the corresponding elevation of others to national prominence and positions of authority and power. In Wolin's words, "The myth of The Founding belongs not to the archetype of Athena springing full-blown from the brow of Zeus but is instead a muted version of the fratricidal story of Romulus."[65] Politics was no longer to be a conversation between citizens about their shared and public lives but, rather, a confrontational relationship of suspicious watchfulness. Since the Federalists won, we may never know whether Americans were fit for another kind of political life, but we can look at the most prominent alternative at the time to glimpse what those possibilities may have been.

Chapter Five

The Anti-Federalists

Men of a Different Faith

At this, the whole community raised their voices and cried aloud, and the people wailed all that night. Then all the sons of Israel grumbled against Moses and Aaron, and the whole community said, "Would that we had died in the land of Egypt, or at least that we had died in this wilderness! . . . Let us appoint another leader and go back to Egypt."

—Numbers 14:1–3

Deeply embedded in the previous chapter is an argument with articulators of the so-called republican thesis on the American founding. These authors—most notably J. G. A. Pocock, Gordon Wood, and Lance Banning—to varying degrees are collectively responsible, along with Wood's teacher, Bernard Bailyn, for the resurrection of the realm of ideas in America's early history; for this they are owed a considerable debt.[1] Insofar as these authors looked for and found a more classically minded mode of political discourse in revolutionary America, they have rendered a great intellectual service by releasing American men and women from the historical determinism that had, in the words of Joyce Appleby, "depicted them as the carriers of ideas that unfolded over time," and in turn placed them in narratives in which they could be seen as "responding discreetly to life's contingencies."[2] Collectively these writers—most specifically Pocock, Bailyn, and Wood—released American historical debate from the myopic question of *who* or what the founders and their opponents *were* and allowed us to start taking seriously what they *said* as well as the historical context in which they said it. It was a dramatic shift in emphasis that the Anti-Federalists themselves would have applauded. Despite this service, however, there is a difficulty, at least in the work of Pocock and Banning, that I think must be acknowledged and that results from their mutual failure to recognize some of the limits of their own partially shared methodology.

In his "Virtue and Commerce in the Eighteenth Century," as he has done elsewhere in various ways, Pocock contends: "Men cannot do what they have no means of saying they have done, and what they do must in part be what they can say and conceive it is."[3] His point, as I understand it, is that our ability to conceive of something is predicated upon our language having the necessary words, ideas, and constructs to describe it in a way that makes sense. Without that mediating function performed by language, the things of the ideas cannot in a cognitive sense exist for us, and therefore how we describe things around us in effect becomes how those things are constituted in our particular realities.[4] The same is then true for our actions and activities to the extent that they are viewed as "things." For example, within Christianity there were separate categories for heretics, sinners, pagans, and heathens, since it would make no sense to say that people living in ignorance of the faith were subject to the methods of evaluation and judgment that the faith applied to those who knew what was expected of them. In other words, you cannot be something that you cannot call by name.

Thus, in a world where "most of the inherited structure of eighteenth-century political thought persisted in America for years after 1789 . . . [thereby producing] a structured universe of classical thought [that] continued to serve as the intellectual medium through which Americans perceived the political world, and [provided] an inherited political language [that] was the primary vehicle for expression of their hopes and discontents,"[5] men could not possibly be "liberals" for the simple reason that they did not have the language to describe themselves and their behavior as such, if Pocock is correct.[6] Yet, as intriguing and useful as this mode of argumentation is, there is a serious question that must be raised in terms of its ability to stand apart from other forms of analysis, insofar as it seems to lack even an elemental theory of change.

Clearly the intellectual framework developed by Pocock owes a significant debt to the work of Clifford Geertz and Thomas Kuhn insofar as it asks us to "comprehend [every text] within the linguistic, conceptual, and social systems that controlled its creation and reception."[7] In other words, we must see ideologies as cultural systems that operate on political communities in much the same way that Kuhn's notion of a paradigm operated on scientific communities: creating a closed or "normal" system of discourse that subsequently resulted in "puzzle solving." But despite these similarities there is a crucial difference between the nature of Kuhn's work and that of Pocock, in that Kuhn's work, while incisively descriptive, is at its root a theory of change (hence the work's title). Pocock's chief construct, his "Machiavellian moment," on the other hand, is at its root a theory of resisting change, of maintaining the current paradigm against either "anomalies" from alternative ideologies or, more important, internal weaknesses. Pocock writes:

> . . . the "Machiavellian moment" denotes the problem itself. It is a name for the moment in conceptualized time in which the republic was seen as confronting its own temporal finitude, as attempting to remain morally and politically stable in a

stream of irrational events conceived as essentially destructive of all systems of secular stability.[8]

This emphasis on resistance, for Pocock, is embodied in the classical republican struggle between virtue and corruption. In America this becomes the struggle between virtue and commerce.[9] It is a struggle that, he implies, exists hegemonically throughout the history of American political life, up until what he calls the "melodrama of 1973."[10] So, rather than embracing Wood's thesis of the second founding as the "end of classical politics,"[11] or the "repudiation of 1776,"[12] Pocock claims the following:

> But even after the wealth of detail with which Wood's, Pole's, and other analyses have explored the thesis of an implicit abandonment of virtue in Federalist theory, we are not faced with a generation who unanimously made this abandonment explicit . . . the vocabulary of virtue and corruption persisted in American thought, not merely as a survival slowly dying after its tap root was cut, but with a reality and relevance to elements in American experience that kept it alive.[13]

This is in large measure what Pocock means when he tells his readers that "the interpretation put forward here stresses Machiavelli at the expense of Locke."[14] And this is exactly where the problem with Pocock's work on America seems to lie; he has simply replaced one monolithic interpretation of American political thought with another.[15] Everything, it would seem, must be captured within his "republican web," just as for Louis Hartz everything was reducible to liberalism. The fact of the matter is that it does not have to be all or nothing across time—and it would seem that a more appropriate model would be that of Bellah and his associates in *Habits of the Heart,* where it is suggested that various modes of political discourse compete for space in American political life. And, this is largely the response Pocock's work receives from Joyce Appleby as she argues that the concept of ideology as derived from Geertz and implicit in the work of Kuhn had limitations that thwarted its application to nations where "the high level of literacy . . . encouraged the free circulation of printed material [and] neither censorship nor limited access to printing presses existed to inhibit the publication of divergent, even inflammatory, points of view."[16] Despite her general praise for the body of republican work, her critical eye is still perceptive and insightful:

> The conceptual world of the elite permeated all classes, but it could not and did not exclude competing views—views which in time exercised greater interpretive powers for those differently positioned in society. By insisting upon the hegemony of a particular political tradition on theoretical grounds, the republican revisionists have resisted seeing that in pluralistic, uncensored, literate societies, the ideological predispositions of human beings have an opposite effect. Instead of insuring social solidarity, competing ideologies thwart it.[17]

To harken back to the roads metaphor in the prologue, material circumstances and historical experience created opportunities for political invention and the emergence of competing modes of discourse. Just as the events and conditions in America had laid the foundation for the birth of a new and modern form of republicanism, so did they also present certain thinkers with "anomalies" that they felt were important enough to resolve after a period of "extraordinary science" with the construction of an alternative paradigm. This was the tale implicitly told in the two preceding chapters. But just as Kuhn recognized that there were certain problems that could be solved within the old paradigm but not the new one, so we need to recognize that competing languages of political discourse may exist alongside each other in free and differentiated countries, unequal in their explanatory power at any given time but still worthy of consideration, just like Bellah and associates' "second languages."

The second founders may not have been able to refer to themselves as "liberals," but their thought clearly pointed in that direction. Whereas the Revolution produced a revision of the classical model, the second founding generated another model altogether, perhaps by fortune or perhaps by default. It is true that America can never be free from its past, and thus today must still answer to critics who draw on that earlier political language to "embarrass the progress of liberal values in America."[18] It is the thesis of this volume that the linguistic representatives of that republican past are the Anti-Federalists, who revised without releasing the lessons of their classically minded exemplars, at the same time translating their thought for an American audience/public.

In the *German Ideology* Karl Marx tells his readers that "life is not determined by consciousness, but consciousness by life," which we should compare against Pocock's statement that "men cannot do what they have no means of saying they have done." Appleby writes that "the one [statement] does not exclude the other,"[19] which on its face seems like a rather curious assertion. And just like the existentialist assertion that "existence precedes essence," we are left with what might be seen as a proverbial "chicken and egg" question in terms of what comes first, the practice or the idea. Perhaps Alexis de Tocqueville can offer some respite from this potential paradox through his discussion of language in democratic America:

> . . . the continual restlessness of a democracy leads to endless change of language as of all else. In the general stir of intellectual competition a great many new ideas take shape; old ideas get lost or *take new forms* or are perhaps subdivided with an infinite variety of nuances.[20]

The inference here is that it may be possible for people to be doing new things but describing them with old words, thus in effect saying what they have done but doing different things as their new and changing contexts demand. In early American political discourse, both the Federalists and the Anti-Federalists were engaged in this process to some extent, which is why the terminology of "republicanism" becomes so muddled and confusing—it did not seem to mean precisely the same thing from one person or group to the next.[21] Epistemologi-cally speaking, then, it is difficult to say at some fixed historical point that a particular person or group meant a particular thing on the basis of what that term or concept might have meant in some previous context. The best that we can do, it would seem, is to look for general linkages between expressions, arguments, supposed authorial intentions, the particular historical contexts, and the intended and unintended practical outcomes, or desired outcomes, in order to make our judgments.

The Federalists, as represented by Publius, whether in good faith or in bad faith, transformed republican discourse so dramatically from its prior American meaning that they mandated the creation of a new set of linguistic structures and political understandings, and eventually modes of political behavior, that could be collectively referred to only as "liberal."[22] Liberalism, as an alternative political language, quickly superseded in importance the emergent sense, and corresponding language, of republicanism that had been gestating in the minds and political activity of American colonists, that had recently come to term during the Revolution and had been baptized under the Articles of Confedera-tion. Hence republicanism, at least in terms of substantive meaning, was quickly rendered a "second language" of American political discourse. As Appleby put it:

> Liberalism had the power to evoke the behavior it prescribed. National norms acted like a sieve to strain from the fellowship of the liberal-minded those immigrants and native-born Americans who failed to exhibit the energetic qualities of the free and independent man. Having supplied the givens for a worldview, liberalism disappeared into the underground foundations of American thinking.[23]

This language of liberalism was indeed the child of the Federalists, and despite—or perhaps because of—its sociopathic potential, it garnered most of the attention post 1789, thus eclipsing its republican sibling without quite slay-ing it. Republicanism, like the historical republics themselves, was fragile, and in need of protection, nurturing, and an opportunity to overcome its adoles-cent awkwardness; but it lacked the charisma and exuberance of liberalism, and no doubt its hubris as well. It was forced to defend itself against the charges that it was not more like liberalism, and could not do the same sorts of things with a similar grace and expediency, which was quite true. Republican strengths and offerings were different, and more careful. It is perhaps an unfor-tunate fact that the loud and the bold are often victorious because they are loud and bold, and despite their hidden weaknesses or false representations. In a general sense this is why the Anti-Federalist defense of republicanism is problematic and so often misunderstood. Once the Federalists and their agenda had usurped the historical stage with their bold, daring, and all too calculated entrance, there was little the Anti-Federalists could do to regain their audience except either to accept competition on the Federalist level or to assert the dignity of their own program, only to watch it be drowned out in the end.

This is what previous scholars (with a few exceptions) who have written about the Anti-Federalists have never quite understood; they have grouped them together with their opponents and then judged them by the standards of success and failure contained within Federalist/liberal discourse, attempted to make them into bold advocates of an alternative nationalist theory, demonized them in order to make the Federalists shine even more brightly, or made them out to be guileless political innocents who are best seen and not heard. All of these approaches fail to capture the true essence and importance of Anti-Federalist discourse for both the times in which they lived and the political world we inhabit today.

With a few notable exceptions, the scholarly literature on the thought of the Anti-Federalists is mostly truncated or concealed within work focusing on the founding in general, or on some other aspect of early constitutional history. The problem with such approaches, even when the writers are given to sympathetic analysis, is that in treating that body of thought *only* as an appendage of the greater event (which it certainly is), its own context and relevance usually get lost. In other words, part of the theoretical/historical project contained in this volume so far has been to present Anti-Federalism as an extension of a much older, much larger historical/political context that not only predates the ratification debates over the Constitution but also, in metamorphosed form, actually postdates those debates as well. Only by plucking Anti-Federalism from its particularized, and thus rarefied, context does it become possible to understand the fullness of Anti-Federalist political thought in its own right. This having been said, I would like to turn to a brief overview of the academic literature on the Anti-Federalists, and then move rather quickly into my primary discussion of their thought.[24]

The post-Civil War, pre-Charles Beard historians, often called the romantics—George Bancroft, John Fiske, and Andrew McLaughlin, among others[25]—by and large denigrated the Anti-Federalists for their opposition to the Constitution (which, for these historians, was among the greatest political achievements in the history of the world, let alone of America). The Anti-Federalists were called ignorant, shallow, absurd, overly theoretical, lacking in reason, obstructionist, and so on; the judgments on the founders were equally passionate and positive.[26] Given the historical circumstances and the context in which this work took place, it makes sense that scholars would be interested in stressing the unity of the nation and the corresponding dangers associated with those who opposed that unity in thought or deed. Ultimately, however, the polemical and typically ad hominem mode of argumentation found in parts of these works proved to be of very little use in gaining any real insight into the nature of the early historical debates or the temper of the times they sought to explain. Hence, there soon appeared another group of scholars who were decidedly antagonistic to the second founding, and sought to uncover what they thought to be a more realistic picture of the nation's early history, blemishes and all.

Charles Beard and the progressive historians attempted to recast the Anti-Federalists as democrats who had been outmaneuvered by a sly group of would-be aristocrats and "capitalists" who were bent on securing an order more favorable to their particular class interests. Beard took his lead from progressives like Charles Merriam and J. Allen Smith,[27] who were responsible early on for the academic portrayal of the Constitution as a counter-revolutionary document designed by men who were worried about the emerging democratic ethos and power structures in the new nation. To the work of Beard we can add that of Vernon Louis Parrington,[28] who, James Hurston tells us, was "an admirer of Beard [though he] believed that ideas had a life of their own,"[29] which resulted in his depiction of the Anti-Federalists as "agrarian democrats" and of the Federalists as conservatives (though conservative of what we do not know). This, as abundantly noted in the annals of historiography, fit quite well with the Progressive's turn-of-the-century political agenda of trust-busting and democratic empowerment.

But it was not necessarily a correct view of the Anti-Federalists, and subsequently was as flawed as the view of their detractors. I say this because the Progressive agenda called for *national* democratic reforms, as evidenced by their legislative and constitutional program, not to mention their attack on the Supreme Court as undemocratic.[30] The truth is, however, that the quasi-plebiscitary democratic union that the Progressive vision enshrined could never have been imagined by the Anti-Federalists of the eighteenth century. Theirs was a more classically inclined democratic vision of small, face-to-face democratic city-states, or small republics. Furthermore, the depiction of the Federalists as "conservatives" is equally misplaced, especially if Merriam's thesis is at all on the mark. To be conservative, there must be some tradition to conserve; and since the Federalists were certainly not Tories, the question becomes what they were. The answer I have already given is that they were radicals, and though I do not have the time to expand on the point, I think that the style of politics hitherto associated in this volume with the Federalists has much more in common with the Progressives than they perhaps would have wanted to admit.

Richard Hofstadter's contention that "Beard no longer persuades, but he still sets the terms of the debate" is an unfortunate truth. I say "unfortunate" because in his world of the righteous working class and the nefarious big-monied men there was very little room for subtle theorizing or textured understandings of the political world, only the partisan politics of "us" and "them."

The result of Beard's having structured the debate was, as one could guess, the tenacious academic dispute that ensued, conducted in the well-known idiom of "is so/are not." In other words, by claiming that on one side there were small "d" democrats (by that time one of the most powerful political symbols in American culture) and that on the other side there were antidemocratic "conservative" usurpers, and with both sides wanting desperately to lay claim to the "democratic" label/symbol, Beard, if taken seriously, all but ensured that the fundamental historical/political debate in America would take place on terms favorable to his particular political/academic agenda. The trouble with such an agenda, however, is that in the end it was really not much more than a red herring in terms of its usefulness in understanding the political theory and culture of the founding period.

It was not until 1958, with the publication of Forrest MacDonald's *We the People: The Economic Origins of the Constitution,* and later of his 1965 work, *E Pluribus Unum: The Foundations of the American Republic,* that Beard's thesis underwent strict scrutiny on its own economic terms and was found wanting.[31] But more important in terms of this volume, Beard's work underwent a serious theoretical attack by both political theorists and historians of the consensus variety in the 1950s and the 1960s. Among these works the best known, and perhaps one of the four or five most important works in the relatively small area of Anti-Federalist literature, is Cecelia M. Kenyon's "Men of Little Faith: The Anti-Federalists on the Nature of Representative Government."[32] Unfortunately, it is significant because it is a response within the Beardian paradigm that, although opposed to his conclusions, still accepts his categories, thus producing a debate that could be likened to a dispute between Ptolemaic astronomers.

Kenyon, ironically enough, begins her work with the words, "One of the gravest defects of the late Charles Beard's economic interpretation of the Constitution is the limited perspective it has encouraged in those who have accepted it."[33] Her explicit enemy in the essay is the economic determinism that Beard's work posits, and the subsequent pigeonholing of the founders, to the benefit of their Anti-Federalist opponents, that the methodology encouraged. But Kenyon's explicit strategy of rescuing the founders' democratic credentials and withdrawing those of their Anti-Federalist critics is still reminiscent of a heroes-and-villains approach to history. Kenyon is right when she claims that Beard was "more influenced by the Populist and Progressive movements of his own time," and that he associated democracy with "simple majority rule,"[34] but she fails to recognize the gleam in her own eye at the same time. It is her acceptance of the Beardian definition of democracy as nationalist majoritarianism that becomes her enabling critical device for the debunking of Anti-Federalism and the corresponding elevation of Federalist political theory. Her argument rests ultimately on the claim that Federalist constitutionalism was more open to majority rule than one acceptable to the Anti-Federalists could ever have been. In her own words Kenyon makes this point in the following passages:

> These qualities were feared and not admired by the Anti-Federalists. They wanted detailed explicitness which would confine the discretion of Congressional majorities within narrow boundaries.[35]

> They placed even greater emphasis on the structure of government than did the Founding Fathers, and refused to take for granted, as the latter did, that the "genius" of the country was republican, and that the behavior of the men to be placed in office would in general be republican also.[36]

> The Anti-Federalists wanted a more rigid system of separation of powers, more numerous and more effective checks and balances, than the Founding Fathers had provided.[37]

> There was no more confidence in the inherent justice of the will of the majority than there was in its electoral capacity. Since the Anti-Federalists were skeptical that constituent opinion would be adequately reflected in the national legislature, they were less inclined than the Federalists to regard the government as the instrument of the people or of the majority.[38]

> There was, then, no doctrinaire devotion to majoritarianism.[39]

> The Anti-Federalists were not latter-day democrats. Least of all were they majoritarians with respect to the national government.[40]

> The last thing in the world they wanted was a national democracy which would permit Congressional majorities to operate freely and without restraint.[41]

While this strategy may appear a bit cumbersome, it is important, given the prominence of Kenyon's work on the Anti-Federalists, to point out exactly what the nature of her criticism of them was and to ask whether it is pertinent. The problem that becomes apparent on my reading of both her work and of the Anti-Federalists themselves is that she ultimately appears to be attacking a straw man. Yes, she is absolutely right: the Anti-Federalists were not national majoritarians or, to substitute a term, twentieth-century Progressives. And yes, she is also absolutely correct when she criticizes Beard for making them out to be. But Kenyon does not end her argument with this historiographical debate. Instead, she seems explicitly to claim that because the Anti-Federalists were not twentieth-century Progressives, they are doomed to the role of misguided provocateurs or "men of little faith." In other words, Kenyon, while rejecting Beard's historical claims about the Anti-Federalists, is at the same time reinforcing his normative edifice: *If* the Anti-Federalists had been nationalist majoritarians, *then* they would have been worthy of historical prominence. The flip side of the argument, then, is the praise that Kenyon reserves for the Federalists, who, although not quite the Progressives that she no doubt would have liked them to be, were the ones "of 1787–1788 who created a national framework which would accommodate the later rise of democracy."[42] So it is that Beard, while no longer persuading, but still setting the terms of the debate, in 1955 also was still tenaciously fixing the criterion for evaluation.

Although the work of Kenyon and Jackson Turner Main was flawed, there can be no denying the importance of the role they played, along with a small handful of others, in fostering interest in Anti-Federalist thought and its relationship to the second founding. And yet, despite their prominence, no one deserves more credit for the firm establishment of the Anti-Federalist position in the lexicon of American political thought than does the late Herbert Storing. As indicated by the title of his work on the Anti-Federalists, *What the Anti-Federalists Were for,* Storing was the first scholar who attempted to understand the founding through the eyes of the Anti-Federalists rather than the Federalists. Thus he was the first scholar who attempted to come to terms with the positive aspects of their political project rather than simply to reiterate their oppositional position with regard to the Constitution.

But in spite of his obvious historical sympathy, as well as a very strong descriptive analysis of these "other" founding fathers and their ideas, Storing's interpretation is still bound by the limited context from which it originates. In other words, although he goes a long way toward understanding Anti-Federalism "as *it* understood *itself,*" as well as its lasting impact on American political life, Storing still can view it only through the lens of the second founding, and not as the culturally independent and historically prior group of ideas that it really is. Aside from the obvious Pocockian rationale for such an approach—that Anti-Federalism as a set of ideas or as a linguistic entity could not exist until there was a Constitution for it to confront—there is a better, or at least alternative, explanation available that can be outlined briefly.

If for the moment we were to take Marx's position that "life is not determined by consciousness, but consciousness by life" as controlling, then we might be able to make the following supposition: that, unless challenged by an alternative paradigm, existing social and cultural arrangements may in fact remain unarticulated while at the same time providing sufficient intersubjective cues for a stable and comfortable public practice. In other words, it is possible that Anti-Federalism as a cultural matrix (and perhaps called by some other name) preexisted the ratification debates but remained an "unspoken faith." It is possible that, much like the lack of articulation of existing political relationships as independent prior to the Revolution (even though the reality of such a state of affairs was for many colonists already in place), Anti-Federalism existed in some kind of crystallized form, lived but not explicitly defined or theorized, but no less real and important to the life of the community.

And if this was indeed the case, is it not also possible that the Federalists with their nationalist political project caught the Anti-Federalists so off guard that they had to scramble to articulate as forcefully as possible what had hitherto been unspoken, thus finding themselves forced to undertake a defense that they were not at that moment able to make as skillfully as they would have liked? This, I would contend, is not an unusual phenomenon, insofar as many of our deepest commitments as human beings remain undefended, and perhaps even unexamined in any serious way, until they are endangered or confronted with extinction; but this does not preclude their validity. The genius of the Federalists as politicians was their ability to usurp the agenda-setting power of their opponents and to make it appear that Anti-Federalist thought was something new that arose in reaction to that of the Federalists, when in reality it was the other way around.[43] This is the important point of departure that will allow us to see where Storing, as strong as his work is, went wrong.

Storing tells us from the start that he will be using the founding as his historical lens, and he claims that, viewed in the light of the complexity and wide-ranging nature of the ratification debates,

> those who opposed the Constitution must be seen as playing an indispensable if subordinate part in the founding process. They contributed to the dialogue of the American founding. . . . The Anti-Federalists are entitled, then, to be counted among the Founding Fathers, in what is admittedly a somewhat paradoxical sense, and to share in the honor and the study devoted to the founding.[44]

Storing's congratulations to the "losers" would ring rather hollow in most Anti-Federalist ears. In modern literary theory, his introductory remarks would be seen instantly as an act of *erasure,* an act whereby important differences are reduced to the familiar or normalized so that they can be studied within the confines of the existing paradigm rather than functioning as an anomaly with all the potential for disruption such a thing entails à la Kuhn. Few Anti-Federalists would have either desired or accepted such a historical position if one had been offered. They would have seen such an award as a simple case of adding insult to injury.

That last point aside, however, Storing does have an argument to make. Although his work is more comprehensive in its theoretical understandings of the Anti-Federalists than that which preceded it, he still reaches conclusions that ultimately stress the lack of differences between the ratification rivals:

> If the Federalists and Anti-Federalists were divided among themselves, they were, at a deeper level, united with one another. Their disagreements were not based on different premises about the nature of man or the ends of political life. They were not the deep cleavages of contending regimes. They were the much less sharp and clear-cut differences within the family, as it were, of men agreed that the purpose of government is the regulation and thereby protection of individual rights.[45]

What Storing has done in one fell swoop is immediately to cast the second founding as an intentional liberal event. This seems quite spurious in and of itself, but then he subsumes both the Federalists and the Anti-Federalists into that unstable vortex by differentiating them in degree rather than in kind. When he argues in Kenyonesque fashion that the Anti-Federalists "did not fail to *see* the opportunity for American nationhood that the Federalists seized so gloriously, but they could not join in grasping it,"[46] he has effectively rendered the Anti-Federalists as the well-intentioned but weak-willed liberals who could not distinguish between legitimate grants of authority and the unbridled use of power, or "men of little faith." This, unfortunately, mars Storing's well-intentioned attempt at reframing Anti-Federalist thought as an important component of the second founding. His sentiment that "the Anti-Federalist reservations echo through American history; and it is in the dialogue, not merely the Federalist victory, that the country's principles are to be discovered,"[47] while seeming to increase the prominence of the Anti-Federalists, in reality only diminishes it.

Storing's Anti-Federalists are placed in a conversation that assumes away their very real substantive differences about the proper ordering of American political life, and subsequently renders the founding itself a "symposium" rather than a debate. The important difference between the two is that a symposium is a meeting at which the ends are shared but the means are different, and a debate is a clashing where the ends, and probably the means as well, differ. Storing's conclusion, then, that "the Anti-Federalists lost the debate over the Constitution not merely because they were less clever arguers or less skillful politicians but because they had the weaker argument" is really a non sequitur. In order for that to be true, we would need to accept the primacy of the Federalist political doctrine or value schema, which the Anti-Federalists clearly did not.

Although the title of Storing's work is framed as a partial rebuff to the work of Cecelia Kenyon, in reality it is not wholly incompatible with her findings so much as it is with her interpretation of those findings. She, like Storing (later), and like the Progressive and neo-Progressive scholars with whom she quarrels, seems to see the Anti-Federalists only in the narrow context of the ratification debates. Therefore Kenyon is forced intellectually to the position of making the stance one takes with regard to the Anti-Federalists as sort of a "retrospective vote" on the Constitution. Even some who have sought explicitly to defend the Anti-Federalists have done so in a way that limits them to the role of Socratic gadfly, thus still subsuming them into the more general paradigm of the founding, and hence limiting their potential for any sort of positive theoretical import.[48]

Unfortunately, it is only by placing the founding debates into the larger context of American political thought and culture in general, and recognizing Anti-Federalism as what it was—one of "the two political cultures contending for supremacy"[49] in early American politics—that we can understand our political heritage and our political possibilities. In attempting to come to grips with Anti-Federalism as *a* political culture, I am aware that as a term "Anti-Federalism" does not always describe a mutually exclusive or dichotomous category of analysis. But, to borrow a phrase from Herbert Storing, I will be "looking not for what is *common* so much as for what is *fundamental.*"[50] As in any faith there are sects and disagreements, some of them deep as chasms, but that is in the end a sign of life and should not be mistaken, as it often is, for a sign of degeneration or confusion. In the end, Anti-Federalist thought represents a choice between political faiths. The alternative is provided by the Federalists. In the end Anti-Federalist thought must stand or fall to the degree that we are willing to act on the beliefs it inspires.

ANTI-FEDERALIST DISCOURSE: AN AMERICAN SEDER

Psalm 78, titled "The lessons of Israelite history,"[51] exclaims:

> What we have heard and known for ourselves,
> and what our ancestors have told us,
> must not be withheld from their descendents,
> but handed on by us to the next generation; . . .

> He gave our ancestors strict orders
> to teach it to their children;
> the next generation was to learn it,
> the children still to be born,

> And these in turn were to tell their own children
> so that they would put their confidence in God,
> never forgetting God's achievements,
> and always keeping his commandments.

Jaroslav Pelikin distinguishes between tradition and traditionalism by arguing that the former is the "living faith of the dead," and the latter is the "dead faith of the living." Tradition, he implies, should therefore be embraced, and traditionalism should be avoided. But it is the bane of human beings that they forget. Traditions require remembrance, homage through ritual and word, as well as contemporary applications in order to remain useful to new contexts and changing times.

In Judaism one of the most important ways in which lessons are passed from one generation to the next, per the injunction above in Psalms, is through the seder. The most important seder in Judaism is the Passover seder, at which the recital of the traditional Haggadah takes place. The Haggadah is the Passover narrative that details the liberation of the Israelites from slavery, and the exodus that followed emancipation. Aside from its somewhat festive nature, the seder represents a highly ritualized gathering of both religious and political significance. It represents a celebration of freedom and a period of thanksgiving for the Jews' status as God's chosen people, and serves to stir "the spirit of freedom in the hearts of young and old across the centuries."[52]

For Bellah and his associates the secular functional equivalent of the Jewish seder would be the "constitutive narrative," whereby a community of memory tells its story and "offers examples of the men and women who have exemplified the meaning of the community."[53] These rituals and remembrances tie the past, the present, and the future together, and give the lives within those communities of memory sustenance and meaning.

The paradox in American culture, according to Bellah and associates, is that "we live in a society that encourages us to cut free from the past."[54] This in turn gives us a "tradition" that is steeped in forgetting as opposed to remembering. This is not surprising, given the project and recommendation of Publius in the *Federalist Papers*. Madison writes in *Federalist* no. 37:

> The novelty of the undertaking immediately strikes us. It has been shown in the course of these papers that the existing Confederation is founded on principles which are fallacious; that we must consequently change this first foundation, and with it the superstructure resting upon it. It has been shown that the other confederacies which could be consulted as precedents have been vitiated by the same erroneous principles, and can therefore furnish no other light than beacons, which give warning of the course to be shunned.[55]

The message is quite clear: all that has gone before is to be avoided, and whatever remains is to be torn down; the past is of use only insofar as it can be overcome; innovation is our only hope; and so on. Progress comes to demand that we forget our past and begin again, and so the Federalists must tie their promise exclusively to the future that will be if we only listen to them. One writer who has paraphrased this sentiment wrote, "Whatever else we can say about the future, it appears that we can safely take for granted its sophisticated contempt for the rudimentary quality of our present ways."[56] Although not specifically intended for the American framers, the quote manages to capture their fundamental ethos rather well. Given this, it is appropriate that the Anti-Federalists draw their inspiration elsewhere, in a remembrance of the past and not a transcendence.

Anti-Federalist discourse often recalls the Revolution for defense of existing arrangements and incremental modification and for polemical assault on Federalist political theory. In what we might call an American seder, Anti-Federalist writers consistently direct their audience's attention to the immediate past, as well as to the more distant past, to which they feel their Revolution is related, in an attempt to instill "the spirit of freedom in the hearts of young and old across the centuries." The act of recalling the Revolution can sometimes be a very brief allusion in which the reader is asked a question—"For what did you open the veins of your citizens and expend their treasure? For what did you throw off the yoke of Britain and call yourselves independent?"[57]—or an injunction to "guard against all encroachments upon your liberties so dearly purchased with the costly expense of blood and treasure."[58] At other times the recalling can take on greater proportions and frame entire essays, as in the work of Centinel, who begins:

> Incredible transition! the people who, seven years ago, deemed every earthly good, every other consideration, as worthless, when placed in competition with liberty, that heaven-born blessing, that zest of all others; the people, who, actuated by this noble ardor of patriotism, rose superior to every weakness of humanity, and shone with such dazzling luster amidst the greatest difficulties; who, emulous of eclipsing each other in the glorious assertion of the dignity of human nature, courted every danger, and were ever ready, when necessary to lay down their lives at the altar of liberty. . . .[59]

Perhaps the single best extended example, however, is found in the work of Mercy Warren:

> The expense of blood and treasure, lavished for the purchase of freedom, should teach Americans to estimate its real worth, nor ever suffer it to be depreciated by the vices of the human mind. The sons of America ought ever to bear in grateful remembrance the worthy band of patriots, who first supported an opposition to the tyrannic measures of Great Britain. Though some have long since been consigned to the tomb, a tribute of gratitude is ever due to their memory, while the advantages of freedom and independence are felt by their latest posterity.[60]

In each case the eyes of the audience are turned for some period of time back upon recent history and forced to come to terms with the justifications rendered and the losses incurred by the American people in their struggle for independence. It is an important function insofar as time and distance tend to dilute the force and content of historical events. We celebrate and commemorate without an empathy that would give important events and the people who made them the respect and awe they deserve. Without the presence of solemnity that ought to attach to causes that cost many lives and create many hardships, events of magnitude like the American Revolution become easy targets for manipulation by those who would place them in the service of less than worthy ends. So it when a Columbian Patriot eloquently reminds his readers of the sacrifice of the Revolution, and of

> people who have made the most costly of sacrifices in the cause of liberty,—who have braved the power of Britain, weathered the convulsions of war, and waded

thro' the blood of friends and foes to establish their independence and to support freedom of the human mind.[61]

The audience is asked to remember before they act, before they accept what they are being offered. This is far different from a proposition in which the reader is asked to envision what could or will be once the past is transcended or left behind. In this, however, Anti-Federalist discourse is not anti-progress or anti-change, but only anti-forgetting. The past in Anti-Federalist discourse becomes not something to be transcended but, rather, something to be expanded upon and nurtured through history. Given this, it is no wonder that the Revolution takes on religious trappings for writers like the Impartial Examiner, who likens the ratification period to a new time of trial for Americans:

> Shall you, O Virginians; shall you, I say, after exhibiting such bright examples of true patriotic heroism, suddenly become inconsistent with yourselves; and were [fail?] to maintain a privilege so incontestably your due?—No, my countrymen;—by no means can I conceive that the laudable vigor, which flamed so high in every breast can have so far evaporated in the space of five years. I doubt not, but you will in this trying instance acquit yourselves in a manner worthy of your former conduct.[62]

The period after the Revolution, for the Anti-Federalists, is a time of trial, when the faith of the people will be tested to see if they have the desire and the character to finish what they have begun. It is *not* a "critical period" in which certain weaknesses are exploited by American "Grand Inquisitors" to see if the people are willing to trade their freedom for bread. As Philadelphiensis tells it, "Nothing short of pure liberty is consistent with revolution principles; the *temple of freedom* that was raised in America, was intended by Providence. . . ."[63] And he exclaims in an earlier essay, "Horrid thought! that the greatest blessing that God ever bestowed on a nation, should terminate in misery and disgrace. Strange reverse this! that the freemen of America, *the favored of heaven,* should submit to a government so arbitrary in its embryo."[64] And this theme of Americans as the newly chosen people of God, which dates back to the Puritans, is echoed elsewhere:

> . . . our great men . . . might profit much on the present occasion by attending to the history of the Children of Israel, as recorded in that holy book; they did not trust in the promises, which were made them by their heavenly father through his holy prophets; they were restless under the government, which was appointed over them by the Almighty; they were fickle and fond of changing; they were ambitious, and wanted to appear respectable abroad; they must like all the nations, have a king to judge them.[65]

To be chosen, to be special, required, as the Israelites learned all too well, a willingness to suffer and to struggle, to persevere even though it was easier to let someone else do it, even though it meant living with uncertainty from time to time. As Cato warns his fellow citizens, in a voice that could have been borrowed from Machiavelli, "Your fate, and that of your posterity depends on your present conduct—do not give the latter reason to curse you, nor yourselves cause of reprehension . . . leave to your children a fair political inheritance, untouched by the vultures of power, which you acquired by *an unshaken* perseverance in the cause of liberty,"[66] we can hear reverence in his voice. But reverence is not enough, because there are always those whose pride will force them to irreverence, to want to be praised themselves. True reverence must be paid through deeds. In the words of one writer:

> Men, in some countries do not remain free, merely because they are entitled to natural inalienable rights; men in all countries are entitled to them, not because their ancestors once got together and enumerated them on paper, but because, by repeated negotiations and declarations, all parties are brought to realize them, and of course to believe them to be sacred.[67]

As Luther Martin put it, Americans "had *appealed* to the *Supreme being* for his assistance, as the *God of freedom,*"[68] and He had approved their request. It was only fitting, then, the Anti-Federalists thought, to remember that intervention by reminding their brethren of their history, and subsequently asking them whether the current actions they were proposing honored that memory. An interesting question, seeing that the Federalists apparently honored no one but themselves.

ANTI-FEDERALIST DISCOURSE AS A NARRATIVE OF SHAME

Christopher Lasch has written, "When the Jews referred to themselves as the chosen people, they meant that they had agreed to submit to a uniquely demanding set of ethical standards, not that they were destined to rule the world or enjoy special favors from heaven."[69] He goes on to say, "The seventeenth-century Puritan settlers of New England, much indebted to the Old Testament for their conception of a collective identity, understood their mission in the same way."[70] I agree. Furthermore, the argument so far in this volume has been that Puritan theology/ideology, in increasingly secularized and politicized form, greatly influenced American political praxis throughout colonial history and served as the rhetorical touchstone for the American Revolution. This idea is supported in the work of Bailyn and of Wood, as well as in more recent scholarship.[71] The earliest account of this phenomenon is found in the work of Andrew McLaughlin.[72] Among the most important accounts, however, is Edmund Morgan's.[73] His argument, simply put, is that the Puritan notion that "God called no one to a life of prayer or to a life of ease or to any life that added nothing to the common good," resulted in the widespread use of the jeremiad, a sermon decrying the loss of virtue and warning of divine retribution for the sin, which was, in his words, "a rhetorical substitute for adversity."[74] Subsequently, Morgan claims, this ethos was transmitted to the revolutionary generation and served to foster the conception of the Revolution as something of a holy war. Here, however, Morgan argues that although the idea of "an omnipresent angry God" was not as prominent in the thought of the revolutionary generation, they still maintained "the values and precepts derived from it." They located those values in their reading of a history "that attributed the rise and fall of empires to the acquisition and loss of the same virtues that God had demanded of the founders of New England."[75]

The Anti-Federalists were the heirs to that Puritan/Revolution tradition in the post-revolutionary schism between themselves and the Federalists. They were the ones who embraced the Puritan notion of a "calling," whereby they viewed themselves as having been summoned by God through the Revolution to serve the cause of liberty. Since the Revolution had been fought to preserve and enhance the social and political arrangements that had existed prior to the Revolution, the way to illustrate one's thankfulness was to preserve what God had ordained. The Anti-Federalists told their readers to watch the "altar of liberty with attentive assiduity,"[76] then told them of "the *divine founder* of our religion and his beatified followers,"[77] and cautioned them to be wise "by preserving [their] freedom [and proving] that Heaven bestowed it not in vain."[78] They warned against ingratitude, which the readers were told was considered by the Persians to be "an indication of the vilest spirit"; the Persians also believed that it was impossible "for an ungrateful man to love the gods, or even his parents, friends or country."[79]

The earlier emphasis on remembrance, coupled with this sense of a mission, placed the Anti-Federalists ostensibly, if not squarely, in a tradition where "history mattered because it was under divine judgement, not because it led inevitably to the promised land."[80] Political grace (temporal longevity) therefore was earned through a combination of faith and works directed toward the care and nurturing of God's gift of freedom, and accomplished through virtue on the part of the citizenry. It was not the product of audacity.[81] As one writer tells it, "The biblical account of creation taught that order had been originally constituted by God and subsequently sustained solely by His power. If God were to withdraw his power, order would collapse and chaos would follow."[82] For the Anti-Federalists that withdrawal would come when men forgot— which, they believed, the Federalists with their new Constitution had already done.

Whereas the Anti-Federalists can be cast in the quasi-millennialist framework that "served to recall them, again and again, to a painful awareness of their own shortcomings," and subsequently to prod them into an awareness that their having been "chosen" was no guarantee of their ultimate worthiness,[83] the Federalists were the harbingers of another, radically more modern tradition.[84] They were steeped quite heavily in the emergent gospel of "progress," which was marked not by a notion of the millennialist ideal of a "duty to live with faith and hope, in a world that often seemed to give no encouragement to either," but by "the expectation of indefinite, open-ended improvement . . . that can come only by human effort."[85] Wolin captures this difference quite well when he claims, "In *The Federalist*, biblical myth is recast into the language of modern science to warn Americans of their fate if they were to fail to constitute power sufficient to secure order."[86] This substitution of the power of man for the grace of God is known in Christianity as the "sin of pride," or the failure, as a result of hubris, to recognize divine authority. And it is through the trope of a sin of pride that we should, at least in part, read the Anti-Federalist critique of the Federalist political project—in other words, as a narrative of shame.

Cato warns his readers, "beware of those who wish to influence your passions, and make you dupes to their resentments and little interests . . . attach yourselves to measures, not to men."[87] It is advice as difficult to follow as it is easy to agree with. Cato's plea is for American citizens to lead principled lives, and not to let themselves become so enamored of particular people that they are misled by them into fallacious or wrongful acts. Christ's message was "Render unto Caesar that which is Caesar's, and to God what belongs to God,"[88] which is all the more powerful because it follows shortly after the famous passage that exclaims, "You are the light of the world. A city built on a hilltop cannot be hidden. No one lights a lamp to put it under a tub. . . . In the same way your light must shine in the sight of men, so that, seeing your good works, they may give praise to your Father in heaven."[89] But what is Caesar's and what is God's? What homage is due "the city of man" and what is due the "city of God"?

In his essay on the founding fathers and fame, Douglass Adair claims "Most of us in common speech today use the words *honor, glory,* and *fame* as if their meanings were interchangeable,"[90] which he cautions against. He goes on to extol the virtues of *fame* (which is public, looks to the greatest possible audience over time, and consists of actions such that posterity will remember the name of the person who "imposes his will, his ideas, for good or ill, upon history"[91]) as it attached to the founding fathers. What Adair, however, fails to do is to draw any pertinent *normative* distinctions among the three terms that might let us know whether *fame* was what the Founders *ought* to have wanted. Perhaps they ought to have been more interested in *glory,* which Adair defines as a concept that "assumes that He [God] is always watching men and that those men who, conscious that God's eye is continually on them, [will] behave with such piety and goodness in rendering homage to Him [that they will] shine with reflections of His glory."[92] Or perhaps they should have embraced the somewhat lesser idea of *honor,* which builds "into the heart and mind of an individual a powerful personal sense of socially expected conduct, a pattern of behavior calculated to win praise from his contemporaries," and which "acts like conscience for a practicing Christian." Is not the desire for *fame* really the desire for the praise that is owed God as it looks "horizontally in space and vertically in time"?[93] Does not the Bible warn "be careful not to parade your good deeds before men to attract their notice; by doing this you will lose all reward from your father in Heaven"?[94]

Earlier we explored the complex relationship among the individual, the community, and the leadership of the community in the context of a covenant in which each person was linked with the other and all were collectively beholden to God for their fortune. Each soul was like a cosigner on a loan in a covenant with God, in which the failure of the individual could bring ruin to the collective and vice versa. Above all this reciprocal arrangement demanded the virtue of community leaders, who, if they failed the test of virtue, were to be resisted at all costs, under penalty of treason against God. To extrapolate a little, if the reward good leaders brought to their communities was the grace of God in the form of safeguarding their liberties, the punishment for hubris (the quest for *fame*) would clearly be the loss of those liberties and of God's grace. We can view this historically through the narrative of the emancipated Jews as their story is used as a parallel to America's own by Melancton Smith:

> The nation of Israel having received a form of civil government from Heaven, enjoyed it for a considerable period; but at length labouring under pressures, which were brought upon them by their own misconduct and imprudence, instead of imputing their misfortunes to their true causes, and making proper improvement of their calamities, by a correction of their errors, they imputed them to a defect in their constitution.[95]

The result of the Hebrew request for alternative leadership was the enthronement of a vicious king who enslaved them and their families, took their property, and committed most other tyrannical deeds. This, Smith tells us, was the price a nation paid for ingratitude. I asked earlier what price the average citizen would have to pay for the sake of the founders' fame, and in chapter 4 I suggested that at best the price would be banishment to the private sphere; but here the Anti-Federalists are worried about more than that, they are worried about divine judgment being brought upon them by their hubristic leaders. In the words of Samuel, "If civil rulers won't acknowledge God, he won't acknowledge them; and they must perish from the way."[96]

It would be a grave mistake to discount the mystical or spiritual aspects of American republicanism as they were manifested in the idea of communal survival or failure. Sometimes "fortune" cannot be whipped or prodded;

sometimes, rather than building embankments, it is better to build arks. In many "civilized" nations there is a tendency, as time goes on, to downplay the humble beginnings from which a people or a nation emerged, including the faith that not only may have sustained them through dangerous times, but also may have made "civilization" or "progress" possible to begin with. One has to wonder at the statistical validity of Machiavelli's contention that it is "better to be impetuous than circumspect."[97] In any case, the tendency to downplay the role of fate, the gods, or God, and to elevate the role of human beings, is an interesting phenomenon, one that is important for the purpose of Anti-Federalist theory.

When Gordon Wood states that in the early stages of the revolutionary period "the American clergy [was] already deep in the process of working out—in an elaborate manner congenial to their covenant theology—the concept of the Revolution as an antidote to moral decay,"[98] which in turn led to the idea that "God may prove us, whether we be wheat or chaff,"[99] and the notion that "independence thus became not only political but moral,"[100] we are forced to ask what kind of hubris it took to reject the legitimacy that "God" had conferred on the nation's endeavor. This was precisely the question being raised by the Anti-Federalists. They did this first by questioning the Federalist impropriety inherent in the failure to properly remember or appreciate the Revolution and its pedigree of sacrifice, and its relationship to divine or at least extrahuman intervention; and second, by questioning the esteem in which the founders seemed to hold themselves and their ideas.

A Maryland Farmer writes sarcastically:

> What amazing progress in political knowledge have the Americans made in the last ten years! Should they go on improving by such laudable and rapid discoveries, what may we not expect in the course of a few years to come? . . . We talk now with the utmost confidence in our own experience, and an appeal to the history of mankind, is considered as an insult on the sagacity and understanding, of THE CHOICE AND MASTER SPIRITS OF THIS AGE. That we are the wisest people under the sun, seems to be no longer in dispute, and those whose youthful vanity has been flattered, by a transient public applause, think that because they have come into the world, they have therefore all the wisdom and experience, of those who have gone before them.[101]

The reader can glimpse the foundation of the Anti-Federalist critique of Federalist hubris and egoism. These sentiments are also mirrored in the writings of Cincinnatus, who asks, "Will any one believe, that it is because we are become wiser, that in twelve years we are to overthrow every system which reason *and experience* taught us right?"[102] This Anti-Federalist writer stresses remembrance and not simply self-aggrandizement. The political world is not merely the product of our unfettered minds roaming freely from premises to conclusions but, rather, a structured universe in which both problems and solutions must be addressed within a historical/political/moral context that rejects the substitution of some vague conception of "progress" for common sense. This helps to account for a periodic Anti-Federalist theme that warns against the unceasing quest for innovation and tells of the dangers to political life when "there is often as a great a rage for change and novelty in politics, as in amusements and fashions."[103] And Centinel declares:

> . . . a jealousy of innovation confirmed by uniform experience prevails in most communities; this reluctance to change, has been found to be the greatest security of free governments, and the principle bulwark of liberty; for the aspiring and ever-restless spirit of ambition would otherwise, by her deceptive wiles and ensnaring glosses, triumph over the freest and most enlightened people.[104]

It would be a mistake to read such passages as mere conservative reaction on the part of the Anti-Federalists, given the cast placed on this sentiment by the Impartial Examiner, who argues that both "an overweaning fondness for novelty" and a "listless inactivity of mind" are to be avoided by those who wish to have their participation "accord with [their] dignity and reputation, as an independent people."[105] This attempt to find some middle ground is a dominant theme of the Anti-Federalist text, which at many points concedes the need for change while attempting to limit that change in such a way that it reflects the values and theories of the day without giving way to some "brave new world." The sentiment expressed by one writer, that "there is nothing solid or useful that is new,"[106] is in no way representative of or fundamental to the Anti-Federalist political faith. The key is to foster change without forgetting, to improve without transforming, and most of all to move ahead without excluding those who have died, those who are living, or those yet to be born from the ongoing political conversation.

In other words, the Anti-Federalists, like the Congregationalists before them, viewed society as "a covenant between *each* with *all.*"[107] Though often used interchangeably with the idea of a *contract,* a covenant is in fact qualitatively and substantively different. The former implies a legal relationship as embodied in the phrase "quid pro quo," while the latter implies a moral or religious relationship, a solemn agreement between people (members of a group) to act in harmony with their shared ideals. The latter is often a utilitarian device entered into by two or more parties for their mutual benefit and convenience. A covenant, on the other hand, implies a promise to give aid and comfort even when, perhaps especially when, it is not convenient or necessarily of benefit for a particular person or group to do so. Thus, while it is perhaps legally and ethically wrong to break a contract, it is not usually considered a sin—at least not a sin for which anyone but the person or people involved could be considered liable. Breaking a covenant, on the other hand, is to court the wrath of God and to undermine the very foundation of society.

Hence, in American revolutionary cosmology, the British had not simply failed to live up to their agreement; they had in fact broken a sacred covenant with their colonies, thereby forcing the Americans to repudiate them or be found complicit in the eyes of the Divine and face certain defeat and subjugation, just as the early Israelites had. The question then raised in terms of the Federalist "revolution" was whether it sought the spiritual regeneration of America, as the Revolution itself had done,[108] and as the Federalists were claiming it would, or whether that "revolution" was itself a falling away from the covenant brought forth as a *result* of the actual Revolution, and therefore something that had to be resisted full bore.

The answer was not necessarily plain to see, because the Federalists had done their best to adopt a republican idiom and to marginalize the Anti-Federalists in the process (note the controversy over the names of the two parties[109]). But despite that dilemma, there is strong narrative evidence for the latter view: that the Federalists were not well intentioned but mistaken; rather, they were subversive, and therefore morally blameworthy. Such evidence can be found within the Anti-Federalist text when the various writers confront the question of promise breaking and infidelity to oaths already sworn. The most forceful and comprehensive statement on this theme comes from the pen of Vox Populi:

> But is here not a difficulty involved in this matter which is rather hard of removal? Every officer legislative, judicial or executive must be bound by oath or affirmation to support this constitution, and every such officer has taken or must take a solemn oath that he does *truly and sincerely aknowledge, profess, testify and declare that the Commonwealth of Massachusetts* is, and *of right ought to be, a free, sovereign and independent state—and that he will bear true faith and allegiance to the said Commonwealth, and that he will defend the same against traitorous conspiracies and all hostile attempts whatsoever.* . . . . How any *honest* man can take this oath almost every word of which is *emphatical* and at the same hour perhaps take the other I must confess to me is paradoxical: In the first of which he swears *that this Commonwealth is, and of right ought to be, a free, sovereign and independent state, and that he will bear true faith and allegiance to it.* . . . . In the other he swears he will support a constitution which (it appears to me) takes away every idea of *sovereignty* which is worth retaining. How these things can be reconciled is wholly beyond my conception.[110]

This writer was joined in his confusion by others like A Countryman, who claimed that, given the vague parameters of the new Constitution, he could not "see how an honest man will ever be able to take such an oath [to support the state constitution]; for one day he may be bound by oath to observe a law made by his own government, and the next day out comes a law or treaty from the general government, by which he is obliged by oath to do the contrary." He concludes this part of his letter by saying, "It is a serious thing to trifle with an oath."[111] But why, someone might ask, is it serious to trifle with an oath, especially if that oath prevents the facilitation of some supposed greater good for some greater number? There are two Anti-Federalist responses, one that accepts the utilitarian framework and criticizes it from within the paradigm, and one that rejects the paradigm and substitutes another more in line with the ongoing narrative of moral decline.

Luther Martin, in his speech before the Maryland State Assembly in which he outlines his reasons for not signing the final Constitution, even though he was in attendance at the convention, asserts the following logic:

> The same reasons which you *now* urge for destroying our *present* federal government, may be urged for *abolishing the system* which you now propose to adopt; and as the *method prescribed* by the *articles* of confederation is *now totally disregarded* by you, as *little regard* may be shewn by you to the *rules prescribed* for the amendment of the *new system*. . . .[112]

This is simply a utilitarian defense of keeping one's promises, just as the defense of Publius in *The Federalist,* with all its talk of anarchy,[113] was of breaking them. Once we begin to think that "oaths are things to trifle with," where will it end, Luther asks. What can be done to ensure the stability and order that is found wanting in the present system, and is promised in the new, once people come to believe that their word, their loyalty, their promise is simply a question of convenience? The utilitarian version of the argument would then typically conclude with the sentiment that we should keep our promises, because if we do not, then no one else will, thus rendering promises obsolete even though they are a vital component of both public *and* private life. But there is more to the Anti-Federalist critique of not keeping promises or oaths than the basic utilitarian argument; deeply interwoven with criticism like Martin's is the argument made by writers like Cornelius, who questions the damage done to a nation's moral fabric by the easy negation of oaths entailed in ratification of the Constitution:

> If a nation may so easily discharge itself from obligations to abide by its most solemn and fundamental compacts, may it not, with still greater ease do the same in matters of less importance? And if nations may set the example, may not particular States, citizens, and subjects, follow? What then will become of public and private faith? Where is the ground of allegiance that is due government? Are not the bonds of civil society dissolved? Or is allegiance founded only in power? Has *moral obligation* no place in civil government? In mutual compacts, can one party be bound while the other is free? Or, can one party disannul such compact, without the consent of the other?[114]

Taken in toto, Cornelius's series of questions and observations provides the reader with *the* metaphor for the coming age he envisions as a result of this constitutional moment. It will be an age where everything can be, and perhaps ought to be, "forgotten" when it becomes inconvenient or is deemed progressive or forward-looking to do so. Nothing will be certain except power, and that will then become its own justification. Marx in a famous passage told of a modern world "where all that is solid melts into air," and it would seem as though his commentary came rather late. Republican Federalist, assuming ratification, asks, "What must be the consequence of thus destroying public faith and confidence, are these not the principles that bind and cement the community, and that establish them as a body politic?"[115] The answer to the latter, rhetorical question is "yes," and the answer to his first question is that something else must then provide that "cement," seeing as how the Constitution, according to Samuel, "is an open professed resolution, to break a solemn covenant."[116] What that "cement" will be, becomes the basis for a good deal of Anti-Federalist anxiety. The political agenda of the Federalists, as viewed through the lens of the convenantal politics of the Anti-Federalist text, threatened not just the existing order but the whole concept of an uncoerced order altogether. The consequences, as we already know, for breaking a covenant were rightfully severe and consequently feared. To overcome these fears, and the strong arguments against such an overcoming, the temptation had to be made even greater than usual, which apparently it was.

In a similar theoretical context J. Peter Euben claimed: "When men know themselves to be users of history and creators of their own greatness, all accounts of the past, like all quotations of poetic authorities, are self-serving political projections that construct reality rather than give account of it."[117] His point here is that the shift to the idea, however vague it may have been in the early period he was writing about, of "reality" as *socially constructed,* and the corresponding elevation of men and women from "created" to "creator," while liberating in its own right, also brought forth a world where the line between the appearance of the thing and the thing itself became very very blurred. Words, in this emerging world, became empowered to *create* reality (which perhaps they had always done), whereas before they were believed to only be able to *describe* it. Even when words were imprecise, there was always the notion that they were used in an attempt to capture a reality that preexisted them, that there was some "thing" for which the words could only serve as weak substitute (and which they could not replace). Those who sought to use words to distort rather than to describe were deemed reprobates and labeled as dishonest or treacherous. However, the early Sophists changed this perception in the minds of some people and argued that words, while not *creating* reality (they had not moved that far), could be used as "tools" (weapons?) to influence how others viewed reality in a way that was beneficial to the one speaking. In contemporary theory this activity might be described as what Peter Berger has called "cognitive imperialism," which he defines as "the imposition of the people of one world on to another world . . . conversion as opposed to consciousness raising."[118] Such a thing necessarily entails *forgetting.*

While Berger was concerned with the process of modernization and the relationship between "advanced" and "underdeveloped" countries, the terminology in a strange way seems applicable to the Federalist/Anti-Federalist dispute since it took place in the context of competing cultural matrices. One was concerned with "progress" and development at almost any cost, and the other was concerned with preserving an existing cognitive world against the onslaught of the other, not because it was anti-progress but because the conservation of that world was believed necessary for progress to occur. In keeping with the current Anti-Federalist narrative, then, the next line of attack on the Federalist project was over the proper construction, or understanding, of the then existing reality. Here the Anti-Federalists more or less accuse the Federalists of using current "history" to further their own greatness, by constructing an image of recent events that were in reality only "self-serving projections." In other words, the Anti-Federalists attacked the legitimacy of the "critical period" thesis as put forth by Publius.

The "critical period" thesis, which resulted from contemporary assessments and the perspective of the constitutional framers, held that the period following the Revolution was one in which the basic fabric of society itself was tearing apart—anarchy, civil war, foreign invasion, and/or economic collapse were all imminent. America as a nation was suffering from a loss of respect and prestige abroad. Nationalists and soon-to-be Federalists stressed this depiction as a rhetorical device for persuading the nation of the need for a stronger, more efficient, energetic national government. There were no guns involved, but it was coercion nonetheless; and apparently in some measure it worked. The Anti-Federalist critical narrative again and again addresses the validity of this construction of reality. A Plebeian restates the Federalist depiction quite well:

> It is insisted, that the present situation of our country is such, as not to admit of delay in forming a new government, or of time sufficient to deliberate and agree upon amendments which are proper, without involving ourselves in a state of anarchy and confusion. On this head all the powers of rhetoric, and the arts of description, are employed to paint the condition of this country, in the most hideous and frightful colors. We are told, that agriculture is without encouragement; trade is languishing; private faith and credit are disregarded . . . the spirit of licentiousness is rampant, and ready to break over every bound set to it by the government.[119]

He goes on to detail and list the supposed state of affairs in the nation as depicted by the Constitution's supporters and concludes, as anyone would, that "from this high-wrought picture, one would suppose, that we were in a condition the most deplorable of any people upon earth."[120] And if the depiction were true, he would have been right. Historians differ about the actual nature of the post-revolutionary period, and there is a large degree of relativity possible with regard to the time in question; one person's anarchy is another person's participatory democracy. Perhaps the best approach for deciding between the competing constructions of reality is the one proposed by the Plebeian himself, who suggests that we ask people, "What is your condition?" To this query he himself answers rhetorically, "Does not every man sit under his own vine and under his own fig-tree, having none to make him afraid? Does not every one follow his calling without impediments and receive the reward of his industry?"[121] He is followed in this line of thought by Agrippa:

> Let any man look around his neighborhood, and see if the people are not, with very few exceptions, peaceable and attached to government; if the country had ever within their knowledge more appearance of industry, improvement and tranquility; if there was ever more of the produce of all kinds together for the market; if their stock does not rapidly increase; if there was ever a more ready vent for their surplus; and if the average of prices is not as high as was usual in a plentiful year before the war.[122]

Somewhere between the Federalists' depiction of death and destruction and this idyllic vision of an Anti-Federalist is probably the truth. The difference is that the Anti-Federalists do not ask their readers simply to trust them; they ask them, as members of the conversation, to look around and tell their fellow citizens what they see. There is no elaborate construction, no urgency in their position, as Candidus asks, "Can it be supposed that the people, are so savage, and void of every principle of common prudence, that they would abandon all their deliberations in Council, and rush immediately to arms?"[123] The answer is clearly "no." Alfred speaks for most of the Anti-Federalists when he claims, after detailing the wealth of the nation in terms of land and resources, "I cannot be brought to believe that America is in that deplorable, ruined condition which some designing politicians represent; or that we are in a state of anarchy beyond redemption."[124] Although he puts them more enthusiastically, Patrick Henry relays the same thoughts in a speech at the Virginia Ratifying Convention: "No peace—a general cry and alarm in the country—Commerce, riches, and wealth vanished—Citizens going to seek comforts in other parts of the world—Laws insulted—Many instances of tyrannical legislation. These things, Sir, are new to me."[125]

What is the rush? Why the urgency? Perhaps the Americans did not know they were naked. Perhaps, as William Findley claims, the Federalists believed "that nothing, no argument, no opposition can withstand the plea of necessity."[126] Or, as An Old Whig suggests, the Federalists hoped that "like a person in the agonies of a violent disease, who is willing to swallow any medicine, that gives them the faintest hope of relief; the people stood ready to receive the new constitution, in almost any form in which it could be presented to them."[127] This is not an unusual strategy, according to the Federal Farmer, who says, "It is natural for men, who wish to hasten the adoption of a measure, to tell us, now is the crisis—now is the critical moment which must be seized, or all will be lost."[128] But, as he himself claims, and as Centinel points out, "it is the argument of tyrants."[129]

The discourse of the revolutionary period has at this point started to come full circle as the watchful eyes of the American "congregation" are now trained on those who would lead them in a rejection of their current political life in a favor of a new one. But do they come as kindred spirits, as fellow citizens who share both memories of the past and a vision for the future, or do they come as tyrants, or despots, offering salvation and safety in exchange for the freedom and liberties of their brethren, like Dostoyevsky's priest? As the Old Whig thoughtfully warns, "Scarce any people every deliberately gave up their liberties; but many instances occur in history of their losing them forever by a rash and sudden act, to avoid a pressing inconvenience or gratify some violent passion of revenge or fear."[130] In a similar vein the Impartial Examiner cries out:

> . . . of what consequence will that state of congressional pre-eminence be to you, or to your posterity, if either the one, or the other should thereby be reduced to a mere herd of ————? O Great GOD, avert that dreadful catastrophe.—Let not the day be permitted to dawn, which shall discover to the world that America remains no longer a free nation!—O let not this last sacred asylum of persecuted liberty cease to afford a resting place for that fair goddess!—Re-animate each spirit, that languishes in this glorious cause! Shine upon us . . . that in this awful moment we may be conducted safely through the maze of error;—that a firm basis of national happiness may be established, and flourish in undiminished *glory* through all succeeding ages![131]

It is as if the Examiner is crying out for a biblical deliverer, in much the same way the Revolutionaries called upon the deity in their time of trial. But, having won the war, from whom are they to be delivered? From themselves; from their weaknesses, to be sure; but, more than that, from those who would exploit their fears, who would "give them bread" in exchange for their dreadful freedom. The friends of the new Constitution not only claim that without it all is lost, they also claim that with it nothing is impossible. As one writer puts it, "Agriculture is to flourish, and our fields to yield a hundred fold—Commerce is to expand her wings, and bear our productions to all ports in the world—Money is to pour into our country through every channel—Arts and manufacturers are to rear their heads, and every mecanic [sic] find full employ."[132] The choice as presented was between total failure and complete bliss. Is it any wonder that the Anti-Federalists are suspicious? Is it any wonder that they believe the Constitution and the words offered in support of it are but a mask for some far more nefarious and devious plan?

The contemporary African-American literary theorist Houston Baker, Jr., offers an interesting theoretical device that might provide some insight into the nature and depth of Anti-Federalist criticism. In his book *Modernism and*

the Harlem Renaissance,[133] Baker introduces two discursive strategies he believes
were at work in the writings of such early black authors as Booker T. Washington and Zora Neale Hurston. He calls them *the mastery of form* and *the deformation of mastery.* What is of interest here is *the mastery of form,* which contains
within it the idea of a *mask.* Baker argues that many black writers, who were
forced to work within the context of a hostile white society, adopted a literary
survival strategy whereby they would appear to be carrying out familiar and
stereotypical roles for their white audience, while at the same time "hiding"
or "coding" something original and subversive to those familiar and expected
images, which was directed at their radical (black) audience/public. The representative figures here become the minstrels. By *mastering* the expected form and
wearing it as a mask, these discreet subversives were in reality promulgating a
radical message without having to suffer the consequences that such activity in
the turn-of-the-century American South would surely have brought them.

Baker's argument is in reality a provocative, and unacknowledged, left-
wing appropriation of Leo Strauss's work on behalf of "conservative" philosophers.[134] Given this, the use of some version of the *mastery of form* and its *mask*
accompaniment is not necessarily the domain of any particular ideological
camp but, rather, a theoretical tool available to those who seek power from a
minority position, whether they are black separatists or philosopher-kings. I
have spent a little time here because whether the Federalists engaged in this
practice or not, their Anti-Federalist counterparts certainly thought they did;
and since the Federalists could not claim the title of disenfranchised or op-
pressed minority, the question becomes what their purpose in fact was.

The Anti-Federalists found themselves forced not only to engage in a monumental political struggle over theory and principle with the Federalists, but
also to engage in the very time-consuming and highly elusive strategy of unmasking opponents who had sufficiently mastered the political *forms* of the day.
As the Impartial Examiner explains, some people "conceive a fondness for this
species of government, because it is framed in the *republican stile;* and, although
fraught with the seeds of *despotism,* the apparent loveliness of its outward garb
hides all the *deformity* of its inward corruptions."[135] Centinel tells his readers,
"It is only necessary to strip the monster of its assumed garb, and to exhibit it
in its native colors, to excite the universal abhorrence and rejection of every
virtuous and patriotic mind."[136] He goes on to assert that "a good cause does
not stand in need of such means; it scorns all indirect advantages and borrowed
helps, and trusts alone to its own native merit and intrinsic strength . . . it is
knavery that seeks disguise."[137] Finally, in a reply to a Federalist sympathizer,
A Citizen warns "that little dependence can be placed on appearances, and
that the people ought to guard against the cunning and insidious arts, employed
by designing men; for it is evident, that the name which the writer assumes,
and the candor he effects, were purposely designed the better to carry on the
business of deception."[138]

The specter being raised by the Anti-Federalists with this emphasis on deception and usurpation, coupled with their depiction of the Federalists as disconnected from the revolutionary tradition, is clearly one of moral condemnation. The Federalists are portrayed as semi-Godless men for whom oaths are matters of convenience, men who would construct reality so as to incite fear and anxiety in much of the citizenry. They represent a leadership class, bereft of virtue, who through their actions beckon the judgment of a Divine that abhors corruption. This is no simple intrafamilial disagreement between like-minded politicos, but a real, persistent, coherent, and perhaps thoroughly justified political/religious inquisition. It is important to keep in mind that, however illiberal and unpopular Puritan theories of membership might be in contemporary America, there was an explicit duty to cast the unregenerate out of the community when they could not be persuaded to conform to the moral imperatives established by the members. To allow them to stay would mean complicity, and complicity would bring failure to the whole and perhaps to each of its parts. For the Anti-Federalists it was not so much a critical period as it was a time of trial for America. In essence, Samuel Chase claims as much in his speech to the Maryland Ratifying Convention: "The question is the most important that ever came before an assembly for decision. It involves the happiness or misery of millions yet unborn . . . the present and future generations will bless or execrate us. We are at a solemn crisis."[139] These concerns are mirrored as well by Centinel, who also speaks in the dialect of divine sanction or retribution as he challenges his readers:

> You are now called upon to make this decision, which involves in it, not only your fate, but that of your posterity for ages to come. Your determination will either ensure the possession of those blessings, which render life desirable, or entail those evils which make existence a curse: that such are the consequences of a wise or improper organization of government, the history of mankind abundantly testifies.[140]

America's time of trial, the time of the great and ultimately irresistible temptation, was, for the Anti-Federalists, upon the nation and its people. This of itself was not particularly new. Republics constantly existed in tension with temptation, with the seductive lure of the forbidden fruits of untold wealth, power, and fame offered by corruption. What was new, historically speaking, was the speed with which their first major test had come upon them. As Mercy Warren was to note so poignantly through the voice of another, "There is seldom any medium between gratitude for benefits, and hatred to the authors of them; a little mind is hurt by the remembrance of obligations, begins by forgetting, and not uncommonly ends by persecution."[141] Political actors/theorists whose political projects were steeped in the anti-gospel of *forgetting* obviously would reach Warren's final stage all the more quickly. But there is still a question that puzzles: how the Anti-Federalists moved from what could very well have been a political disagreement over the nature and means of political reform to the imputation of corruption, and the virtual demonization of their rivals. To answer this question, we need to turn away from the substantive political program and written defense of the Constitution that the Federalists offered and look through Anti-Federalists' eyes at the context from which the Constitution actually emerged. Here the most appropriate metaphor is *darkness*.

Centinel frames the Anti-Federalist discussion of the Constitutional Convention with a set of biblical passages (John 3:20 and Luke 12:3–4) that open one of his letters:

> For everyone that doeth evil, hateth the light, neither cometh to the light, lest his deeds should be reproved . . .—But there is nothing covered that shall not be revealed; neither hid that shall not be known. Therefore whatsoever ye have spoken in darkness, shall be heard in light: and that which ye have spoken in the ear in closets, shall be proclaimed on the house tops.[142]

Where John Winthrop spoke of a city on the hill that would be a beacon, a bright and shining example for the world to see, the Anti-Federalists perceived the framers as operating under the cloak of darkness and secrecy, in the world of the Devil, not of God. Given the prominence of many of the members of the Convention, the Anti-Federalist attacks or imputations of evil were often quite restrained and only hinted at treachery. Patrick Henry, for instance, claims:

> I believe it would have given more general satisfaction, if the proceedings of that Convention had not been concealed from the public eye. This Constitution authorizes the same conduct. There is not an English feature in it. The transactions of Congress may be concealed a century from the public, consistently with the Constitution. This, Sir, is a laudable imitation of the transactions of the Spanish treaty. We have not forgotten with what a thick veil of secrecy those transactions were covered.[143]

Yet others, like Sydney, were less careful and offered up a picture of a long-standing plot of a covey of powerful men to subvert the fundamental basis of American political life:

> If we take a retrospective view of the measures of Congress who have their secret journals, the conduct of their officers, at home and abroad, acting under an oath of secrecy, as well as of individuals who were intimately connected with them, from the year 1780 to the last convention, who also acted under an injunction of secrecy (and whose journals have not been published even to this day, but will no doubt continue buried in the dark womb of suspicious secrecy), we can scarcely entertain a doubt but that a plan has long since been framed to subvert the confederation.[144]

Finally, there were those who were seemingly fearless and far more blunt in their assessment of the Convention's strong attempt to maintain the privacy of their proceedings. Luther Martin and Centinel, respectively, write:

> For this purpose, in a time of profound peace, to shut themselves up in mystery and darkness; to keep all their deliberations an absolute secret from their constituents, who were to be effected thereby; to prevent the publication of their journals; to deprive the free citizens of America every means of information. . . .[145]

> If you are in doubt about the nature and principles of the proposed government, view the conduct of its authors and patrons; that affords the best explanation, the most striking comment. The evil genius of darkness presided at its birth, it came forth under the veil of mystery, its true features being carefully concealed, and every deceptive art has been and is practicing to have this spurious brat received as the genuine off-spring of heaven born liberty.[146]

While it is true that the Convention defended its conduct with the argument that secrecy allowed for a freer discussion in which candor could replace overt posturing for the sake of public praise or the avoidance of blame, it is equally true that explanation is not necessarily a proper substitute for justification. As Cato would ask, "is the power of thinking, on the only subject important to you, to be taken away, and if per chance you should happen to dissent from Caesar, are you to have Caesar's principles crammed down your throats . . . ?"[147] Earlier Cato had proclaimed, "to the astonishment of mankind, your legislatures have concerted measures for alteration, with as much ease as an individual would make a disposition of his ordinary affairs."[148] By making secret and hidden that which is supposed to be public and shared, the members of the Convention have taken on the characteristics of tyrants who act as though the public sphere is their private domain. There is no way to see the language of *darkness* used to describe the process as anything other than biblical in its idiom and accusatory in its reach. The framers, to the Anti-Federalists, once again are not just politically mistaken, they are sinful; and the document that is produced from their union bears the mark of the darkness from which it was produced.

By now the ground leading to the conclusion that the members of the Convention acted outside of their granted authority is well trod. Within the Anti-Federalist text there are repeated imputations of impropriety, and accusations that the Articles of Confederation had been illegitimately bypassed and the legitimate process of amendment ignored in the construction of the Constitution. Denatus captures the essence of the position succinctly: "I renounce it [the Constitution] entirely, because, in my opinion, it was composed without any legal authority. As far as I can learn, the express purpose of the convention was, to revise and amend, the articles of the union."[149] But to fixate on the purely legal questions would be to miss the point altogether; the Anti-Federalists' critique of the Constitution was not procedural, but moral and theoretical. They were not contending in good Hartzian fashion over technique or means, but over ends. And neither was the debate simply an ideological struggle between conservatives and progressives; it was cosmological and theological. Throughout the Anti-Federalist text writer after writer picks up thematically the words of Cato—"Attach yourselves to measures not men." Beware, they tell their readers, of the use of "great names" in the debates over ratification. Do not be tempted merely because Washington and Franklin, or other such men, appear to be intimately connected with the document.[150] A Georgian tells of this phenomenon and provides an unmistakable warning:

> Though this new federal constitution, I believe was framed and intended for the good of the United States, and, as we are well aware, was assented to by the political saviours of our country, to whom all deference and respect is due, yet the sacredness of these illustrious characters has not been sufficient nor able to prevent several articles from creeping into the said constitution, which, by their different constructions and great latitude given them, an American Sylla or Augustus Octavianus, might one day or other make serviceable to his ambition . . . to the utter subversion of our SACRED FREEDOM.[151]

While giving praise to the framers, the Georgian's subtext here is rather explicit and clear—the Constitution carries with it the seeds of crucifixion, of a potential executioner who will destroy what is sacred and, one must suppose, install something profane. Rather than enduring a final judgment, it would be better to incur anarchy, and to begin over again, than it would be to give in to the "artful and designing men." Centinel goes so far as to claim:

> Infinitely preferable would be occasional wars to such an event [the instillation of despotism that would result from ratification of the Constitution]; the former, although a severe scourge, is transient in its continuance, and in its operation partial, but a small proportion of the community are exposed to its greatest horrors, and yet fewer experience its greatest evils; the latter is permanent and universal misery, without remission or exemption.[152]

The despot is the man of hubris, or pride, who renders himself like God, and those who worship other men are guilty of the same sin. For the Anti-Federalists the founders' quest for *fame,* as opposed to *glory* or even honor, brought with it potential damnation for the community. Men must not forget Yahweh was a jealous God. In a world that stresses *remembrance,* it becomes imperative to resist those who would *forget.*

ANTI-FEDERALIST DISCOURSE AS REPUBLICAN THEORY

Despite the argument so far of an Anti-Federalism that transcends the historical confines of the ratification period, it would be difficult to ignore, in any strong account of that thought, the cathartic role those debates played in lending a semblance of theoretical coherency to it. The most succinct summation of Anti-Federalist thought with regard to the Constitution and the *political* alternatives to it is Storing's *What the Anti-Federalists Were for*. Within the Anti-Federalist text itself there are some who go so far as to make neat lists of specific Anti-Federalist positions with regard to each objectionable section of the new Constitution.[153] Rather than sifting through all of those arguments point by point, I would like to construct a general theoretical model of the intellectual threads that bind Anti-Federalist thought together. In other words, I want to illustrate as much as possible what enables us to talk about "Anti-Federal*ism*" rather than the Anti-Federalists.

For scholars like Kenyon and Storing, what ultimately tied the Anti-Federalists together was their collective fear of government, or their extralibertarian impulses. But that view does not comport very well with the picture painted above. There the Anti-Federalists were representative of those who believed in John Winthrop's "federal freedom," the freedom to do that which is right. This is clearly something very different from the freedom to do everything except that which is wrong, which a liberal or libertarian embraces. The Anti-Federalists envisioned a world with positive obligations to remember. The paradigm they were resisting offered them a world where it was all right, and perhaps even necessary, simply to forget those ideals that made one's life more cumbersome.

It was not, then, government that they feared, but corrupt or detached government. Their fear was the fear of loss, of becoming detached from their sense of self and their continuity with the past that made that self possible to begin with. This ideal is captured in the Anti-Federalist theory of society put forth by Agrippa, who, in contradistinction to the sort of standardized "state of nature" theory associated with classical liberalism of the Hobbesian variety, posits the following account of social formation:

> It is common to consider man at first as in a state of nature, separate from all society. The only historical evidence, that the human species ever actually existed in this state, is derived from the book of Gen. There, it is said, that Adam remained a while alone. While the whole species was comprehended in his person was the only instance in which this supposed state of nature really existed. Ever since the completion of the first pair, mankind appear as natural to associate with their own species, as animals of any other kind herd together. Wherever we meet with their settlements, they are found in clans. We are therefore justified in saying, that a state of society is the natural state of man. Wherever we find a settlement of men, we find also some

appearance of government. The state of government is therefore as natural to mankind as a state of society.[154]

In contemporary political thought this view of social formation will compete with a more liberal view on the basis of the "encumbered-self v. the unencumbered-self," with communitarians like Michael Sandel arguing on behalf of the former and contract theorists like John Rawls positing the latter.[155] Agrippa's argument is that aside from one historical instance, which is documented only in the most mythical of ways, the community is prior to the individual and to what later became known as the state. The community is the context in which the individual is constituted. He or she is a social or "encumbered" being rather than a presocial or "unencumbered" being, an Aristotelian "political animal." This, interestingly enough, is also the first tenet of civic republicanism. Perhaps the most eloquent, as well as the most cautionary, expression of this ideal is delivered by Socrates in Plato's *Crito* when he argues that outside of the community that gave him life and constituted his "soul," he would cease to exist and might as well be dead.

While the Socratic case is admittedly extreme, it does help us get at a key difference between Federalist and Anti-Federalist political theory. In the Federalist hierarchy the community is replaced by the nation through an act of reason and will, as argued in chapter 4. The problem, however, with such a shift is that it is ultimately atheoretical or impossible within the context of republicanism because of the latter's emphasis on both extensive citizen participation in the construction and care of the public sphere, and the shared values and mores that enable such an endeavor in the first place, the existence of which is unfortunately context dependent. In other words, the Federalist nation-state cannot hope to produce republican sentiments or manners because it is historically ancillary to, and conceptually separate from, the concept of community that functions as the social and political prerequisite of republican government.

Madison knew this, as evidenced by his theoretical constriction of the substantive category of citizenship to a smaller and smaller group of people at the national level. In turn, under the guise of seeking "republican remedies for republican defects," he transformed the context of political life from the local to the national level. This transformation subsequently left the republican citizens of the earlier period "unencumbered," since they now were neither involved in any significant way with the construction of the public sphere, nor located in a community with specific enough borders to have any but the most general values and mores. To simplify this point a little, it was as if in the earlier period the citizens had all been "children" of a particular "family" that, as families do, shared certain core characteristics, values, and goals, along with a love that linked them to each other in a way that none of them could be linked with others outside of their circle. But in the later period each "family" was separated and its members placed in an "orphanage," where there was still a commonality of sorts, but now it was more distant, less specific, and empty of the fraternal love found within one's own family. Here the best that could be achieved was "solidarity," and the worst was indifference. Thus, in Madison's world the average "citizens" may be safe, dry, and fed, but they are still in effect "homeless," and ultimately alone.

Anti-Federalist theory, on the other hand, recognizes that the size and nature of the political community are intimately linked with its possibilities (perhaps the Federalists also recognize it, but in the context of a different end). The Anti-Federalist theorists understand that *fraternity*, a higher-order good than *solidarity* (because the latter is implicit in the former, whereas the latter does not imply the former[156]), was the product of familiarity and closeness in both a physical sense (proximity) and a conditional sense (a rough equality of condition, or a shared way and standard of life). This point is captured clearly by Cato:

> It may be suggested . . . that whoever is a citizen of one state, is a citizen of each, and that therefore he will be as interested in the happiness and interest of all, as the one he is delegated from; but the argument is fallacious, and, whoever has attended to the history of mankind, and the principles which bind them together as parents, citizens, or men, will readily perceive it. These principles are, in their exercise, like a pebble cast on the calm surface of a river, the circles begin in the center, and are small, active, and forcible, but as they depart from that point, they lose their force, and vanish into calmness.[157]

That "calmness" is in reality what the Federalists, and more specifically Publius, seek through the dissipation of "forcible activity," by the transfer of power from the local to the national level. The first aspect of their strategy as outlined above was to present the various republican "families" (states) as dysfunctional and in need of "therapy" or repair; the second aspect was to offer their services as political therapists via the Constitutional Convention; and the final aspect of their strategy was the cure, which consisted in the consolidation of the states, or their "normalization." In other words, the communities that served as the context for American republicanism had to be circumvented and subsequently replaced by the national government, in substance if not in form. The theoretical implications of this are quite serious, in that having removed the context in which republican government was possible in order to supplant it in the hierarchy with the nation-state, the bonds that held the citizens together were about to be broken, and the citizens more or less cast out on their own. Thus Sheldon Wolin can argue that "there was an important sense in which the new constitution signified that insofar as Americans would surrender or modify the rights they had in their state politics they would, in part, be leaving civil society for a state of nature."[158] And it is in light of this idea of Americans being *reduced* or *degraded* to a state of *individualism*, rather than elevated to it, that we ought to read Anti-Federalist critiques of the Constitution and many of its provisions.

The great New York Anti-Federalist George Clinton wrote:

> I would ask whether in the establishment of this new Government, we find such a religious adherence to Compact—Has it not originated and grown into what it is from motive of political expediency? Has it not been submitted to upon this occasion alone? Have not all the measures that have introduced it and that are now bringing into action been in the force of compact, in direct violation of solemn plighted faith?[159]

We can see here the sense of violation expressed, the sense that something sacred and valuable is being diminished and done away with, in complete disregard for the culture and faith embodied within it. This pathos is made even more problematic insofar as for the Anti-Federalists the radical remaking of the country through the consolidation of the states into a general government represents the destruction of the essence of American strength. As Patrick Henry put it:

> This was a severe conflict. Republican maxims were then esteemed—those maxims, and the genius of Virginia, landed you safe on the shore of freedom. On this awful occasion, did you want a Federal Government? Did federal ideas possess your minds? Did federal ideas lead you to the most splendid victories? I must repeat again the favorite idea, that the genius of Virginia did, and will again lead us to happiness. To obtain the most splendid prize, you did not consolidate. You accomplished the most glorious ends, by the assistance and the genius of your country [state]. Men were taught by that genius, that they were fighting for what was most dear to them.[160]

This, too, is a key republican theme: that the strength of a country, or in this case a state, is often the product of its unique organization and particular brand of virtue. Corruption and crisis, in republican theory, result when the people of the nation fail to consistently return to first principles, and thus fail to renew the source of their strength and energy. Once the sense of mission is gone, once the links between generations are severed, and people come to think of themselves as disconnected over time, if not in space, the inspiration and meaning of success become blurred and the larger ends for which the action was undertaken are discarded as power and victory become the ends themselves rather than the means for preserving a particular way of life and a particular people.

The fear here that the particular will give way to the general at the expense of unique, cherished, and meaningful ways of life in which the people of the various states and local communities had found solace and happiness is played out thematically in two ways in terms of the Anti-Federalist critique of the

Constitution. First there is the line of argument that suggests the new national government will be too distant and detached from local circumstances to understand the people's specific and particular needs; second there is the line of argument that suggests the national government will be involved too intimately with local affairs for which it lacks the appropriate subtleties and sensibilities. These fears are simply two sides of the same coin; in the first instance the fear is akin to a sin of omission, and in the second it is the functional equivalent of a sin of commission. Here social theorist Peter Berger's injunction takes on Anti-Federalist trappings when he argues, in a voice that they might have used against the Federalists:

> A theorist can never say I know the truth—or I want to save you. Cognitive respect implies an injunction to be skeptical of any outsider's claim to superior knowledge of an insider's world. What people say about their own social reality must always be taken with great seriousness.[161]

One of the most important contexts in which this line of argument is revealed lies in the Anti-Federalist critique of the form and substance of the emergent brand of representation embodied in the new Constitution. Aside from the ever-present criticism that the size of the representation (one representative for every thirty thousand) is simply too small, there is the more substantive republican criticism that the representatives will "forget where they came from." Cornelius asserts:

> They will be far removed, and long detained, from the view of their constituents. Their general conduct will be unknown. Their chief connections will be with men of the first rank in the United States, who have been bred in affluence at least, if not the excess of luxury. They will have constantly before them the enchanting example of Ambassadors, other publick Ministers, and Consuls from foreign courts, who, both from principles of policy, and private ambition, will live in the most splendid and costly style. Men are naturally enough inclined to vie with each other. Let any body of men whatever be placed, from year to year, in circumstances like these. . . . And then, let any one judge, whether they will long retain the same ideas, and feel themselves under equal restraints.[162]

In the 1950s the sociologist C. Wright Mills came to refer to this sort of phenomenon as the "iron law of oligarchy" at work, by which he meant to describe the process through which interests, for him specifically class interests, came to congeal horizontally across groups rather than vertically within groups. In other words leaders would come to share the values of other leaders, and members would be left basically without the representation of the like-minded leaders they had originally sought. Here the problem would be enhanced because of the spatial and temporal dislocation that would make accountability

even harder to impose. The often-repeated indictments of the "federal or national city," the "10 miles square" that would become the seat of the new
government, where "the doors [would be opened] for withdrawing from the
state governments entirely, [which in turn might be] very alluring and pleasing
to those anti-republican men who prefer a place under the wings of courts,"[163]
can be read without too much interpretive damage as injunctions against the
distance from home both in the physical sense and in the sense of "home" as
a state of mind or way of thinking about the political world. Although he was
referring to the militia, the sentiments of Aristocrotis are every bit as applicable
to the new national government as a whole, and the legislature in particular,
when he writes of a fear of people "who will not be attached to any particular
place."[164]

Detachment from particular circumstances and local contexts, which for
Publius was to result in an enlarged field of vision for the representatives and
other members of the new national government, in a so-called release from
parochialism, for the Anti-Federalists meant a release from the only legitimate
restraints a republic had: its mores and inculcated public habits or manners.
Patrick Henry speaks on this in the context of taxation:

> Must I give my soul—my lungs to Congress? Congress must have our souls. The
> State must have our souls. This is dishonorable and disgraceful. These two coordi-
> nate, interfering unlimited powers of harassing the community, is [sic] unexampled:
> It is unprecedented in history: They are the visionary projects of modern politicians:
> Tell me not of imaginary means, but of reality; This political solecism will never tend
> to the benefit of the community.[165]

Once the local community is devalued, the primary source of American values
is lost, thereby opening up the political world to a sort of boundlessness where,
according to A Farmer speaking in the analogous context of the fall of Rome,

> . . . the most subtle disquisitions of a metaphysical nature became the universal rage—
> the more incomprehensible—the more obstinately were they maintained, and in
> fine, the canonized Austin or Ambrose, (I forget which) closed his laborious enquir-
> ies, with this holy position—*that he believed, because is was impossible.*[166]

The writer here clearly is arguing against the sort of mindless, utopian theorizing in which people are sometimes prone to engage, in which speculative
logic and constructions of "cities in speech" replace concrete realities, and
existing ways of life, in acts of superimposition that lay waste to vital and living
political cultures. Here we face the worst sort of "cognitive imperialism," in
which no respect is given to existing arrangements and understandings, and the
arrangements replacing them are not even "laboratory tested." Wolin makes a

similar point with his claim that the Constitution deserves to be called "revolutionary" because it "broke with the established direction of political development and available political experience . . . ," and proposed "a constitution without a political culture distinctive to it."[167] As radical as that strategy was, however, under the argument made in chapter 2 it would still have been supportable had the intention been to "clear away the obstacles to community"; but the problem for Federalist political theory was that "community" had in fact become the obstacle they sought to clear away. The shift outside of the local context to discover "T"-truths, and the replacement of local political understandings and foundations, led A Farmer to argue:

> The melancholy truth is, that the internal institutions of an extensive empire signify nought—the principle [sic] convenience, the rights and interests of a part must give way to what is called the good of the whole, unhinges every species of just and equal government, because it is a principle that has no limits.[168]

Anti-Federalist political thought as a political theory of the particular, which is limited and bounded by local consensus and agreement, is reflected, then, in the concept of representation as described by Luther Martin:

> . . . upon *just principles of representation,* the *representative* ought to *speak* the sentiments of his *constituents,* and ought to vote in the same manner that his constituents would do (as far as he can judge) provided his constituents were acting in *person,* and had the same knowledge and information with himself.[169]

Representatives, for the Anti-Federalists, must speak the local political language and must defend the rights of the community to govern itself from the encroachment of the national government in much the same way suggested in the discussion of Whig political theory in chapter 3. The only way in which those representatives are allowed to legislate for the "general welfare" is if it is also the "mutual" welfare (not something that invades local political autonomy but something designed to protect that autonomy, and that of the other political societies involved). Under no circumstances does republican political theory, or its Anti-Federalist counterpart, allow representatives to legislate in such a way that preexisting political decisions of the state are open to modification that will render them uniform.

Recalling the Revolution, Agrippa reminds his readers:

> The contrary principle of local legislation by the representatives of the people, who alone are to be governed by the laws, has raised us to our present greatness; and an attempt on the part of Great-Britain, to invade this right, brought on the revolution, which gave us separate rank among nations. We even declared, that we would not be represented in the national legislature, because one assembly was not adequate to the purposes of internal legislation and taxation.[170]

The differences between states were not considered by the Anti-Federalists as something that needed to be overcome but, rather, as something to be praised and safeguarded from centralizers. Local, particular knowledge (common sense) was the basis for a properly constructed political order, both as a practical matter and as a moral matter. The former is evidenced in the following passage from Cato, who writes with a prescient nod toward Lincoln:

> But whoever seriously considers the immense extent of territory comprehended within the limits of the United States, together with its variety of climates, productions, and commerce, the difference of extent, and number of inhabitants in all; the dissimilitude of interest, morals and policies, in almost everyone, will receive it as an intuitive truth, that a consolidated republican form of government therein, can never *form a perfect union, establish justice, insure domestic tranquility, promote the general welfare, and secure the blessings of liberty to you and your posterity,* for to these objects it must be directed: this unkindred legislature therefore, composed of interests opposite and dissimilar in nature, will in its exercise, emphatically be, like a house divided against itself.[171]

Failure to take notice of the differences—or, more important, any attempt to overcome them rather than to structure a polity that is able to live with those differences, without the need to coerce them out of the system or engage in the process of erasure or normalization—raises the following specter, as depicted by A Farmer:

> In a *national* government, unless cautiously and fortunately administered, any disputes will be the deep-rooted differences of interest, where part of the empire must be injured by the operation of a general law; and then should the sword of government be once drawn (which Heaven avert) I fear it will not be sheathed, until we have waded through that series of desolation . . . in order to bring so many separate states into uniformity.[172]

Far from being pessimistic millennialist railings, and ignoring for now the prescience of their position that we can know through hindsight, the Anti-Federalists here have a not-too-distant past from which to draw a surfeit of historical examples to support *their* theoretical position on behalf of diversity, and their subsequent opposition to uniformity. There were also plenty of contemporary examples from which to draw important inferences. In the words of An Old Whig:

> Uniformity of opinion in science, morality, politics or religion, is undoubtedly a very great happiness to mankind; and there have not been wanting zealous champions in every age, to promote the means of securing so invaluable a blessing. If in America we have not lighted up the fires to consume Heretics in religion, if we have not persecuted unbelievers to promote a unity of faith, in matters which pertain to our

final salvation in a future world, I think we have all of us been witness to something very like the same spirit, in matters which are supposed to regard our political salvation in this world.[173]

The "spirit" to which he is referring here is a frequent Anti-Federalist complaint that derives from both a theoretical sensibility concerning political liberty and a more specific set of circumstances whereby Anti-Federalist writers argued that their writings were being censored by printers who were sympathetic to the new Constitution or had been intimidated into publishing only positive works. Furthermore, there are periodic allusions to Federalist attempts to discern the actual identities of Anti-Federalist writers for the purpose of constructing some sort of early American "enemies list."[174] This interesting issue aside, however, the true thrust of Anti-Federalist theory on this point is that attempts to render the world uniform or unified by fiat are not only theoretically difficult or lacking in cultural support but also, and more important, are anathema to the project of stability itself. In the words of A Farmer:

> My countrymen, preserve your jealousy—reject suspicion, it is the fiend that destroys public happiness. I know some weak, but very few wicked men in public confidence; and *learn* this most difficult and necessary lesson:—That on the preservation of parties, public liberty depends. Whenever men are unanimous on great public questions, whenever there is but one party, freedom ceases and despotism commences. The object of a free and wise people should be to balance parties, that *from the weaknesses of all you may be governed by the moderation of the combined judgements of the whole, not tyrannized ever by the blind passions of a few individuals.*[175]

Although modern predispositions and attitudes may lead us to read the discourse contained in the passages above as a liberal defense of individual rights of conscience, to do so would be a mistake. The defense of diversity here is steeped in respect for groups or communities of people who share a set of beliefs and a way of life, and is set in opposition to a *national* majoritarianism or general will that would strip away differences and forge a monolithic unity in its wake. To grasp this idea more firmly, it becomes imperative that the reader seek out those numerous passages within Anti-Federalist discourse that defend "police powers," and subsequently serve to dispel even further the quasi-libertarian mythology that has enveloped the Anti-Federalists in a good deal of the scholarly literature.

Agrippa lays out plainly, immediately following his summary of the reasons for the Revolution, that the best sort of government for securing the goals of the Revolution is a federal republic in which "each state reserves the right to itself of making and altering its laws for internal regulation, and the right of executing those laws without any external restraint. . . ."[176] He bases this argument on his observation that under a system of general (national) laws, "Unhappiness would be the uniform product . . . for no state can be happy, when the laws contradict the general habits of the people, nor can any state retain its freedom, while there is a power to make and enforce such laws."[177] Just as people *love* most that which is close to them, so the Anti-Federalists, in good republican fashion, claim that people also *know* best what is close to them. James Monroe asked:

> Can a legislature be organized upon such principles as to comprehend the territory lying between the Mississippi, the St. Lawrence, the Lakes, and the Atlantic ocean, with such variety of soil and climate, contain within it all the vital parts of a democracy, and those provisions which the wisdom of the ages has pointed out as the best security for, and be at the same time a strong, efficient, energetic government?[178]

The Anti-Federalist answer is "no." "A wise legislator should possess a precise knowledge of the situation and interests of all the territory and of the state of society, manners, and dispositions of the people within it committed to his care."[179] This intimate and precise knowledge of local needs and dispositions is difficult for a representative a thousand miles from home, let alone for a member of Congress who has never been, nor cares to go, there. Cato's point is well taken as he elaborates upon his "pebble analogy," arguing that "although we acknowledge the same national denomination, we lose the ties of acquaintance, habits, and fortunes, and thus by degrees, we lessen our attachments, till, at length, we no more than acknowledge a sameness of species."[180] Just as the Puritan Congregationalists acknowledged a shared *denomination,* but opted for local churches that were self-governed, with occasional synods to discuss points of mutual concern, so the Anti-Federalists theorize a similar kind of political construct as the basis for their political covenant.

Coinciding with the Anti-Federalists' argument from local circumstances that produces their theoretical persuasion with regard to internal police, is the Anti-Federalist argument concerning the local construction of justice itself. The rejection of overtly transcendent standards of judgment noted earlier, much like Luther's (and, more important, Calvin's) rejection of papal authority in another historical period, leaves Anti-Federalism without appeal, so to speak. The task of forming and passing judgments in relationship to the "Word" (Scripture) was left to each church (community) in its capacity as sovereign, and therein it was delegated to the elect, who for the Anti-Federalists at appointed times become the members of a jury. In this way the nihilistic reductionism of a moral relativism is avoided because there are still transcendent standards that dictate right and wrong, but those standards are interpreted through the lens of the existing local context and covenant.

It is unclear how the defense of a trial by a jury of one's peers can be construed as a liberal, much less a libertarian, construct when conceptually it seems to exude a communitarian/republican ethos. The logic that suggests a group of average citizens are best able to protect the inalienable rights of one of their fellow citizens in the typically complicated situation of a court of law—rather than, say, a professional jury or a supreme tribunal designed explicitly for that purpose—is elusive at best. The defense of local juries is steeped in an ethic of communal caring, in which they are seen as interpreting legal questions concerning individuals fraternally and with an eye toward their shared conceptions of both the good life and justice. Decisions can be rendered that take into account intangible variables that are available only to people who share not just proximity but also a kindred spirit. They enable citizens to guard their rights and liberties through the care they take of others'. Local juries are also able to distribute communal justice, which is meant to be harsh on those who violate its norms and values. Overall, this brand of justice is also designed to insulate the membership of a particular community from the erroneous moral decisions, and varying interpretations of justice, that some, like the members of a distant government, might try to impose upon them.

Thus, when the Anti-Federalists launch their frequent attacks on the Supreme Court's power to hear appeals on both *law* and *fact,* it is in the framework of defending local conceptions of justice, *and* the members of a particular community, from outsiders who do not share in the local moral and legal vocabulary. This reiteration of the principle of closeness is explored by The Federal Farmer:

> . . . the trial of facts in the neighborhood is of great importance in other respects. Nothing can be more essential than the cross examining of witnesses, and generally before the triers of the facts in question. The common people can establish facts with much more ease with oral rather than written evidence; when trials are removed to a distance from the homes of the parties and witnesses, oral evidence becomes intolerably expensive, and the parties must depend on written evidence, which to the common people is expensive and almost useless; it must frequently be taken ex parte, and very seldom leads to the discovery of truth.[181]

The Federal Farmer confirms the importance of the jury trial in Anti-Federalist theory in the following passages:

> The jury trial, especially politically considered, is by far the most important feature in the judicial department in a free country, and the right in question is far the most valuable part, and the last that ought to be yielded, of this trial. Juries are constantly and frequently drawn from the body of the people, and freemen of the country; and by holding a jury's right to return a general verdict in all cases sacred, we secure to the people at large their just and rightful control of the judicial department. . . . It is true, the freemen of a country are not always minutely skilled in the laws, but they have common sense in its purity. . . . The body of the people, principally bear the burdens of the community; they out of right ought to have a control in its important concerns, both in making and executing the laws.[182]

The trial by jury is very important in another point of view. It is essential in every free country, that common people should have a part and a share of influence, in the judicial as well as the legislative department. To hold open to them the offices of senators, judges, and offices to fill which an expensive education is required, cannot answer any valuable purposes for them; these, and most other offices of any considerable importance, will be occupied by the few.[183]

The Anti-Federalist defense of juries, then, is a defense not only of local justice or the expression of a communal ethic of care, but also of citizen participation in the formation and distribution of that justice. Jury duty becomes an avenue of republican participation to be preserved against the attempt by the Federalist court system to centralize and professionalize the political realm beyond the reach of the average person. The very idea that a court sitting in some distant place could be allowed, without the firsthand, personal experience of the local jurors, to listen to appeals of *fact* is incomprehensible to the Anti-Federalist mind. In the words of a democratic Federalist, "the word *appeal*, if I understand it right, in its proper legal signification includes the *fact* as well as the *law,* and precludes every idea of a trial by jury."[184] The same writer concludes, speaking on behalf of many of his friends, by asking rhetorically, concerning the Constitution's failure to ensure trial by jury—"what refuge shall we then have to shelter us from the iron hand of arbitrary power!"[185]

This question becomes the Anti-Federalist/republican mantra for their attack on most Constitutional provisions, as well as their justification for the repeated call for a Bill of Rights. It is not refuge from power or politics that they seek, but from *arbitrary* power, where *arbitrary* means either power in which they cannot participate or power that they cannot hold close and keep a watchful eye on. The Anti-Federalists emphasize *jealousy,* not *suspicion,* because the former springs from love—perhaps overbearing at times, but love nonetheless. The latter, however, springs from distrust and fear. Publius stresses the latter. It is this jealous love of communal liberty, of the republican independence of the citizen, of the public happiness those two elements conspire to make possible, and of the possibilities the overall combination holds that Anti-Federalist theory seeks to defend against encroachment. Within their theoretical narrative there appear various lines of attack on the power and reach of the new government and its institutions, but in the end these partially disparate lines of argument all are representative of the same general fear: the loss of effective republican citizenship through the progressive diminution of the liberties and activities through which such citizenship is ultimately realized. Here the short list of protected rights would include the right of communal self-determination associated with the sovereignty of the state governments from above, the property rights necessary to preserve republican independence, and the political and social rights that allow for meaningful action on the part of the citizen, leading to the possibility of public happiness and the subsequent personal and communal transformation spoken of earlier.

Among the most frequently cited fears in Anti-Federalist discourse is the power of the new national government to levy internal taxes on the people and property of the various states. It was well known that the power to tax and spend for the general welfare was among the defining marks of a sovereign government. It was also one of the ways in which the members of particular regimes sapped the resources necessary for effective citizenship. The extent of this fear is captured at length by Brutus, who writes what, in the context of taxation, could really be a metaphor for the new national government embodied in the Constitution as a whole:

> This power, exercised without limitation, will introduce itself into every corner of the city, and country—It will wait upon the ladies at their toilet, and will not leave them in any of their domestic concerns; it will accompany them to the ball, the play, and the assembly; it will go with them when they visit, and will, on all occasions, sit beside them in their carriages, nor will it desert them even at church; it will enter the house of every gentleman, watch over his cellar . . . it will take cognizance of the professional man in his office, or his study; it will watch the merchant in the counting-house, or in his store, it will follow the mechanic to his shop, and in his work, and will haunt him in his family . . . it will be a constant companion of the industrious farmer in all his labour . . . it will light upon the head of every person in the United States. To all these different classes of people, and in all these circumstances, in which it will attend them, the language in which it will address them, will be GIVE! GIVE![186]

When taken in light of other provisions, like the Necessary and Proper Clause and the Supremacy Clause, it becomes clear to the Anti-Federalists that the new government's reach will be only a question of its grasp and its will. While this does not necessarily mean that the power will be used tyrannically, it does imply a threat. It is important to remember that according to the theory of the Revolution, "free people were not those who were merely spared actual oppression, but those who have a constitutional check upon the power to oppress."[187] The seemingly unlimited potential for congressional invasion into the details of one's life by men George Mason described as "little concern'd and unacquainted with their effects and consequences,"[188] gives Cato Uticensis cause to claim:

> Consider that if you pass the Federal Constitution in toto, you subject yourselves to see the doors of your houses, the impenetrable castles of freemen, fly open before the magic wand of an exciseman, and, that, if you should resent and punish the insolence of office, the daring brutality of the publican, perhaps offered to the wife of thy bosom, you will be dragged for trial before a distant tribunal, and there, perhaps, condemned without enjoying the benefit of a jury from your vicinage, your inalienable right as a freeman.[189]

While these railings against taxation may take on libertarian overtones in 1993, they are actually steeped in the republican ideology of independent citizenry in 1787. To possess property was to be free from the bounds of necessity, or to be independent in the fullest possible sense of the term (not dependent upon anyone or anything). This independence had been the prerequisite for civic virtue since the time of Aristotle's *Politics*. To be overly taxed was to lose one's independence, and thus one's standing as a capable republican citizen.

Interwoven with the power to tax, for the Anti-Federalists, was the increase in the size as well as the scope of the national government through the creation of an ever-increasing number of offices and administrators. Aside from the obvious arguments concerning the ever-increasing costs via taxation that cannot help but accompany the rise of a national bureaucracy, the Anti-Federalist argument against the increase in administrative positions carries with it a deep-seated ideological objection to the brand of politics such an increase brings with it. In chapter 2 I referred to the notion of a "politics of technique," which replaced the sort of public political activity historically associated with active republican citizenship and public happiness with the idea of politics by experts, or politics by administration. The effect of such a transformation was more or less to send the citizens back to private life. In their own way the Anti-Federalists are confronted with this same phenomenon, whose implications are described polemically by Centinel, who writes of "the institution of lucrative, needless offices to provide for the swarms of gaping, almost famished expectants, who have been campaigning it for ten years without success against our inestimable state constitution, as a reward for their preserving toils, but particularly for their zeal on the present occasion, and also as a phalanx to tyranny."[190] Put less dramatically by Alfred, the same issue becomes a simple set of questions that bear directly on the future of republicanism and public happiness in American political life:

> Will the new system, which really comprehends an imperium in imperis, be administered at a less expense than, we now experience? Can we create new *offices* without an accumulation of expenses? Shall we enjoy a greater degree of political freedom and happiness under the proposed plan? If *these* and other advantages are not quite evident, we ought to be extremely cautious, how we change our condition. Systems may be very specious in theory; but fail us in practice. Government is a science which consists more in experience than in notional knowledge.[191]

The upshot of this line of criticism is the rejection of expert knowledge as controlling in political life. Instead, Anti-Federalist theory substitutes a nonpejorative notion of *common sense*. A Friend of the Republic claims that "honest affection for the general good and common qualifications are sufficient— Administration has always been best managed, and the public liberty best secured, when plain honesty and common sense alone governed public affairs."[192] Furthermore, the idea, implicit in the *Federalist,* that somehow good administration can replace the need for civic virtue is attacked by the Anti-Federalist writer from Dutchess County, who argues that even the most tyrannical government be, and often is, administered quite well![193]

The growth of boundaryless power, if not unlimited power, coupled with the growing concerns that political activity was soon to be restricted to the domain of so-called experts or administrators, generated a profound sense of loss among Anti-Federalists. Their fears of tyranny and disenfranchisement were heightened by the grant of power that allowed Congress to bring a standing army into existence. Whereas the other aspects of the Constitution could be argued about in terms of their meaning and potential for harm, Anti-Federalist theory and its republican counterpart had no qualms about this provision. Standing armies in times of peace had forever been the bane of republics, and their very existence was taken as a sign of collapse and corruption. A Farmer describes the institution as being "like the locusts and caterpillars of Egypt; they bear down all before them—and many times, by designing men, have been used as an engine to destroy the liberties of the people."[194] In other places the Anti-Federalists warn not so much against the potential for armed tyranny as they do about what would later be called the military industrial complex (here writ small), the army being described as eating out the subsistence of the nation with a hunger that grows ever more insatiable. In other places the members of the army are derided as dregs of society, what Marx would call the lumpenproletariat, who were propertyless and without virtue, and who would be quite enamored of the power, prestige, and pay of military duty as opposed to some more demanding and productive industry.

All of these ideas taken together show a group of people who were desperately afraid of losing their birthrights, of losing control over the creation they had helped to make, and of going back. "Progress" was upon them, in need of nurturing and help, but not wholesale change. Thus the Anti-Federalists did not fail to recognize the potential inherent in America as empire; they knew what price that greatness would elicit and deemed it too high. Somerset Maugham once said, through a Buddhist monk that he created, "that the path to salvation was as narrow and sharp as the razor's edge." It was not a thought that John Calvin would have disputed. The question the Anti-Federalists worried about was not how we organize our polity for order and greatness but how we organize our polity for public happiness and political salvation. Agrippa's claims that "freedom is necessary for industry" and that "in absolute governments, the people, be the climate what it may be, are in general lazy, cowardly, turbulent, and vicious to an extreme"[195] are but his way of saying that without the sense of attachment and empowerment that comes with public participation, there can be no virtue, and without virtue there can be no happiness.

This is the theoretical thread that ties Anti-Federalist thought together. It is the notion that the Constitution as a centralizing, ultimately disempowering, document will leave them bereft of their power to save themselves, that it will ultimately, in the words of Hannah Arendt, "banish the citizens from the public realm into the privacy of their households, and demand of them that they mind their own private business."[196] This would certainly be a torturous existence for a people who believed their individual chance for redemption was tied intimately to their shared public life. Self-government for the Anti-Federalists was not just a mechanistic device to ensure the safety of their fortunes, it was an opportunity to transform themselves and expand their circle of concerns while encouraging others to do the same. Political participation for the Anti-Federalists became an end to be pursued as well as a means. The Federal Farmer wrote, in the context of defending frequent rotation in office, that

> . . . on the one hand, by this rotation, we may sometimes exclude good men from being elected. On the other hand, we guard against those pernicious connections, which usually grow up among men left to continue long periods in office, we increase the number of those who make laws and return to their constituents; and thereby spread information, and preserve a spirit of activity and investigation among the people.[197]

And Melancton Smith explained:

> If the office is to be perpetually confined to a few, other men of equal talents and virtue, but not possessed of so extensive an influence, may be discouraged from aspiring to it. The more perfectly we are versed in political science, the more firmly will the happy principles of republicanism be supported. The true policy of constitutions will be to increase the information of the country, and disseminate the knowledge of government as universally as possible. If this be done, we shall have, in any dangerous emergency, a numerous body of enlightened citizens, ready for the call of their country.[198]

Each of the traditional Anti-Federalist fears listed above can be reduced to a fear of dependency or tenantry, and the potential loss of republican citizenship and philosophy. Free speech, freedom of the press, the right to trial by jury, and rotation in office are all ultimately freedoms that demand public participation from those who possess them. If you had no desire to participate in political life, or if you thought it was unimportant or time-consuming, why would you place yourself in the position of holding and participating in yearly elections or having to sit on juries? Anti-Federalists were unwilling to allow "some heaven-born PHAETONS amongst [them], who like the son of Apollo, think themselves entitled to guide the chariot of the sun"[199] to rule them. Standing armies, an expanded bureaucracy, and fears of taxation are emblematic of a people who are concerned that they may end up detached from the most important decisions of their lives and the lives of those they hold dear. The Anti-Federalists knew, just as the Puritans knew, that mutual watchfulness requires physical as well as ideological closeness. They sought to preserve public happiness, and the local communities and state sovereignty that made it possible. They were not men of little faith ultimately, but men with different values, which in turn required a different political theory to sustain them. In the conclusion I will try to explain why their loss ultimately may have been our loss as well.

Conclusion
Fruitful Heresy

Here too the context seems to contaminate the form, only the misery here is the misery of happiness . . . an unhappiness that doesn't know its name, that has no way of telling itself apart from genuine satisfaction and fulfillment since it has presumably never encountered this last.

—Fredric Jameson

Thomas Jefferson as a postmodern protagonist might have looked around in the early months of 1801 and thought about the desirability of repeating American history a few times, doing certain things differently each time, comparing the results, and then choosing the best possible course of events. He might have thought along the same lines as Milan Kundera's Tomas, whose realization that such experimentation, strictly speaking, was impossible, led him to the conclusion that "history is as light as individual human life, unbearably light." But Jefferson was no such character; he was first and foremost a political man, with political tasks to carry out in a context that he may or may not have found desirable. To call the election of his administration and platform, as powerful as the event was, a "revolution" is a mistake. The genie was already out of the bottle, and America would never be the same. Claude Bowers wrote at the conclusion of his great work on Jefferson and Hamilton, and their historic struggle that "The eighteenth century witnessed their Plutarchian battles; the twentieth century uncovers at the graves at Monticello and in Trinity Churchyard—but the spirits of Jefferson and Hamilton still stalk the ways of men—still fighting."[1]

He was right. But their struggle, unlike that between Federalists and Anti-Federalists a few years earlier, was not Promethean in its import, because in the end it took place within a shared, although viciously contested, nationalist framework. Whatever Jefferson may have been in 1776, by 1801 he was president of the national government and acted accordingly. In 1781 he wrote in a good Anti-Federalist idiom:

Those who labor in the earth are the chosen people of God, if ever he had a chosen people, whose breasts he has made his peculiar deposit of virtue. It is the focus in which he keeps alive that sacred fire, which otherwise might escape from the face of the earth. Corruption of morals in the mass of cultivators is a phenomenon of which no age or nation has furnished an example. It is the mark set on those, who not looking up to heaven, to their own soil and industry, as does the husbandman, for their subsistence, depend for it on the casualties and caprice of customers. Dependence begets subservience and venality, suffocates the germ of virtue, and prepares fit tools for the designs of ambition.[2]

A few years later, in a similar mode, he claimed that his essential principles of government included the following:

Equal and exact justice to all men, of whatever state or persuasion, religious or political; peace, commerce, and honest friendship, with all nations—entangling alliances with none; the support of state governments in all their rights, as the most competent administrations for our domestic concerns and the surest bulwarks against anti-republican tendencies . . . .[3]

And, in defense of the Louisiana Purchase, he claimed in a more Madisonian dialect, "But who can limit the extent to which federative principles may operate effectively? The larger our association, the less it will be shaken by local passions."[4]

Jefferson's context had changed; he was a strong champion of democracy, agrarianism, civic virtue, republican education, and so on, but in the end he was also a realist, a practical political man, more so than a political theorist.[5] The world that Jefferson defended in his early work (1781), the world that Daniel Shays and his men were fighting to preserve in 1786,[6] and the world for which the Anti-Federalists attempted to provide a theoretical rationale—a world of industrious, independent, republican citizens who worked their land, traded some goods, and participated in the public life of their communities through the church and the town hall—had by the end of the eighteenth century given way to another. It was in the end Hamilton's vision that in large measure carried the day. As someone once said in Washington, Hamilton has no memorial, whereas Jefferson has many (unless you count the city itself). In other words, Jefferson may be the one we remember with fondness, and he may be the one we esteem, but it is Hamilton to whom our actions pay homage.

While the depiction of Jefferson and his followers as engaged republicans fighting a rearguard action against entrenched Federalist politicians and political theory is very interesting, and historically important, it is also tangential to the point.[7] Just as the nationalists had managed to set the agenda and structure the choice opportunities during the Constitutional Convention by introducing the Virginia Plan as their working model, so the ratification of the Constitution and Jefferson's participation in national politics implied a set of conceptual, linguistic boundaries that limited the theoretical and the practical possibilities of Jeffersonian politics. Jefferson was forced to stake out a position within the nationalist paradigm rather than in *opposition* to it, as his Anti-Federalist predecessors and fellow travelers had done. His political agenda, no matter how radical or democratic in comparison with Hamilton's, could never be truly revolutionary. The best Jeffersonian government could probably yield, within the paradigm out of which it was compelled to operate, was an early version, powerful though it was, of democratic progressivism. The elitist politics associated with Hamiltonian/Federalist political thought fell before the high and egalitarian Jeffersonian tide, but a fertile, siltlike residue of Hamiltonian thought remained. Jefferson may have been able to weave back together the cultural fabric of the Revolution in his reestablishment of the idea of Americans as "born equal," but Hamilton's ghost would forever tell those same Americans that there was no reason for them to remain that way.

In Hamilton's *Report on Manufactures* (1791), in which he defended the rise of commercial manufacturing in America against charges leveled at it by republicans who saw in it the seeds of European luxury, class distinctions, and therefore political corruption, American readers, perhaps without noticing it, are treated to an exemplary piece of modern political discourse. Rather than looking at the content of the essay, the reader should notice the form it takes, and its approach to questions of public policy and political life. Glancing at Jefferson's assertion that "Those who labor in the earth are the chosen people of God," the reader should see an absolutism, a principled position that resists the sense of moral and political compromise associated with liberalism's implicit assumption that all life-style choices deserve the same basic protections if not respect. I raise the question here not to enter into that volatile debate but, rather, to illustrate the nature of the emergent ideological shift that was taking place, and that is represented in Hamilton's essay, which near its close argues in the following way:

> In the course of the preceding illustrations, the products of equal quantities of the labor of the farmer and the artificer have been treated as if equal to each other. But this is not to be understood as intending to assert any such precise equality. It is merely a manner of expression, adopted for the sake of simplicity and perspicuity. *Whether the value of the produce of the labor of the farmer be somewhat more or less than that of the artificer, is not material to the main scope of the argument, which hitherto, has only aimed at showing that the one, as well as the other, occasions a positive argumentation of the total produce and revenue of the society* [emphasis mine].[8]

Under Jefferson's formulation, "those who labor[ed] in the earth" did so *not* because it added to the "total produce and revenue of the society" but because it was the way in which the laborer "keeps alive that sacred fire." In Hamilton's equation the spiritual or moral term has dropped out, leaving only questions of efficiency and production. It was not that Jefferson had failed to realize the potential economic gains associated with manufactures, because those were evident to all who had even a passing familiarity with European civilization. But Jefferson also realized the costs of such an economy, both to the moral fabric of the citizenry and to the political life of the nation. He understood the costs because he had seen them firsthand in his travels abroad on behalf of the early government, and he wrote about them in letters of 1785:

> Let us view the disadvantages to sending a youth to Europe. To enumerate them all, would require a volume. I will select a few. If he goes to England, he learns drinking, horse racing, and boxing. These are the peculiarities of English education. The following circumstances are common to education in that, and the other countries of Europe. He acquires a fondness for European luxury and dissipation, and a contempt for the simplicity of his own country; he is fascinated with the privileges of the European aristocrats, and sees, with abhorrence, the lovely equality which the poor enjoy with the rich in his own country.[9]

> . . . the solitude of my walk led me into a train of reflections on that unequal division of property which occasions the numberless instances of wretchedness which I had observed in this country and is to be observed all over Europe.[10]

Those observations, the first set of which goes on for two pages, listing every decadence known at the time, can be coupled with his earlier assertion in the *Notes:*

> The mobs of great cities add just so much to the support of pure government, as sores do to the strength of the human body. It is the manners and spirit of a people which preserve a republic in vigor. A degeneracy in these is a canker which soon eats to the heart of its laws and constitution.[11]

Together, they provide the reader with a enlightening view of early Jeffersonian convictions and beliefs, not to mention a brief insight into Jeffersonian political philosophy. Where Hamilton was worried about the nation "getting ahead," Jefferson was worried about maintaining what it had.

Jefferson may have later won the election, but by then the American paradox was already in place. The tendency to view Hamilton and Jefferson as mutually exclusive competitors for the American soul, where the former prods and entices us into covetous behavior by promising untold riches and power if we just *forget,* and the latter holds out the promise of redemption and political salvation if we only *remember,* is ultimately mistaken. It is mistaken, I believe, for at least two reasons. First, the battles of the soul are fought within it; the best the political world can do is to offer up a social and ideological context that encourages certain kinds of behavior while frowning on others, thus making virtue easier and corruption more difficult to choose. Second, Jefferson was a paradoxical man who, while asserting the fundamental superiority of the farmer in his fields, also embraced Francis Bacon as one of "the three greatest men that have ever lived."[12] It is difficult to reconcile the Jefferson of the often pastoral or idyllic *Notes* and the Jefferson who is singing the praises of a scientist whose core ambition was the Great Insaturation, with its project of restoring man to a position of mastery over the natural world. Leaving this aside, however, and returning to the question of the soul, my point is that Americans are in many respects duplicitous beings: on the one hand we cherish the idea of equality and community, but on the other we yearn for individual distinction and power. Both, perhaps unfortunately, are part of the American psyche. The former values were nurtured and protected by pre-Constitution constitutional arrangements, and the latter values, if not encouraged by the Constitution and its nationalism, were at the very least given by them the space they needed in order to grow. That space was provided by the erosion of former mediating structures like the township, the municipalities, and the states, of which Alexis de Tocqueville spoke so glowingly in his work.[13]

Thus, try as he might to reestablish those structures and empower citizens once again, in the end Jefferson could only control, contain, and direct "the monster";[14] but he could not, and probably did not want to, "slay" it. And so, to steal a phrase from Michael Oakeshott as a metaphor for Jeffersonianism, "a plan to resist planning, may be better than its opposite, but it belongs to the same style of politics." Jefferson would not have the fact that he had been president of the United States inscribed on his tombstone, but neither would he have wished, as the Anti-Federalist Rawlins Lowndes did, to have "no other epitaph than to have inscribed on his tomb, here lies the man that opposed the constitution, because it was ruinous to the liberty of America."[15]

AMERICAN KITSCH

In chapter 5 I borrowed an argument from Sheldon Wolin that asserted, in effect, that by voiding the state constitutions, the national Constitution had broken the bonds of civil society and returned Americans to the status of individuals in a state of nature. This idea was consistent with the Federalist project of remaking America as a national or commercial republic, as depicted in the writings of Publius. The end result of Publius's new *national* theorization of republicanism was the dramatic reduction in state and local political sovereignty, as well as the corresponding diffusion of the powers and responsibilities of citizenship as those duties and most of the power devolved on the members of the new national regime. As a result of losing both the local context in which their citizenship and participation made sense, and the corresponding political power itself, most Americans were forced to devote their time and interests to the pursuit of private rather than public goods. People were prod-ded into the privacy of their homes slowly but surely. This precipitated the rise of American individualism and its ideological counterpart liberalism, which, according to Louis Hartz and others, eventually came to dominate American political discourse and American political life. Shorn of their public role in a shared communal life, where the guiding trope had been *fraternity*, the vast majority of Americans were now situated in private roles, seeking to maximize their personal happiness and interests, where the guiding trope eventually be-came *competition*.

In a political world where individuals vie with one another for scarce re-sources that serve as both the means to individual self-fulfillment and symbols of individual success, all actions that either are benevolent or aim at the com-mon good are suspected as a pretext for a hidden personal agenda or mocked as foolish. Harkening back to Kundera's discussion of *totalitarian kitsch,* where he claimed that by "totalitarian, what I mean is that everything that infringes on kitsch must be banished for life," we can see how post-Constitution politi-cal life could be said—however ironically, given Kundera's object of criti-cism—to generate its own brand of *totalitarian kitsch.* Here, however, it would not be *every display of individualism* that would be banished but every display of something other than individualism.

The constitutional vortex drew unto the national government the power and responsibility for American public life, leaving only private life in its wake. That private life of competition and mutual suspicion in turn transformed the institutional role of government in America from arbiter of the common good and forum for public happiness to facilitator of private interests and protector of individual rights. Thereafter, virtually all major political struggles would be about access to the system and equal protection for one's interests. In other words, political life in America came to consist in clearing away the obstacles to individualism, whereas before it had consisted in clearing away the obstacles to community. The first such struggle, as noted above, took place between the Jeffersonians and the Federalists, not as a struggle between republicans and liberals but as a struggle between egalitarians and elitists. Hamiltonian elitism was vanquished, but it was done in the spirit, if not the name, of Federalist individualism. Subsequently Jeffersonian democratic reforms, wealth redistri-bution plans, and attempts to secure land for as many people as wanted it, while certainly consistent with republican ideology, are probably better seen as hedges against the kind of rabid inequality that would make any sort of rough equality of opportunity impossible. The yeoman farmer has equal potential as a liberal symbol or as a republican one. Jefferson knew that, given the destruc-tion of more traditional avenues to personal fulfillment (participation in public life), some form of equality of opportunity was essential to maintain political equilibrium and avoid the sordid and degenerated politics of Europe.

The politicians, movements, and ideas that followed in the Jeffersonian tradition came to engage in this strategy again and again, and with greater and greater degrees of political self-consciousness. Jeffersonian as well as Anti-Federalist discourse came to be used, often with good intentions, by various politicians and movements in American politics from the oxymoronic perspective of a *national* community, *not* in order to regain the sense of community and local empowerment but to further what had quickly become the only acceptable agenda: making the country safe for individualism. Minimally, any list of such movements would have to include Lincoln's abolitionism and support for free labor, Radical Republicanism, late-nineteenth- and early-twentieth-century populism, Progressivism, trade unionism, democratic socialism, the women's suffrage movement, the New Freedom, the New Nationalism, the New Deal, the Fair Deal, the New Frontier, and the Great Society.

While I realize that I am painting with a rather broad brush here, it seems to me that, given the time and space, a sound case could be made that none of these sometimes massive, and even radical, reorientations of American politics ever fundamentally challenged American individualism in the name of community. Instead, each of them fought, sometimes valiantly, in different ways to preserve or enhance American liberalism, whether through the passage of the Fourteenth Amendment, busting the trusts, shutting down the factories with strikes, regulating the workplace, instituting the welfare state, or ending poverty in America. All of these are worthwhile projects when viewed in historical isolation, because each attempted to come to grips with serious, and typically deadly, problems in the lives of average or less-than-average Americans within what had to seem like the only possible political framework. But when these programs are taken together, the picture is perhaps not as worthwhile, because what they indicate collectively is the sickly constitution of the model, which is always in need of large-scale political doctoring, and the corresponding increase in the duties and responsibilities of the national government to provide the care. Thus the national government draws still more power unto itself and increases the centralization of its operations even more. Correspondingly, it depends more than ever on administration by experts. This phenomenon pushes Americans deeper into the solitude of their private lives and affairs, rendering them more detached from any notion of a shared world, and less aware of any personal responsibilities they might have for its survival.

So it is that in 1956, after a good many of the movements and programs mentioned above had had an opportunity to run their course, and had in their own ways buttressed the equality of opportunity and the American individualism that it served, C. Wright Mills could write:

> The powers of ordinary men are circumscribed by the everyday worlds in which they live, yet even in these rounds of job, family, and neighborhood they often seem

driven by forces they can neither understand nor govern. . . . The very framework of modern society confines them to projects not their own, but from every side, such changes now press upon the men and women of mass society, who accordingly feel that they are without purpose in an epoch where they are without power. But not all men are in this sense ordinary.[16]

The question we must ask is why, with the massive efforts and whole-scale national programs meant to include people and expand their power, we ended up in 1956 with "men and women of mass society, who accordingly feel that they are without purpose in an epoch where they are without power"? Why would another writer of the same period, although ultimately of a different political persuasion, claim that "a specter is haunting the modern mind, the specter of insecurity?"[17] It is in the answer to these questions that I believe we can find the relevance of Anti-Federalism for modern American political thought.

THE WEIGHT OF RAGGED DICK

Dick left the counting-room, hardly knowing whether he stood on his head or his heels, so overjoyed was he at the sudden change in his fortunes. Ten dollars a week to him was a fortune, and three times as much as he had expected to obtain at first. Indeed he would have been glad, only the day before, to get a place at three dollars a week. He reflected that with the stock of clothes he had now on hand, he could save up at least half of it, and even then live better than he had been accustomed to do; so that his little fund in the savings bank, instead of being diminished, would be steadily increasing. Then he was to be advanced if he deserved it. It was indeed a bright prospect for a boy who, only a year before, could neither read, nor write, and depended for a night's lodging upon the chance hospitality of an alley-way or old wagon. Dick's great ambition to "grow up 'spectable" seemed likely to be accomplished after all.[18]

As the characters of another hundred Alger novels had done, Ragged Dick had overcome poverty and despair to rise to the American middle class, and he had been able to do so because "in this free country poverty is no bar to a man's advancement." As powerful as that last idea is for American political culture, and as easy a target as it can sometimes be for those who would like to challenge the substantive reality of its claim, it is not the part of "Algerism" on which I would like to focus for the purposes of this volume. This is why I have quoted at length the section above rather than some other passage designed to reify the ideal of equality of opportunity in America. What I would like the reader to notice in the passage above are the goals that Alger has helped to cement at the apex of American society. Respectability was a function of one's job, income, savings, and wardrobe; and one's future happiness was linked only to advancement, and the corresponding addition to those items that it implied. This is evidenced by Dick's thoughts: "Henceforth he meant to press onward, and rise as high as possible"; he could "afford to leave Mott street now . . . and live in a nicer corner of the city." His friend Fosdick tells him that "you must drop that name [Ragged Dick] and think of yourself now as Richard Hunter, Esq., . . . a young man on his way to fame and fortune";[19] the reader is invited to follow in Dick's footsteps. The government, on the other hand, is invited to make sure that stories like Dick's remain possible.

While most readers should have no particular quarrels with the goals of a decent job, a nice place to live, some money in the bank, and the opportunity for advancement, they should notice what is missing from that construction of "respectability": a public persona, or the duties of citizenship. One of Ragged Dick's mentors, Mr. Whitney, sums up his (and, one must assume, the public's) expectations of Dick: "I hope, my lad, you will prosper and rise in the world." But are these enough to sustain us as full human beings? The answer, I am afraid, is "no." And this is also the answer implicit in Anti-Federalist discourse. Hannah Arendt is right, I believe, when she claims:

> To live an entirely private life means above all to be deprived of things essential to a truly human life: to be deprived of the reality that comes from being seen and heard by others, to be deprived of an "objective" relationship with them that comes from being related to or separated from them through the intermediary of a common world of things, to be deprived of the possibility of achieving something more per-manent than life itself. The privation of privacy lies in the absence of others; as far as they are concerned, private man does not appear, and therefore it is as though he did not exist. Whatever he does remains without significance and consequence to others, and what matters to him is without interest to other people.[20]

In other words, we are reduced to part of the mass—insignificant, inter-changeable, and for the most part unmemorable. Linda Loman cries to her sons and to the audience at the conclusion of Arthur Miller's classic American tragedy, *Death of a Salesman,* regarding her husband, Willy, "Attention must finally be paid to such a man!" Despite the pity and perhaps even empathy we might have for Willy Loman, we should ask her "why?" What was his life devoted to, that we care for him and his fate? When we ask What service did he perform? What deeds did he do? What was his quest? the answers to these questions are all the same: "none." There is no outstanding reason to pay attention to Willy Loman, or any of the Willy Lomans of the world, of whom there are no doubt thousands to every Ragged Dick. But that does not matter, for in the end we have no reason to pay attention to Dick either: he, like Willy, "remains without significance and consequence to others, and what matters to him is without interest to other people." Both of their lives will pass in relative obscurity with regard to those around them.

This commentary, however, should not be taken to mean that only through

Odysseus-like acts can a person earn recognition and remembrance. George Bailey, in the film *It's a Wonderful Life,* earned such remembrance and respect without leaving his home town, holding public office, or doing anything of singular greatness. But he lived his life among others, and he contributed to the public world in a committed and meaningful way. In return he was made a better person, and so were those around him. But is a "wonderful life" still possible in a world steeped in the social religion of individualism and shrouded as a result in a "specter of insecurity"? If not, what is to be done?

LIGHTNESS AND WEIGHT

There are limits to what can be accomplished politically and socially within the framework of individualism, a fact that was perhaps Hartz's most important contribution to our understanding of American political thought. Some of those limits are good and necessary insofar as America has no Gulag. Some of them, however, are stifling and stagnating. One writer has suggested that American liberals sometimes have a conceptual difficulty as a result of their individualist myopia in distinguishing between a convent and a concentration camp.[21] What this preoccupation—one might even say neurosis—has meant for American politics since the ratification debates has been that the solutions to our problems have not only had to be respectful of liberal individualism and equality of opportunity but typically also have had to promise to foster more of the same. The cure for what ails America has usually been *more* individualism, *more* opportunity, *more* freedom. But while Americans were progressively freed from want, from fear, from any real restraints on their life choices, they were also freed from their political and communal moorings. They were set adrift, not free from loneliness or anomie. Even in the 1960s, when the image of the "organization man" came under fire and the pathos of Willy Loman was challenged, the individualism remained. The cure for the white-collar or one-dimensional world, for some in the youth movement, was experimentation with new forms of what Robert Bellah and associates call "expressive individualism." But that, too, eventually proved empty and light, not to mention conformist in its own way. Friedrich Neitzsche may have been more fun at a party than John Locke, but both ultimately sent people home alone. Yet there were other voices.

In 1962, before the generation of students, intellectuals, and political activists were in the throes of the "will to power," a group of radicals called Students for a Democratic Society (SDS) met in Michigan and issued a document titled the *Port Huron Statement.* Though typically thought of as the forerunner of the New Left, there is a good argument to be made (though only suggested here) that this particular document is in fact better thought of in relationship to the early modern civil rights movement and groups like CORE, SNCC, and the SCLC, not to mention the sociological and political movements associated with David Riesman, Louis Hartz, and Robert Nisbet. Whatever its place in terms of the political zeitgeist of the twentieth century's middle age, the *Port Huron Statement,* perhaps unconsciously, speaks to Americans in a partly borrowed political idiom that is quite old and, according to some, perhaps even a dead language—Anti-Federalism.

Framing the argument in terms of the Declaration of Independence, they return to its roots and argue against a purely liberal interpretation: "This kind of Independence does not mean egoistic individualism—the object is not to have one's way so much as it is to have a way that is one's own."[22] The *Statement* describes the situation at hand: "Loneliness, estrangement, isolation describe the vast distance between man and man today. These dominant tendencies cannot be overcome by better personnel management, nor by improved gadgets."[23] And their goals are stated thus:

> As a *social system* we seek the establishment of a democracy of individual participation, governed by two central aims: that the individual share in those social decisions determining the quality and direction of his life; that society be organized to encourage independence in men and provide the media for their common participation.[24]

Rather than arguing for yet more individualism, SDS was arguing for more responsibility, for more activity, and for decentralization. Rather than embracing exclusively the more traditional left-wing credo that thought redistribution of wealth and resources would somehow create a more sustaining and meaningful political order for human beings, they were arguing for an order in which the value of participation in public life was not only utilitarian but also meaningful in itself. They would, as they said, "look outwards to the less exotic but more lasting struggles for justice."[25] Although much less conservative and religious than their Anti-Federalist and Puritan ancestors, these students shared a general political theory with them of decentralization, political participation, and rejection of the politics of administration. Although their project fell victim to the ideological rips and tears of the decade, not to mention the degeneration into violence and extra-American forms of political discourse, they did represent, at least for a time, a viable alternative to both the establishment and the less productive political alternatives that followed it.

The Anti-Federalist voice in American political discourse that in the 1960s was so radical that J. Edgar Hoover and the FBI haunted the members of SDS until Hoover's death, had refused to offer the traditional progressive response of *more* individualism in the face of a despondent American polity. In fact, it offered just the opposite, as did the Anti-Federalists themselves. The cure for the specter of insecurity was not more individual *liberation* or freedom from community, but more *liberation* for community. Like alcoholics who as time goes by need more and more alcohol to sustain the same level of intoxication, so has individualism in America consumed more of its own political elixir, only to find that it cannot solve all of the problems that drove it to drink in the first place. This does not mean that individualism itself is not good—it is—but it is meaningful only within an appropriate context of a shared life. Although we cannot "go home again," even if we want to, Anti-Federalist discourse offers Americans a theoretical language with which to start their own political conversations in the 1990s, as it did in the 1960s. It is a language that is often deeply submerged within our political consciousness, but one that offers a good deal of potential for finding what we seem to be missing. Can it be done?

In his provocative and richly argued book *Human Scale,* Kirkpatrick Sale contends that "size matters," as he introduces his readers to the "beanstalk principle."[26] His thesis is that there is an appropriate size for everything, from bedrooms, to schools, to communities, and that violations of the "beanstalk principle" lead to paralysis, breakdown, and even failure. If American political society has outgrown its ability to allow people to live without the "specter of insecurity" and the suspicion, loneliness, and spiritual longing that accompany it, if community empowerment, decentralization, and citizen participation in public life—which are not part of the present order—cannot be made reality, perhaps we are lost. But the question remains—can we do it? Since we have the language within us, since it is not foreign to this land, the answer is that we have a better chance of doing it than we do of adopting some more distant political model. But can we do it?

When confronted with a similar query, Sale said that he was reminded of the man who, when asked for directions on how to get to the post office, thought a bit and replied, "Well I wouldn't start from here."[27] The Federalists were a hardy breed, and those who have followed in their wake are even stronger. The resistance in America to anything that challenges the liberal model is fierce. If it were not for the fact that something else creeps through now and again in our "second languages," I would not recommend that we try—but it does, and so I do. The road has perhaps diverged, or will soon; it is a trail down which we rode once, a long time ago, and on which we have traveled occasionally since then. It is less traveled than the one we are on—but perhaps that is an advantage. Sometimes "being" is less light at one time than it is at others.

Notes

INTRODUCTION

1. Bernard Bailyn, *The Ideological Origins of the American Revolution* (Cambridge, Mass.: Harvard University Press, 1967); Gordon Wood, *The Creation of the American Republic, 1776–1787* (Chapel Hill: University of North Carolina Press, 1969); J. G. A. Pocock, *The Machiavellian Moment* (Princeton: Princeton University Press, 1975).

2. For example, see John Patrick Diggins, "Comrades and Citizens: New Mythologies in American Historiography," *American Historical Review* 90 (June 1985): 614–649; and J. G. A. Pocock, "Between Gog and Magog: The Republican Thesis and the *Ideologia Americana*," *Journal of the History of Ideas* 48, no. 2 (1987): 325–346.

3. Don Herzog, "Some Questions for Republicans," *Political Theory* 14, no. 3 (1986): 475.

4. Ibid., p. 473.

5. Ibid., p. 477.

6. Ibid., p. 481.

7. Ibid., p. 484.

8. Ibid., p. 487.

9. Frank Bryan and John McClaughry, *The Vermont Papers: Recreating Democracy on a Human Scale* (Post Mills, Vt.: Chelsea Green, 1989).

10. See Students for a Democratic Society, *The Port Huron Statement* (Port Huron, Mich.: SDS, 1962).

11. See Twelve Southerners, *I'll Take My Stand* (Baton Rouge: Louisiana State University Press, [1930] 1990).

12. Herzog, "Some Questions for Republicans," p. 490.

13. Cass Sunstein, "Beyond the Republican Revival," *Yale Law Journal* 97 (1988): 1539–1590; Morton J. Horwitz, "Republicanism and Liberalism in American Constitutional Thought," *William and Mary Law Review* 29 (1987): 57–74, and "History and Theory," *Yale Law Journal* 96 (1987): 1825–1835; Frank Michelman, "Law's Republic," *Yale Law Journal* 97 (1988): 1493–1537, and "The Supreme Court 1985 Term Forward: Traces of Self-Government," *Harvard Law Review* 100, no. 4 (1986): 4–77; Suzanna Sherry, "Civic Virtue and the Feminine Voice in Constitutional Adjudication," *Virginia Law Review* 72 (1986): 543–616.

14. Sunstein, "Beyond the Republican Revival," p. 1541.

15. Michelman, "Law's Republic," p. 1506.

16. Ibid., p. 1526.

17. Michelman, "The Supreme Court 1985 Term," pp. 24–36.

18. Ibid., p. 16.

19. Sherry, "Civic Virtue and the Feminine Voice in Constitutional Adjudication," p. 580.

20. Carol Gilligan, *In a Different Voice* (Cambridge, Mass.: Harvard University Press, 1982).

21. Sherry, p. 580.

22. Ibid., p. 584.

23. Ibid., p. 593.

24. Cecelia M. Kenyon, "Men of Little Faith: The Anti-Federalists on the Nature of Representative Government," *William and Mary Quarterly,* 3rd ser., 12 (January 1955), pp. 3–43.

25. Jackson Turner Main, *The Antifederalists* (New York: W. W. Norton, 1974).

26. Louis Hartz, *The Liberal Tradition in America* (New York: Harcourt Brace Jovanovich, [1954] 1983).

27. Herbert Storing, *What the Anti-Federalists Were for* (Chicago: University of Chicago Press, 1981).

28. "Speeches of Rawlins Lowndes in the South Carolina Legislature," in *The Complete Anti-Federalist,* edited by Herbert Storing 7 vols. (Chicago: University of Chicago Press, 1981). Rather than using Storing's numbering system for identifying various Anti-Federalist essays, I will use the volume number followed by the page. This citation would be 5:157.

29. Joshua Miller, *The Rise and Fall of Democracy in Early America, 1630–1789* (University Park: Pennsylvania State University Press, 1991).

30. Andrew C. McLauglin, *The Foundations of American Constitutionalism* (New York: New York University Press, 1932).

31. Ellis Sandoz, *A Government of Laws* (Baton Rouge: Louisiana State University Press, 1990).

32. Wilson Carey MacWilliams, *The Idea of Fraternity in America* (Berkeley: University of California Press, 1973); Donald Lutz, *The Origins of American Constitutionalism* (Baton Rouge: Louisiana State University Press, 1988); Robert Bellah, *The Broken Covenant* (New York: Seabury Press, 1975); Sanford Kessler, "Tocqueville's Puritans: Christianity and the American Founding," *Journal of Politics* 54, no. 3 (August 1992): 776–792; Edmund S. Morgan, *Puritan Political Ideas: 1588–1784* (Indianapolis: Bobbs-Merrill, 1965).

33. Michael Lienesch, *New Order of the Ages* (Princeton: Princeton University Press, 1988); Robert W. Hoffert, *A Politics of Tension* (Boulder: University of Colorado Press, 1992); Russell Hanson, *The Democratic Imagination in America* (Princeton: Princeton University Press, 1985); Peter Onuf, *Statehood and Union* (Bloomington: Indiana University Press, 1987); and Cathy D. Matson and Peter Onuf, *A Union of Interests* (Lawrence: University Press of Kansas, 1990).

34. Hoffert, *A Politics of Tension,* p. 13.

35. Ibid., p. 35.

36. Ibid., p. 192.

37. Ibid., p. xvi.

38. Lienesch, *New Order of the Ages,* p. 8.

39. Ibid., p. 139.

40. Ibid., p. 150.

41. Ibid.

42. Ibid., p. 141.

43. Ibid., p. 134.

44. Ibid.

45. Ibid., p. 124.

46. Ibid., p. 162.

47. Ibid., p. 81.

48. See MacWilliams, *The Idea of Fraternity in America,* for an extended treatment of this theme.

Prologue: A Crisis of Faith

1. Michael Walzer, *The Company of Critics* (New York: Basic Books, 1988), p. 17.

2. See Joshua Miller, *The Rise and Fall of Democracy in Early America, 1630–1789* (University Park: Pennsylvania State University Press, 1991).

3. George Steiner, *In Bluebeard's Castle* (New Haven: Yale University Press, 1970), p. 140.

4. Milan Kundera, *The Unbearable Lightness of Being* (New York: Harper & Row, 1984), pp. 222–224.

5. Ibid., p. 248.

6. Ibid., pp. 248–249.

7. Ibid., p. 250.

8. Ibid.

9. Ibid., pp. 251, 252.

10. Aside from Miller, see Michael Lienesch, *New Order of the Ages* (Princeton: Princeton University Press, 1988); Robert Hoffert, *A Politics of Tension* (Boulder: University of Colorado Press, 1992); Russell Hanson, *The Democratic Imagination in America* (Princeton: Princeton University Press, 1985); and Herbert Storing, *What the Anti-Federalists Were for* (Chicago: University of Chicago Press, 1981).

11. See Quentin Skinner, *The Foundations of Modern Political Thought,* 2 vols. (Cambridge: Cambridge University Press, 1978); J. G. A. Pocock, *Politics, Language, and Time* (New York: Atheneum, 1971), and "Verbalizing as a Political Act: Towards a Politics of Speech," *Political Theory* 1, no. 1 (February 1973): 27–45.

12. Alexis De Tocqueville, *Democracy in America,* translated by George Lawrence, edited by J. P. Mayer (New York: Harper & Row, [1835] 1988), p. 506.

13. Ibid.

14. Ibid., p. 507.

15. Ibid.

16. Ibid., p. 508.

17. Ibid.

18. Louis Hartz, *The Liberal Tradition in America* (New York: Harcourt Brace Jovanovich, 1983), ch. 1, esp. p. 20.

19. Ibid., pp. 3–6.

20. Ibid., p. 6.

21. Ibid.

22. Ibid., p. 10.

23. Ibid.

24. Tocqueville, *Democracy in America,* chs. 4 and 5; quote is from p. 512.

25. Other works with which I would group Hartz's include Sebastian de Grazia, *The Political Community* (Chicago: University of Chicago Press, 1948); C. Wright Mills *White Collar* (New York: Oxford University Press, 1951), and *The Power Elite* (Oxford:

Oxford University Press, 1956); William H. Whyte, Jr., *The Organization Man* (New York: Simon & Schuster, 1956); Paul Goodman, *Growing up Absurd* (New York: Vantage Books, 1962); Robert Nisbet, *The Quest for Community* (San Francisco: ICS Press, 1953); and Herbert Marcuse, *One Dimensional Man* (Boston: Beacon Press, 1964).

26. Hartz, *The Liberal Tradition in America,* p. 11.

27. For a detailed theoretical account of the loss of those mediating structures, see Nisbet, *The Quest for Community.* See also de Grazia, *The Political Community,* ch. 6, in which the author goes so far as to pair passages from Tocqueville's *Democracy in America* and Emile Durkheim's *Suicide* (Glenco, Ill.: Free Press, [1897] 1951) that compare in an almost uncomfortable manner with one another.

28. For an earlier and more extended treatment of this idea, see Christopher M. Duncan, "Tyrants and Witches in the American Cold War as Seen by Arthur Miller," *Michigan Journal of Political Science* no. 14 (Winter 1991–1992): 1–17.

29. Daniel Boorstin, "Our Unspoken National Faith: Why Americans Need No Ideology," *Commentary* 15, no. 4 (April 1953): 327–337.

30. Hartz, *The Liberal Tradition in America,* p. 32.

31. Ibid.

32. Ibid.

33. Benjamin Barber, *The Conquest of Politics* (Princeton: Princeton University Press, 1988), pp. 18–19.

34. Hartz, *The Liberal Tradition in America,* p. 287.

35. Ibid., p. 308.

36. For the most thorough development of Barber's thought on this subject, see his *Strong Democracy* (Berkeley: University of California Press, 1984).

37. Robert Bellah, Richard Madsen, William Sullivan, Ann Swindler, and Steven Tipton, *Habits of the Heart* (New York: Harper & Row, 1984), ch. 1.

38. Ibid., ch. 2, esp. pp. 27–35.

39. Ibid., p. 20.

40. Ibid., p. 6.

41. Ibid.

42. Ibid., p. 7.

43. Ibid., p. 23.

44. Ibid., p. 26.

45. Ibid., p. 24.

46. Ibid., p. 16.

47. Ibid., p. 143.

48. Ibid., p. 6.

49. Ibid., p. 48.

50. Ibid., p. 151. See also p. 38, where the authors claim that "involvement in public affairs is the best antidote to the pernicious effects of individualistic isolation," as well as the concluding chapter (11) on transforming American culture.

51. Ibid., pp. 152–155.

52. Ibid., p. 153.

53. Ibid., p. 154.

54. Ibid.

55. Ibid.

56. Ibid., p. 155.

57. See Gordon Wood, *The Creation of the American Republic, 1776–1787* (New York: W. W. Norton, 1972), for the most thorough historical treatment of this process.

CHAPTER 1: PURITAN THEOLOGY AS POLITICAL LIBERATION

1. Hannah Arendt, *The Human Condition* (Chicago: University of Chicago Press, 1958), ch. 2.

2. See Robert Hoffert, *A Politics of Tension* (Boulder: University of Colorado Press, 1992), esp. ch. 1.

3. Glenn Tinder, *The Political Meaning of Christianity* (Baton Rouge: Louisiana State University Press, 1989), p. 150.

4. Roberto Mangabeira Unger, *Knowledge and Politics* (New York: The Free Press, 1984), p. 253.

5. Philip Abbott, *Seeking Many Inventions: The Idea of Community in America* (Tennessee: The University of Tennessee Press, 1987), p. 173.

6. Ibid., p. 174.

7. Cf. John of Salisbury, *Policraticus: The Statesmen's Handbook,* Bk. 4, ch. 2; Thomas Aquinas, *Summa Theologica,* Ia IIae, q. 96, a.5. For a fine secondary discussion see Ewart Lewis, "The Contribution of Medieval Thought to the American Political Tradition," *American Political Science Review* 50, no. 2 (December, 1956): 462–474.

8. Lewis, p. 464.

9. John Calvin, *The Institutes of the Christian Religion* (Chicago: Henry Regency Comp., [1536] 1949.)

10. Ibid., pp. 45–47.

11. Michael Walzer, *The Revolution of the Saints: A Study in the Origins of Radical Politics* (New York: Atheneum, 1968), p. 19.

12. Ibid., p. 54.

13. Calvin was so taken with this ideal that in 1537, in his own covenanted city of Geneva, he prodded the entire population into making a public profession of faith in which the citizens swore to obey the Ten Commandments and at the same time swore their loyalty to the city itself; see Walzer, *Revolution of the Saints,* pp. 55–56; and J. T. McNeill, *The History and Character of Calvinism* (New York: Oxford University Press, 1954), p. 142.

14. Ibid., p. 57.

15. Calvin, *Institutes.*

16. Walzer, *Revolution of the Saints,* p. 116.

17. Ibid., p. 119.

18. Ibid., p. 121.

19. Ibid., p. 123.

20. Ibid., p. 130.

21. Ibid., p. 51.

22. John Calvin, "Institutes of the Christian Religion," quoted in William Ebenstien, *Great Political Thinkers: Plato to the Present,* 4th ed. (New York: Holt, Rienhart and Winston, 1969) p. 326.

23. Walzer, *Revolution of the Saints,* p. 73.

24. Ibid.

25. Calvin, *Institutes,* p. 4.

26. Walzer, *Revolution of the Saints,* p. 38.

27. Ibid., p. 40.

28. Ibid.

29. Stephen Junius Brutus (a pseudonym), *A Defense of Liberty Against Tyrants,* trans. Julian Franklin (New York: Pegasus, [1579] 1969), p. 143. For debates concerning the true identity of the author, see Ernest Barker, "The Authorship of the *Vinidiciae Contra Tyrannos,*" *Cambridge Historical Journal,* III, no. 2 (1930): 164–181.

30. Brutus, *Defense,* p. 144.

31. J. W. Allen, *The History of Political Thought in the Sixteenth Century* (London: The Dial Press, Inc., 1928). Allen argues that the contribution of the *Defense* to political thought was in its stress on the rights of local communities to political independence, which foreshadowed the notion of a federal system later by Americans, especially in the period of the first American founding (pp. 320–331).

32. Ernest Barker, *Church, State and Study* (London: Methuen, 1930). Here Baker illustrates the strong similarities between the content of the *Defense* and Locke's *Second Treatise of Government* (pp. 72–108). For another argument that links the *Defense* to English political life see E. Armstrong, "The Political Theory of the Huguenots," *English Historical Review,* 4 (January 1889): 13–40.

33. Brutus, *Defense,* p. 147.

34. If, as Ernest Baker suggested, there were significant similarities between the *Defense* and Locke's *Second Treatise* we might want to ask at some later point if those similarities require us perhaps to re-read Locke as arguing for something substantively different than the rigid liberal individualism he has been so closely associated with, and perhaps see him in the light of the more communitarian/religious sentiments of the *Defense.*

35. Brutus, *Defense,* p. 150.

36. Ibid., p. 154.

37. Ibid., p. 155.

38. Ibid.

39. Ibid., p. 156.

40. Calvin, *Institutes,* p. 132.

41. Walzer, *Revolution of the Saints,* p. 24.

42. Thomas Hobbes, *Leviathan* (New York: Liberal Arts Press, 1958), p. 92.

43. For an overview of this period see John Herman Randall, Jr., *The Making of the Modern Mind* (New York: Columbia University Press, [1926] 1976), esp. chs. 6–14.

44. Crane Brinton, *Anatomy of Revolution* (New York: Vintage, 1938).

45. Perry Miller, "The Marrow of Puritan Divinity," *Publications of the Massachusetts Historical Society* 32 (1937): 248.

46. Ibid., p. 251.

47. Ibid., pp. 251–254.

48. Ibid., p. 263.

49. In a passage taken from the "Confession of the Brethren Arrested at Trieste, 1539, and *The Five Articles,* attributed to Hans Denk, located in Will and Ariel Durant, *The Age of Reformation* (New York: Simon & Schuster, 1957), p. 129, the risks attributed to Anabaptist thought are evident when the question is raised as to whether Christians can be magistrates. The answer given was no: "Christ was invited to be a king, but he fled. We follow him in this for the kingdom of Christ is not of this world. . . . Because the government of the world is of the flesh and that of a Christian according to the spirit."

50. The most important work here is Norman Pettit, *The Heart Prepared* (New Haven: Yale University Press, 1966).

51. In 1618 the Synod of Dort was called for the purpose of judging the views of Jacobus Arminius, who had rejected the doctrine of unconditional election and had asserted that man, by his own will, could assist in the process of salvation. The Synod resulted in the declaration of Arminius' thought being declared heretical; subsequently he was tortured, and two hundred ministers who had embraced his teachings were deposed and driven from the Church.

52. Pettit, *The Heart Prepared,* pp. 17 and 101; see also Wilson Carey MacWilliams, *The Idea of Fraternity in America* (Berkeley: University of California Press, 1973), ch. 5, esp. p. 121.

53. Pettit, *The Heart Prepared,* pp. 98–99.

54. For Puritans there was no way to God other than through interpretation of the scripture or the Word, and this was only possible within a congregation of members all seeking the same goal. Antinomianism in its root sense means opposed to the law. In theology it is the opinion that the moral law is not binding upon Christians who are under the law of grace. It is associated with direct revelation and therefore stood in opposition to the entire foundation of the Puritan community. This is the crime with which Anne Hutchinson would eventually be punished and exiled from Massachusetts Bay Colony. For a documentary discussion of the period see David Hall, *The Antinomian Controversy 1636–1638* (Middleton, Conn.: Wesleyan University Press, 1968); and for a discussion about the Hutchinson case in particular see Edmund Morgan, "The Case Against Anne Hutchinson," *New England Quarterly* 10 (1937): 675–697; and Edmund Morgan, *The Puritan Dilemma* (New York: Little Brown and Co., 1958).

55. See MacWilliams, *Idea of Fraternity,* p. 123, where he talks of a covenant designed to produce a "common soul."

56. Walzer, *Revolution of the Saints,* pp. 30–45.

57. Reprinted in Michael B. Levy, *Political Thought in America,* 2nd ed. (Chicago: The Dorsey Press, 1988), pp. 11–12.

58. MacWilliams claims that "improvement in man and his condition required the development of external substitutes which would compensate for the will's defect," *Idea of Fraternity,* p. 121. Whatever else those substitutes might be they are in essence part of the political world.

59. Levy, *Political Thought,* p. 13.

60. Ibid.

61. Ibid., pp. 13–14.

62. MacWilliams discusses this framework in the language of interlocking fraternities that bind people with different roles and positions to one another, *Idea of Fraternity,* p. 136. And in a recent article John Schaar suggests that modern debates between liberals and communitarians over the tension between liberty and community might be reconciled by the conception of authority suggested in the work of John Winthrop, see Schaar, "Liberty/Authority/Community in the Political Thought of John Winthrop," *Political Theory* 19, no. 4 (November 1991): 493–518.

63. What Benjamin Barber might call the "conquest of politics by philosophy;" see his *The Conquest of Politics* (Princeton: Princeton University Press, 1988).

64. The dangers of this (for me) can be seen in the recent work of Roberto Unger,

Politics (Cambridge: Cambridge University Press, 1987).

    65. Morgan, *Puritan Dilemma,* p. 85.

    66. Ibid., p. 93.

    67. Ibid.

    68. Donald S. Lutz, *Popular Consent and Popular Control* (Baton Rouge: Louisiana State University Press, 1980), p. 25.

    69. Cf. St. Augustine, *City of God* (classical).

    70. Edmund Morgan, *Visible Saints* (New York: New York University Press, 1963), pp. 1–4.

    71. Morgan, *Puritan Dilemma,* p. 89.

    72. Vernon Louis Parrington, *Main Currents in American Thought,* Volume I (New York: Harcourt, Brace, and Company, Inc., 1930).

    73. Joshua Miller, *The Rise and Fall of Democracy in Early America, 1630–1789* (University Park: The Pennsylvania State University Press, 1991), ch. 2.

    74. Ibid., pp. 28–29.

    75. Ibid., p. 28.

    76. Abbott, *Seeking Many Inventions,* p. 174.

    77. Morgan, "Case Against Anne Hutchinson," p. 648.

    78. MacWilliams, *Idea of Fraternity,* p. 144.

    79. Miller, *Rise and Fall of Democracy,* p. 49.

    80. Morgan, *Visible Saints,* p. 66.

    81. Ibid., p. 67.

    82. Ibid., p. 88.

CHAPTER 2: POLITICAL LIBERATION AS AMERICAN THEOLOGY

    1. Ferdinand Tönnies, *Community and Society* (1887).

    2. Jane J. Mansbridge, *Beyond Adversary Democracy* (Chicago: University of Chicago Press, 1983).

    3. Ferdinand Tönnies, *Critique of Public Opinion* (1922).

    4. Mansbridge, *Beyond Adversary Democracy,* ch. 3.

    5. Hannah Arendt, *The Human Condition* (Chicago: University of Chicago Press, 1958), ch. 2.

    6. Michael Walzer, *The Revolution of the Saints* (New York: Atheneum, 1968), pp. 318–319.

    7. Crane Brinton, *The Anatomy of Revolution* (New York: Vintage, 1938).

    8. See Michael Lienesch, *New Order of the Ages* (Princeton: Princeton University Press, 1988), p. 134.

    9. See Philip Abbott, *Seeking Many Inventions* (Tennessee: University of Tennessee Press, 1987). In his introductory remarks Abbott faults modern political commentators like Truman and Dahl for by and large collapsing all forms of public association into a calculus of "marginal utility" (p. 16).

    10. Robert Nisbet, *The Quest for Community* (San Francisco: ICS Press, 1990), p. 18.

11. Michael Walzer, "A Particularism of My Own," *Religious Studies Review* 16, no. 3 (July 1990): 193–195.

12. Michael Oakeshott, "Rationalism in Politics," in his *Rationalism in Politics and Other Essays* (Indianapolis: Liberty Press, 1991), p. 26.

13. Gilbert Meilaender, "A View from Somewhere: The Political Thought of Michael Walzer," *Religious Studies Review* 16, no. 3 (July 1990): 200.

14. Ibid.

15. Hannah Arendt, *On Revolution* (New York: Penguin Books, 1965), pp. 121–122.

16. Ibid., pp. 122–124.

17. Ibid., pp. 124–125.

18. Julien Benda, *The Treason of the Intellectuals* (New York: W. W. Norton, [1928] 1956).

19. Louis Hartz, *The Liberal Tradition in America* (New York: Harcourt Brace Jovanovich, [1955] 1983); Richard Hofstadter, *The American Political Tradition and the Men Who Made It* (New York: Vintage, [1948] 1974); John P. Diggins, *The Lost Soul of American Politics* (Chicago: University of Chicago Press, 1984).

20. The most comprehensive and contextually accurate work on Locke to date is Richard Ashcraft, *Revolutionary Politics and Locke's Two Treatises of Government* (Princeton: Princeton University Press, 1986), in which it is argued that Locke was firmly entrenched in the republican school along with Algernon Sydney, Harrington, and others. For a more concise rendering of the same basic argument, see Ashcraft's "Revolutionary Politics and Locke's *Two Treatises of Government:* Radicalism and Lockean Political Theory," *Political Theory* 8, no. 4 (November 1980): 429–485. For a view of Locke as primarily a religious thinker, see John Dunn, *The Political Thought of John Locke* (Cambridge: Cambridge University Press, 1969). The chief work in the vein of Locke as liberal individualist thinker from a critical perspective rather than the apologetic position is C. B. Macphearson, *The Political Theory of Possessive Individualism* (Oxford: Oxford University Press, 1962).

21. Forrest MacDonald, *Novus Ordo Seclorum* (Lawrence: University Press of Kansas, 1985), pp. 10–13.

22. Caroline Robbins, *The Eighteenth-Century Commonwealthman* (Cambridge, Mass.: Harvard University Press, 1959).

23. Macphearson, *The Political Theory of Possessive Individualism*.

24. Hugh R. Trevor-Roper, *The Gentry, 1540-1640* (London: Cambridge University Press, 1953).

25. J. G. A. Pocock, "Machiavelli, Harrington, and English Political Ideologies in the Eighteenth Century," *William and Mary Quarterly* 3d ser., 22 (1965): 548–583.

26. Ibid., pp. 565–566. I quote Pocock at such length here because I have yet to come across a more coherent and relatively compact description of country Whig thought.

27. See Max Weber, *The Protestant Ethic and the Spirit of Capitalism* (New York: Scribners, [1905] 1958).

28. Gordon Wood, *The Creation of the American Republic, 1776–1787* (New York: W. W. Norton, [1969] 1972), p. 108.

29. Ibid., p. 111.

30. See Bernard Bailyn, *The Ideological Origins of the American Revolution* (Cambridge, Mass.: Harvard University Press, 1967), ch. 4.

31. Ibid., esp. pp. 110–115. See also Pauline Maier, "John Wilkes and American

Disillusionment with Britain," *William and Mary Quarterly* 3d ser., 20 (1963): 373–395.

32. Bailyn, *Ideological Origins of the American Revolution,* p. 160.

33. Thomas Paine, "Common Sense," in *The Thomas Paine Reader,* edited by Michael Foot and Isaac Kramnick (New York: Penguin, 1987), p. 65.

34. Ibid., p. 66.

35. For a comprehensive review of this vast body of literature, see Robert E. Shalope, "Republicanism and Early American Historiography," *William and Mary Quarterly* 3d ser., 39 (1982): 334–356.

36. Clifford Geertz, *Interpretation of Cultures* (New York: Basic Books, 1973); Kenneth Burke, *The Philosophy of Literary Form* (Baton Rouge: Louisiana State University Press, 1941); and Erik Erikson, *Young Man Luther* (New York: W. W. Norton, 1958).

37. Shalhope, "Republicanism and Early American Historiography," p. 355.

38. Oakeshott, "Rationalism in Politics," p. 16.

39. Arendt, *The Human Condition,* p. 40.

40. Ibid.

41. Oakeshott, "Rationalism in Politics," p. 26.

42. Hannah Fenichel Pitkin provides a useful corrective and extension to the more severe possibilities of Arendt's position in her essay "Justice: On Relating Private and Public," *Political Theory* 9, no. 3 (August 1981): 327–352. See especially her argument at p. 347.

43. Arendt, *On Revolution,* pp. 60–61.

44. Arendt, *The Human Condition,* p. 68.

45. Arendt, *On Revolution,* p. 127.

46. In *The Portable Thomas Jefferson,* edited by Merrill D. Peterson (New York: Penguin, 1988). p. 4.

47. Ibid., p. 399.

48. Ibid., p. 414.

49. Though this sentiment is expressed in various places in Jefferson's writings, I borrowed it from the title page of Benjamin Barber's *Strong Democracy* (Berkeley: University of California Press, 1984).

50. Oakeshott, "Rationalism in Politics," p. 29.

51. Ibid., p. 15.

52. Ibid., p. 11.

53. Quoted in Arendt, *On Revolution,* p. 131.

54. Found in *Documents of American Constitutional and Legal History,* edited by Melvin I. Urofsky (New York: Alfred A. Knopf, 1989), pp. 6–7. I have modernized the spellings to improve the readability of this document and any that follow where such a change would not be detrimental to the document or in any way seriously alter its meaning.

55. Ibid., pp. 10–11.

56. Ibid., p. 12.

57. Donald S. Lutz, *Popular Consent and Popular Control* (Baton Rouge: Louisiana State University Press, 1980), pp. 27–29.

58. Cited in Fredrick L. Richardson, "Early American Political Authority, 1773–1778" (Ph.D. diss., Brandeis University, 1973), taken from Samuel Huntington, *Political Order in Changing Societies* (New Haven: Yale University Press, 1968), p. 96. See also G. R. Elton, *The Body of the Whole Realm* (Charlottesville: University Press of Virginia, 1969); and J. R. Pole, *The Seventeenth Century* (Charlottesville: University Press of Virginia, 1969) and *Political Representation in England and the Origins of the American Republic* (London: Macmillan, 1966).

59. Lutz, *Popular Consent and Popular Control,* p. 25.

60. Michael Zuckerman, "The Social Context of Democracy in Massachusetts," *William and Mary Quarterly* 3d ser., 25, no. 4 (1968): 523–544; see also his *Peaceable Kingdoms* (New York: Alfred A. Knopf, 1970).

61. Zuckerman, "Social Context," p. 527.

62. Mansbridge, *Beyond Adversary Democracy,* p. 25.

63. For a solid discussion of this phenomenon, see Jack P. Greene, *The Quest for Power* (Chapel Hill: University of North Carolina Press, 1963); see also Jackson Turner Main, *The Upper House in Revolutionary America, 1763–1788* (Madison: University of Wisconsin Press, 1967); and Michael Kammen, *Deputyes and Libertyes* (New York: Alfred A. Knopf, 1969).

64. For documentation of this, see Robert E. Brown, *Middle-Class Democracy and the Revolution in Massachusetts* (Ithaca, N.Y.: Cornell University Press, 1955).

65. Quoted in Wood, *The Creation of the American Republic,* p. 25.

66. See Bernard Bailyn, *Pamphlets of the American Revolution,* 2 vol. (Cambridge, Mass.: Harvard University Press, 1965), for a substantial though still partial collection of such works. See also the excellent collection of founding era writings in *American Political Writing During the Founding Era, 1760–1805,* edited by Charles S. Hyneman and Donald S. Lutz, 2 vols. (Indianapolis: Liberty Press, 1983).

67. Probably the most comprehensive attempt to grasp the Declaration in all its various facets is Garry Wills, *Inventing America* (New York: Doubleday, 1978). Before that, the standard work on the origins of the Declaration was Carl Becker, *The Declaration of Independence* (New York: Harcourt, Brace, 1922).

68. Arendt, *On Revolution,* ch. 3, esp. pp. 126–128. There are many other ways in which scholars have read that particular passage. The reader is referred to Herbert Lawrence Ganter, "Jefferson's *Pursuit of Happiness* and Some Forgotten Men," *William and Mary Quarterly,* 2nd ser., 16 (1936): 422–434, 558–585, which is a fine review of all the early literature concerning the passage. For more recent discussions and controversies, see Wills, *Inventing America;* Arthur M. Schlesinger, "The Lost Meaning of 'The Pursuit of Happiness,' " *William and Mary Quarterly* 3d ser., 21 (1964): 325–327; and, for a critical view of those two, see Ronald Hamowy, "Jefferson and the Scottish Enlightenment: A Critique of Garry Wills's *Inventing America: Jefferson's Declaration of Independence,*" *William and Mary Quarterly* 3d ser., 36 (1979): 503–523. All of these interpretations basically ignore the view outlined here, and thus Arendt's as well, preferring to focus on either the idea of personal and private happiness as being left alone by government, or the role of government in ensuring the happiness of the general population.

69. See Pocock, "Machiavelli, Harrington, and English Political Ideologies in the Eighteenth Century."

70. John Locke, *The Second Treatise of Government* (Indianapolis: Bobbs-Merrill, [1690] 1952), p. 139.

71. Ibid., p. 119.

72. All citations from the Declaration of Independence are taken from a reprinted photograph of the original.

73. See John Marshall's majority opinion in *Barron* v. *Baltimore,* 7 Pet. 243, 8 L.Ed. 672 (1833).

74. Arendt, *On Revolution,* p. 130.

75. Urofsky, *Documents of American Constitutional and Legal History,* vol. 1, pp. 37–38.

76. Ibid., p. 35. (This represents the view of Urofsky.)

77. See Plato, *The Republic*, book II.

78. Urofsky, *Documents of American Constitutional and Legal History*, vol. 1, p. 43.

79. This, however, should not be taken to mean that Jefferson or republican thought in general believed that justice was simply a question of opinion or preference. There was still God, and there was still the idea of a universal moral code; but, like their Puritan forerunners, American republicans believed that interpretation of that universal code was a communal responsibility.

CHAPTER 3: AMERICAN POLITICAL REFORMATIONS

1. Fredrick Richardson, "Early American Political Authority, 1773–1778" (Ph.D. diss., Brandeis University, 1973), p. 213.

2. Gordon Wood in ch. 5, "The Nature of Representation," of his *The Creation of the American Republic* (New York: W. W. Norton, [1969] 1972), describes in great detail the microlevel companion to this transfer of authority from England to the state legislatures by pointing out the dramatic change that took place not just in who could rightfully represent, but also in how representation itself was supposed to function. In simplified form, he argues that the conception of representation in America had turned 180 degrees from the representative as "trustee," à la Edmund Burke, to the notion of the representative as "delegate," which the modern literature typically associates with John Stuart Mill. In Wood's words, "The elected members would be, in other words, 'an exact epitome of the whole people,' 'an exact miniature of their constituents.' " For what is still the most comprehensive discussion on the various understandings of "representation," see Hannah Fenichel Pitkin, *The Concept of Representation* (Berkeley: University of California Press, 1967).

3. Gordon Wood, *The Radicalism of the American Revolution* (New York: Alfred A. Knopf, 1992), p. 4.

4. Ibid., p. 5.

5. Ibid., p. 23.

6. Ibid., p. 27.

7. Ibid., pp. 240–241.

8. Alexis de Tocqueville, *Democracy in America*, translated by George Lawrence, edited by J. P. Mayer (New York: Harper & Row, [1825] 1988), p. 57.

9. Ibid., p. 506.

10. Fisher Ames, "Dangers of American Liberty," in *Works of Fisher Ames*, vol. 2, edited by Seth Ames (New York: Burt Franklin, 1971), p. 349.

11. Ibid., p. 354.

12. Wood, *The Radicalism of the American Revolution*, p. 369.

13. There are numerous sources that capture this progression, including Bernard Bailyn, *The Ideological Origins of the American Revolution* (Cambridge, Mass.: Harvard University Press, 1967); and Wood, *The Creation of the American Republic*. The most succinct account is probably Edmund Morgan, *The Birth of the Republic 1763–89* (Chicago: University of Chicago Press, 1956). The two best accounts of this period in terms of the democratization process are Pauline Maier, *Resistance to Revolution* (New York: Vintage, 1974); and E. P. Douglass, *Rebels and Democrats* (Chapel Hill: University of North Carolina Press, 1955).

Also see Merrill Jensen, *The Articles of Confederation* (Madison: University of Wisconsin Press, 1940).

14. This argument is made by Joshua Miller in his *The Rise and Fall of Democracy in Early America, 1630-1789* (University Park: Pennsylvania State University Press, 1991), esp. ch. 3. He coins the term "conservative democrats" to make his point.

15. Kenneth Janda, Jeffrey Berry, and Jerry Goldman, *The Challenge of Democracy* (Boston: Houghton Mifflin, 1991), p. 77.

16. William Keefe, Henry Abraham, William Flanigan, Charles O. Jones, Morris Ogul, and John Spanier, *American Democracy* (New York: Harper & Row, 1990), p. 35.

17. David V. Edwards, *The American Political Experience* (Englewood Cliffs, N.J.: Prentice Hall, 1988), p. 30.

18. Everett Carll Ladd, *The American Polity* (New York: W. W. Norton, 1987), p. 76.

19. Susan Welch, John Gruhl, Michael Steinman, and John Comer, *American Government* (St. Paul, Minn.: West Publishing, 1988), p. 30.

20. See Michael Lienesch, *New Order of the Ages* (Princeton: Princeton University Press, 1988), p. 139; and Robert Hoffert, *A Politics of Tension* (Boulder: University of Colorado Press, 1992).

21. John Fiske, *The Critical Period of American History, 1783–1789* (Boston: Houghton Mifflin, [1888] 1901), pp. 98–99.

22. Merrill Jensen, *The New Nation* (New York: Alfred A. Knopf, 1950), pp. xii–xiii.

23. See Tocqueville, *Democracy in America,* vol. 1, chs. 3, 5, and esp. 7, dealing with the nature of public opinion in the United States, Tocqueville's fear of unanimity, and his sentiments on the tyranny of the majority.

24. Louis Hartz, *The Liberal Tradition in America* (New York: Harcourt Brace Jovanovich, [1955] 1983), ch. 1.

25. For a discussion of this phenomenon that uses the American presidency as its focal point, see Philip Abbott, *The Exemplary Presidency* (Amherst: University of Massachusetts Press, 1990).

26. There has been some very interesting work done along these lines in the field of literary criticism. See, for example, Barbara Harlow, *Resistance Literature* (New York: Metheun, 1980), which talks about the subversive side of literature and the dangers to specific counterhegemonic movements implicit in adopting "literary forms identified with the oppressor culture." For an intriguing discussion of the duplicitous lengths to which those engaging in such a project are driven in a uniquely American context, see Houston Baker, Jr., *Modernism and the Harlem Renaissance* (Chicago: University of Chicago Press, 1987).

27. For an interesting parallel, see Thomas Kuhn, *The Structure of Scientific Revolutions* (Chicago: University of Chicago Press, 1962).

28. Jean-Paul Sartre, *Being and Nothingness,* translated by Hazel Barnes (New York: Washington Square Press, 1956), ch. 2.

29. *The Orestes Plays of Aeschylus,* translated by Paul Roche (New York: Mentor, 1962), p. 192.

30. Donald Lutz, *Popular Consent and Popular Control* (Baton Rouge: Louisiana State University Press, 1980), p. 50.

31. Ibid., pp. 160–161.

32. For discussions concerning the specific states and their differences during this period, see Allan Nevins, *The American States During and After the Revolution, 1775–1789*

(New York: Macmillan, 1924); Jackson Turner Main, *The Sovereign States, 1775–1783* (Madison: University of Wisconsin Press, 1973); Peter S. Onuf, *The Origin of the Federal Republic* (Philadelphia: University of Pennsylvania Press, 1983); Willi Paul Adams, *The First American Constitutions* (Chapel Hill: University of North Carolina Press, 1980); Lutz, *Popular Consent and Popular Control;* and Jensen, *The New Nation* and *The Articles of Confederation.*

33. Hannah Arendt, *On Revolution* (New York: Penguin Books, 1965), pp. 174–175.

34. For an interesting discussion of the similarities and differences between Arendt's conception of early American institutions and Tocqueville's, see Suzanne D. Jacobitti, "Individualism and Political Community: Arendt and Tocqueville on the Current Debate in Liberalism," *Polity* 23, no. 4 (1991): 585–604.

35. Tocqueville, *Democracy in America,* p. 59.

36. Ibid., p. 63.

37. Miller, *The Rise and Fall of Democracy in Early America,* p. 80.

38. Tocqueville, *Democracy in America,* p. 69.

39. Arendt, *On Revolution,* p. 212. In point of fact Arendt surprisingly makes little out of America's first founding under the Articles of Confederation, and in doing so ignores a constitution that does not readily fit with her model. For an interesting discussion of this phenomenon that pits Arendt against Nietzsche in the struggle over the nature of modernity, see Dana R. Villa, "Beyond Good and Evil: Arendt, Nietzsche, and the Aestheticization of Political Action," *Political Theory* 20, no. 2 (May 1992): 274–308.

40. See Donald Lutz, "The Relative Influence of European Writers on Late Eighteenth-Century American Political Thought," *American Political Science Review* 78, no. 1 (1984): 189–197.

41. The citations to Montesquieu's *The Spirit of the Laws* (1748) are taken from an abridgment in *Great Political Thinkers: Plato to the Present,* edited by William Ebenstein, 4th ed. (New York: Holt, Rinehart and Winston, 1969), p. 434.

42. Ibid., p. 435.

43. Ibid.

44. All citations concerning the Articles of Confederation are taken from *The Constitution of the United States: Case Summaries,* 11th ed., edited by Edward Smith (New York: Barnes & Noble, 1974), pp. 28–36.

45. Jensen, *The Articles of Confederation,* p. 117.

46. Jean-Jacques Rousseau, *The Social Contract,* translated by Maurice Cranston (New York: Penguin, 1983), p. 60.

47. Jensen, *The Articles of Confederation,* p. 124.

48. Ibid., p. 243.

49. Tocqueville, *Democracy in America,* p. 88.

50. Max Farrand, ed., *The Records of the Constitutional Convention 1787,* 4 vols. (New York: W. W. Norton, [1911] 1974).

51. For a very readable historical overview of this period, see Page Smith, *The Constitution* (New York: Quill Paperbacks, 1980).

52. Hartz, *The Liberal Tradition in America,* p. 10.

53. Forrest MacDonald, *Novus Ordo Seclorum* (Lawrence: University Press of Kansas, 1985), p. 143.

54. Charles A. Beard, *An Economic Interpretation of the Constitution of the United States* (New York: Free Press, [1913] 1986).

55. For an overview of this school of historical thought, see Richard Hofstadter, *The*

Progressive Historians (New York: Knopf, 1968).

56. Beard, *An Economic Interpretation of the Constitution of the United States,* p. 19.

57. See Robert E. Brown, *Charles Beard and the Constitution* (Princeton: Princeton University Press, 1956); and Forrest MacDonald, *We the People* (Chicago: University of Chicago Press, 1958).

58. Richard Hofstadter, *The Progressive Historians,* p. 225.

59. Hartz, *The Liberal Tradition in America;* Richard Hofstadter, *The American Political Tradition and the Men Who Made It* (New York: Vintage Books, [1948] 1974); Brown, *Charles Beard and the Constitution;* Daniel Boorstin, *The Genius of American Politics* (Chicago: University of Chicago Press, 1953); John Diggins, *The Lost Soul of American Politics* (Chicago: University of Chicago Press, 1984); and, so that the reader is aware that there are fundamental differences within these rough categories, John Diggins, "Consciousness and Ideology in American History: The Burden of Daniel J. Boorstin," *American Historical Review* 76 (1971): 99–118; Isaac Kramnick, "Republican Revisionism Revisited," *American Historical Review* 87, no. 3 (1982): 629–664; and Joyce Appleby, *Liberalism and Republicanism in the Historical Imagination* (Cambridge, Mass.: Harvard University Press, 1992).

60. Hartz, *The Liberal Tradition in America,* p. 78.

61. Diggins, *The Lost Soul of American Politics,* p. 68.

62. James Madison, Alexander Hamilton, and John Jay, *The Federalist Papers,* edited by Isaac Kramnick (New York: Penguin Books, [1788] 1988), pp. 122–128.

63. Thomas L. Pangle, *The Spirit of Modern Republicanism* (Chicago: University of Chicago Press, 1988); Christopher Bruell, "A Return to Classical Political Philosophy and the Understanding of the American Founding," *Review of Politics* 53, no. 1 (Winter 1991): 173–186; Thomas West, "Leo Strauss and the American Founding," *Review of Politics* 53, no. 1 (Winter 1991): 157–172; Walter Berns, *Taking the Constitution Seriously* (New York: Simon & Schuster, 1987); Robert Webbing, *The American Revolution and the Politics of Liberty* (Baton Rouge: Louisiana State University Press, 1988); David F. Epstein, *The Political Theory of the Federalist* (Chicago: University of Chicago Press, 1984); Martin Diamond, "Democracy and *The Federalist:* A Reconsideration of the Framers' Intent," *American Political Science Review* 53, no. 1 (March 1959): 52–68.

64. For an understanding of Leo Strauss's own particular project, the reader is directed to the following of his works: *The City and Man* (Chicago: University of Chicago Press, 1964); *Natural Right and History* (Chicago: University of Chicago Press, 1950); *Persecution and the Art of Writing* (New York: Free Press, 1952); *Liberalism, Ancient and Modern* (Ithaca, N.Y.: Cornell University Press, 1968).

65. West, "Leo Strauss and the American Founding," p. 158.

66. Diamond, "Democracy and *The Federalist,*" p. 55.

67. Ibid.

68. Ibid., p. 56.

69. Ibid., pp. 56–57.

70. Ibid., p. 68.

71. Ibid.

72. West, "Leo Strauss and the American Founding," p. 161.

73. For a very interesting argument along these lines, see Michael Walzer, "Philosophy and Democracy, *Political Theory* 9 (August 1981): 379–399.

74. Merrill Jensen, *The New Nation* and "The Idea of a National Government During the American Revolution," *Political Science Quarterly* 58, no. 3 (1944): 356–379; Jackson

Turner Main, *The Anti-federalists* (New York: Norton, 1961); Forrest MacDonald, *Novus Ordo Seclorum;* Douglass Adair, "Fame and the Founding Fathers," in *Fame and the Founding Fathers* edited by Trevor Colbourne (New York: W. W. Norton, 1974); Stanley Elkins and Eric McKitrick, "The Founding Fathers: Young Men of the Revolution," *Political Science Quarterly* 76, no. 2 (1961): 181–216; John P. Roche, "The Founding Fathers: A Reform Caucus in Action," *American Political Science Review* 55, no. 4 (December 1961): 799–816; Wood, *The Creation of the American Republic.*

75. Forrest MacDonald, *E Pluribus Unum* (Indianapolis: Liberty Press, 1965), p. 371.

76. Jensen, "The Idea of a National Government during the American Revolution," p. 357.

77. For a good overview of this event, see Richard H. Kohn, *Eagle and Sword* (New York: Free Press, 1975), esp. ch. 2.

78. Elkins and McKitrick, "The Founding Fathers: Young Men of the Revolution," p. 203.

79. Ibid.

80. Kohn, *Eagle and Sword,* p. 10.

81. Adair, "Fame and the Founding Fathers," pp. 4–8.

82. Ibid., pp. 10–11.

83. Ibid., p. 12.

84. For an overview, see Page Smith, *The Constitution,* ch. 6.

85. Roche, "The Founding Fathers: A Reform Caucus in Action," p. 799. Italics added.

86. Ibid., p. 800.

87. Ibid., p. 801.

88. Ibid., p. 803.

89. Ibid.

90. Ibid., p. 804.

91. Ibid., p. 815. The reader should note that the quote is inverted slightly, in that the last clause actually appeared first in the essay. This does not change the meaning of the passage in any significant way. Italics added.

92. MacDonald, *Novus Ordo Seclorum,* p. 144.

CHAPTER 4: THE FAITH OF THE FEDERALISTS

1. "An Address of the Subscribers Members of the Late House of Representatives of the Commonwealth of Pennsylvania to their Constituents," in *The Complete Anti-Federalist,* edited by Herbert J. Storing (Chicago: University of Chicago Press, 1981), 3.2.3. (The numbering system is Storing's and refers to the volume, place within the volume, and paragraph, respectively.)

2. Sheldon Wolin, *The Presence of the Past* (Baltimore: Johns Hopkins University Press, 1990), p. 87.

3. Ibid., pp. 88–89.

4. Ibid., pp. 90–91.

5. Kramnick, *Federalist* no. 1, p. 87.

6. Ibid., *Federalist* no. 2–no. 5.

7. Ibid., *Federalist* no. 6 and no. 7.

8. Ibid., *Federalist* no. 7–no. 10.

9. Ibid., *Federalist* no. 11–no. 13.

10. Ibid., *Federalist* no. 15–no. 20.

11. Ibid., *Federalist* no. 20, p. 172 (emphasis in the original).

12. Ibid.

13. Ibid., *Federalist* no. 21, p. 174.

14. Ibid.

15. Edmund S. Morgan, *Inventing the People* (New York: Norton, 1988), p. 262.

16. Joshua Miller, *The Rise and Fall of Democracy in Early America* (University Park: Pennsylvania State University Press, 1991), ch. 5. Miller argues that "the Federalists' great accomplishment in political theory was to establish an unmediated relationship between the national government and the people that, ironically, discourages democracy," p. 106.

17. Alexis de Tocqueville, *Democracy in America,* translated by George Lawrence, edited by J. P. Mayer (New York: Harper & Row, [1835], 1988), p. 604.

18. Charles A. Beard, *An Economic Interpretation of the Constitution of the United States* (New York: Free Press, [1913] 1986), ch. 6.

19. Kramnick, *Federalist* no. 10, p. 123.

20. Ibid.

21. Ibid.

22. Ibid., p. 124.

23. Ibid.

24. Ibid., p. 126.

25. Ibid., p. 125.

26. Ibid., p. 126.

27. Ibid.

28. It was the historian Douglass Adair who first elaborated on the relationship between the work of Hume and of Madison in his essay "The Tenth Federalist Revisited," in the collection of his essays titled *Fame and the Founding Fathers* edited by Trevor Colbourne (New York: W. W. Norton, 1974). This citation from Hume is taken from that essay at p. 98.

29. Kramnick, *Federalist* no. 10, p. 127.

30. Ibid.

31. Ibid.

32. Although I do not want to deal with it in the body of the text, there is a very important recent contribution to the interpretive literature surrounding the second founding in general and the *Federalist* in particular: Bruce Ackerman, *We the People* (Cambridge, Mass.: Harvard University Press, 1992). In this book (the first volume of an intended three) Ackerman constructs a theoretical model that he calls "dualist democracy" (ch. 1) in order to explain the theory of *The Federalist Papers.* The basic argument is that the founders established a democratic system that allowed the voice of the people to be heard in a collective fashion through the making of the Constitution and its subsequent amendments, and the voice of the virtuous representatives to be heard during periods of "normal politics." The argument concerning the *Federalist* is based on the idea that the founders "recognized that much of American politics would lack the quality of mobilized deliberation they associated with the spirit of the Revolution" (p. 165). In other words, the extreme context of the Revolution had made virtuous behavior the norm during that period, but once the war was over and the tension was released, that virtuous spirit dissipated and the people returned to

their private (factional) affairs. Thus what Publius intended post Revolution was "to design a system that, given the available human materials, will do as good a job as possible in re-creating the kind of public-spirited deliberation that the People themselves can attain only during rare constitutional crises" (p. 186). This was, of course, to be found in the new national government and Madison's virtuous representatives. The expansion of the republic in *Federalist* no. 10 is then interpreted by Ackerman as a way of creating so many voices that the representative will be left free to choose what he or she thinks is right, since there will be no clear-cut "general will" to listen to. He describes this in the following manner: "the aim of constitutional science is to check and balance competing factions to allow the Peo-ple's representatives leeway to deliberate and pursue the public good" (p. 224). While I think that Ackerman's argument may have some important descriptive merit, what troubles me is the normative import that runs through his work. For him it is good that "normal politics" are left to the "experts," and furthermore, he sees, wrongly, no discrepancy be-tween this new political order and the goals of the Revolution itself (ch. 8).

33. Kramnick, *Federalist* no. 10, p. 128.

34. Ibid.

35. On this point see Hannah Arendt's discussion in her *On Violence* (New York: Harcourt Brace Jovanovich, 1969), where she claims, along with Jouvenel, "that to suppose that majority rule exists only in democracy is a fantastic illusion . . . political institutions are manifestations of power which petrify and decay as soon as the living power of the people ceases to support them," pp. 40–41.

36. Kramnick, *Federalist* no. 44, p. 286.

37. Kramnick, *Federalist* no. 22, p. 179.

38. Arendt, *On Violence,* p. 42.

39. Jean-Jacques Rousseau, *The Social Contract,* translated by Maurice Cranston (New York: Penguin, 1983), p. 72.

40. Kramnick, *Federalist* no. 22, p. 182.

41. See Michael Lienesch, *New Order of the Ages* (Princeton: Princeton University Press, 1988), p. 124, for a discussion of the varying approaches to history pursued by the Federalists and their political opponents.

42. See Gordon Wood, *The Creation of the American Republic* (New York: W. W. Norton, [1969] 1972), ch. 12, on this point.

43. Kramnick, *Federalist* no. 51, p. 320.

44. For the best historical/contextual discussion of this very important theoretical subtlety, see Gordon Wood's discussion of John Adams in "The Relevance and Irrelevance of John Adams," in his *The Creation of the American Republic,* ch. 14.

45. Kramnick, *Federalist* no. 51, p. 320.

46. Niccolo Machiavelli, *The Prince,* translated by George Bull (New York: Penguin, 1982), pp. 131–133.

47. Kramnick, *Federalist* no. 78, p. 437.

48. Ibid., pp. 438–439.

49. Ibid., p. 439.

50. Arendt, *On Revolution,* p. 200.

51. Kramnick, *Federalist* no. 78, p. 440.

52. Ibid.

53. See Michael Walzer, "Philosophy and Democracy," *Political Theory* 9 (August 1981): 379–399.

54. Kramnick, *Federalist* no. 78, p. 440.

55. On this point see Kramnick, *Federalist* no. 79.

56. Kramnick, *Federalist* no. 78, p. 442.

57. In Ralph Lerner, *The Thinking Revolutionary* (Ithaca, N.Y.: Cornell University Press, 1987) pp. 91–136.

58. Ibid., p. 92.

59. Ibid.

60. Ibid., pp. 93–118. The reader should keep in mind that the jury was always intended and defended on localist grounds, since it was to render justice according to their shared and particular community standards, not some transcendent or nationalized sense.

61. Ibid., p. 94.

62. Ibid., p. 104.

63. Ibid., p. 98.

64. Wolin, *The Presence of the Past,* p. 87.

65. Ibid.

CHAPTER 5: THE ANTI-FEDERALISTS

1. J. G. A. Pocock, *The Machiavellian Moment* (Princeton: Princeton University Press, 1975), "Languages and Their Implications: The Transformation of the Study of Political Thought," in his *Politics, Language and Time* (New York: Atheneum, 1971), and "Virtue and Commerce in the Eighteenth Century," *Journal of Interdisciplinary History* 3 (1972): 119–134; Gordon Wood, "Rhetoric and Reality in the American Revolution," *William and Mary Quarterly* 3d ser., 23 (1966): 3–32; and *The Creation of the American Republic, 1776–1787* (New York: W. W. Norton, [1969] 1972); Lance Banning, "Republican Ideology and the Triumph of the Constitution, 1789 to 1793," *William and Mary Quarterly* 3d ser., 31 (1974): 167–188, and *The Jeffersonian Persuasion* (Ithaca, N.Y.: Cornell University Press, 1978); Bernard Bailyn, *The Ideological Origins of the American Revolution* (Cambridge, Mass.: Harvard University Press, 1967).

2. Joyce Appleby, *Liberalism and Republicanism in the Historical Imagination* (Cambridge, Mass.: Harvard University Press, 1992), p. 3.

3. Pocock, "Virtue and Commerce in the Eighteenth Century," p. 122.

4. On this point see Peter Berger and Thomas Luckmann, *The Social Construction of Reality* (New York: Doubleday, 1966), who argue, "Man is biologically predestined to construct and inhabit a world with others. This world becomes for him the dominant and definitive reality. Its limits are set by nature, but once constructed, this world acts back upon nature . . . man produces reality and therefore himself" (p. 183).

5. Banning, "Republican Ideology and the Triumph of the Constitution," p. 173, and *The Jeffersonian Persuasion,* p. 92.

6. On this point see Pocock's *The Machiavellian Moment,* where he contends: ". . . new and dynamic forces, of government, commerce, and war, presented a universe which was effectively superseding the old but condemned the individual to inhabit a realm of fantasy, passion, and *amour-propre.* He could explain this realm, in the sense that he could identify the forces of change that were producing it; he could identify and pursue the goals proposed to him by his passions and fantasies; but he could not explain himself by locating himself as a real and rational being within it. The worlds of history and value therefore

extruded one another, and what would later be described as the alienation of man from his history had begun to be felt" (p. 466). In the language of the more recent communitarian literature, the dilemma being posed by Pocock is that of the idea of an "un-situated-self."

7. See Joyce Appleby, "Republicanism in Old and New Contexts," in her *Liberalism and Republicanism in the Historical Imagination,* p. 330.

8. Pocock, *The Machiavellian Moment,* p. viii.

9. Ibid., ch. 14.

10. Ibid., p. 548. The reader should keep in mind that the work was published in 1975.

11. Wood, *The Creation of the American Republic 1776–1787,* pp. 606–615.

12. Ibid., pp. 519–524.

13. Pocock, *The Machiavellian Moment,* pp. 526–527.

14. Ibid., p. 545.

15. See Daniel T. Rodgers, "Republicanism: The Career of a Concept," *Journal of American History* 79 (June 1992): 11–38.

16. Appleby, *Liberalism and Republicanism in the Historical Imagination,* p. 286.

17. Ibid., p. 287.

18. Ibid., p. 290.

19. Ibid.

20. Alexis de Tocqueville, *Democracy in America,* translated by George Lawrence, edited by J. P. Mayer (New York: Harper & Row, [1835] 1988), p. 478. Emphasis added.

21. For attempts to come to grips with this phenomenon and an extended discussion of the nature and structure of early American republican discourse, see George M. Dutcher, "The Rise of Republican Government in the United States," *Political Science Quarterly* 55, no. 2 (1940): 199–216; Cecelia M. Kenyon, "Republicanism and Radicalism in the American Revolution: An Old Fashion Interpretation," *William and Mary Quarterly* 3d ser., 19, no. 2 (1962): 153–182; Willi Paul Adams, "Republicanism in Political Rhetoric Before 1776," *Political Science Quarterly* 85, no. 3 (1970): 397–421; and Donald Lutz, *Popular Consent and Popular Control* (Baton Rouge: Louisiana State University Press, 1980), ch. 1.

22. Among the best discussions of this transformation from a conspiratorial perspective is Wood's *Creation of the American Republic,* where he claims: "Considering the Federalist desire for a high-toned government filled with the better sorts of people, there is something disingenuous about the democratic radicalism of their arguments, their continual emphasis on the popular character of the Constitution, their manipulation of Whig maxims, their stressing of the representational nature of all parts of the government, including the greatly strengthened executive and Senate. In effect they appropriated and exploited the language that more rightfully belonged to their opponents" (p. 562).

23. Appleby, *Liberalism and Republicanism in the Historical Imagination,* pp. 10–11.

24. For a more detailed review of the literature, the reader should see James H. Hurston, "Country, Court, and Constitution: Antifederalism and the Historians," *William and Mary Quarterly* 3d ser. 38 (July 1981): 337–368. The author also presents a very interesting argument that attempts to synthesize the competing views through the now much-used distinction between country and court, Whiggery à la Pocock.

25. George Bancroft, *History of the Formation of the Constitution of the United States of America* (New York: D. Appleton & Company, 1982), pp. 382–397; John Fiske, *The Critical Period of American History* (Boston: Houghton Mifflin, [1888] 1901), pp. 370–400; Andrew

McLaughlin, *The Confederation and the Constitution 1783–1789* (New York: Harper, 1905), pp. 289–329.

26. See Hurston, "Country, Court, and Constitution: Antifederalism and the Historians," pp. 341–343. For their views on the framers, see ch. 2 of this volume.

27. Charles E. Merriam, *A History of American Political Theories* (New York: Macmillan, 1903); J. Allen Smith, *The Spirit of American Government* (New York: Macmillan, 1907). I say "academic portrayal" because this argument, as we will see, was first made by the Anti-Federalists themselves quite frequently.

28. Vernon Louis Parrington, *Main Currents in American Thought,* vol. 1 (New York: Harcourt, Brace, 1930).

29. Hurston, "Country, Court, and Constitution: Antifederalism and the Historians," p. 344.

30. See Richard Hofstadter, *The Age of Reform* (New York: Vintage Books, 1955).

31. MacDonald's contribution was to assert with hard data that some basic economic similarities existed between the representatives of both the Federalists and the Anti-Federalists—that is, both "realty" and "personality" were represented in both groups in numbers too significant to make that distinction useful for rejecting the null hypothesis of no discernible economic differences. MacDonald's own work, however, was seriously challenged by neo-Progressive scholars like Jackson Turner Main, *The Anti-federalists* (New York: W. W. Norton, 1961); and Robert Rutland, *The Ordeal of the Constitution* (Norman: University of Oklahoma Press, 1966). Although Main's work is important in terms of the ongoing debate over the ascriptive characteristics of the Anti-Federalists as well as the Federalists, and as such is a work that has seriously called into question MacDonald's revision of the Beard thesis, it is in the end not as important for understanding Anti-Federalist political thought or ideology as is the work of Kenyon and Storing (see below). Hence I will not give the work the extended treatment it no doubt deserves here, but will simply say that on my reading of Main's text, he renders the Anti-Federalists the functional equivalent of a "liberal" interest group fighting for position and power with other such groups. The major difference between his work and that of the consensus historians, including (with reservations) MacDonald, is that his normative foundation is distinctively pro-Anti-Federalist. But this distinction does not really take Main very far from the "weak-willed liberals" thesis put forth by Kenyon; rather, it serves to reinforce that view with the amendum that the Anti-Federalists and not the Federalists are deserving of our praise.

32. Cecelia M. Kenyon, "Men of Little Faith: The Anti-Federalists on the Nature of Representative Government," *William and Mary Quarterly* 3rd ser., 12 (January 1955): 3–43. See also Benjamin Fletcher Wright, *Consensus and Continuity 1776–1787* (New York: W. W. Norton, 1958); Linda Grant DePauw, *The Eleventh Pillar* (Ithaca, N.Y.: Cornell University Press, 1966); and Clinton Rossiter, *1787* (New York: Macmillan, 1966).

33. Kenyon, "Men of Little Faith," p. 3.

34. Ibid., p. 5.

35. Ibid., pp. 21–22.

36. Ibid.

37. Ibid., p. 23.

38. Ibid., p. 35.

39. Ibid., p. 37.

40. Ibid., p. 42.

41. Ibid., p. 43.

42. Ibid.

43. The best historical discussion of this process is found in Wood's *The Creation of the American Republic,* pt. V, pp. 471–564; see also Banning, *The Jeffersonian Persuasion,* ch. 4; and Forrest MacDonald, *E Pluribus Unum* (Indianapolis: Liberty Press, 1965), ch. 7.

44. Herbert Storing, *What the Anti-Federalists Were for* (Chicago: University of Chicago Press, 1981), p. 3.

45. Ibid., p. 5.

46. Ibid., p. 6. Emphasis added.

47. Ibid., p. 72.

48. See Michael Lienesch, "In Defence of the Anti-Federalists," *History of Political Thought* 4 (February 1983): 65–87. Here the author argues in a vein similar to Storing's that the Anti-Federalists should be considered among the founding fathers, and that their teachings might be used to provide a more conservative brand of reform, one that depends more on tradition than on the modern conception of change and progress as synonymous.

49. Lutz, *Popular Consent and Popular Control,* p. 202.

50. Storing, *What the Anti-Federalists Were for,* p. 6. Emphasis added.

51. *The Jerusalem Bible: Reader's Edition* (New York: Doubleday, 1968), pp. 744–747.

52. The quote is taken from *Encyclopedia of Jewish Concepts,* edited by Philip Birnbaum (New York: Hebrew Publishing Company, 1991), p. 432. The book also informed this brief discussion.

53. Robert Bellah, Richard Madsen, William Sullivan, Ann Swindler, and Steven Tipton, *Habits of the Heart* (New York: Harper & Row, 1984), p. 153.

54. Ibid., p. 155.

55. Kramnick, *Federalist* no. 37, p. 243.

56. See Christopher Lasch, *The True and Only Heaven* (New York: W. W. Norton, 1991), p. 48.

57. "Letters of Cato," in *The Complete Anti-Federalist,* edited by Herbert J. Storing, 7 vols. (Chicago: University of Chicago Press, 1981), vol. 2, p. 107. Hereafter all citations to Anti-Federalist essays, unless otherwise noted, will be from the Storing collection, and will be cited in the following manner: Storing, name of the essayist or title given by the editor, volume:page. Thus the above item would subsequently read Storing, "Letters of Cato," 2:107.

58. Storing, "Essays by a Georgian," 5:135.

59. Storing, "Letters of Centinel," 2:171.

60. Storing, "Mercy Warren: *History of the Rise, Progress and Termination of the American Revolution,*" 6:240.

61. Storing, "A Columbian Patriot," 4:272.

62. Storing, "The Impartial Examiner," 5:184.

63. Storing, "Philadelphiensis," 3:119. Emphasis added.

64. Ibid., 3:110. Emphasis added.

65. Storing, "A Countryman," 6:82.

66. Storing, "Letters of Cato," 2:105. Emphasis added.

67. Storing, "Letters from the Federal Farmer," 2:325.

68. Storing, "Objections of the Non-Signers of the Constitution: Luther Martin," 2:61. Emphasis added.

69. Lasch, *The True and Only Heaven*, p. 47.

70. Ibid.

71. Bailyn, *The Ideological Origins of the American Revolution*, pp. 32–33, 140, 303; Wood, *The Creation of the American Republic*, pp. 7–8 and ch. 3, esp. pp. 107–124, where he talks about a Christian Sparta; Joshua Miller, *The Rise and Fall of Democracy in Early America* (University Park: Pennsylvania State University Press, 1991). See especially Ellis Sandoz, *A Government of Laws* (Baton Rouge: Louisiana State University Press, 1990); and Donald Lutz, *The Origins of American Constitutionalism* (Baton Rouge: Louisiana State University Press, 1988).

72. Andrew McLaughlin, *The Foundations of American Constitutionalism* (New York: New York University Press, 1932).

73. Edmund S. Morgan, "The Puritan Ethic in the American Revolution," *William and Mary Quarterly* 3d ser., 24 (1967): 3–43.

74. Ibid., pp. 5–6.

75. Ibid., p. 6.

76. Storing, "The Impartial Examiner," 5:187.

77. Storing, "Philadelphiensis," 3:131. Emphasis added.

78. Storing, "Letters of Agrippa," 4:90.

79. Storing, "Mercy Warren," 6:241.

80. Lasch, *The True and Only Heaven*, p. 47.

81. See Michael Lienesch, *New Order of the Ages* (Princeton: Princeton University Press, 1988), p. 141.

82. Sheldon Wolin, "Montesquieu and Publius: The Crisis of Reason and *The Federalist Papers*," in his *The Presence of the Past* (Baltimore: Johns Hopkins University Press, 1990), p. 109.

83. Lasch, *The True and Only Heaven*, p. 47. The reader should be aware that the general narrative drawn from Lasch in this section is not specifically directed at the discussion for which it is being used here.

84. For an interesting discussion of the Anti-Federalists and Federalists in light of contemporary arguments over modernity and postmodernity, where the Anti-Federalists are described as modern and the Federalists as postmodern, see Fredrick M. Dolan, "Anti-Federalist Hermenutics; or, The American Critique of Reason," paper delivered at American Political Science Association's annual meeting, Washington, D.C., 1991.

85. Ibid., pp. 47–48.

86. Wolin, "Montesquieu and Publius: The Crisis of Reason and *The Federalist Papers*," pp. 109–110.

87. Storing, "Letters of Cato," 2:105–106.

88. Matthew 5:22–23.

89. Matthew 5:14–16.

90. Douglass Adair, "Fame and the Founding Fathers," in *Fame and the Founding Fathers*, edited by Trevor Colbourne (New York: W. W. Norton, 1974), p. 9.

91. Ibid., pp. 10–11.

92. Ibid., p. 9.

93. Ibid., pp. 9, 10.

94. Matthew 6:1.

95. Storing, "Speeches by Melancton Smith," 6:152.

96. Storing, "Essay by Samuel," 4:196.

97. Niccolo Machiavelli, *The Prince,* translated by George Bull (New York: Penguin, 1982), p. 133.

98. Wood, *The Creation of the American Republic,* p. 114.

99. Ibid., p. 115.

100. Ibid., p. 117.

101. Storing, "Essays by a Farmer," 5:16–17.

102. Storing, "Essays by Cincinnatus," 6:20. Emphasis added.

103. Storing, "Letters from the Federal Farmer," 2:329.

104. Storing, "Letters of Centinel," 2:196.

105. Storing, "The Impartial Examiner," 5:175.

106. Storing, "Essays by a Farmer," 5:17.

107. Storing, "The Impartial Examiner," 5:175. Emphasis added.

108. On the use of this language see Wood, *The Creation of the American Republic,* pp. 118–124.

109. On this point of contention see Storing, "Letters from the Federal Farmer," 2:258–259; "Essays by Candidus," 4:136; "A Countryman," 6:75–76; "The Impartial Examiner," 5:191; "Luther Martin," 2:47; and "Melancton Smith," 6:151.

110. Storing, "Essays by Vox Populi," 4:51. Emphasis in the original.

111. Storing, "A Countryman," 6:83–84.

112. Storing, "Mr. Martin's Information to the General Assembly of the State of Maryland," 2:42. Emphasis in the original.

113. Although a constant theme of the *Papers,* see *Federalist* no. 15 as a good example. Hamilton writes: ". . . there are material imperfections in our national system and that something ought to be done to rescue us from impending anarchy."

114. Storing, "Essay by Cornelius," 4:140. Emphasis added.

115. Storing, "Letters of a Republican Federalist," 4:173.

116. Storing, "Essay by Samuel," 4:196.

117. J. Peter Euben, "The Battle of Salamis and the Origins of Political Theory," *Political Theory* 14, no. 3 (1986): 360.

118. Peter L. Berger, *Pyramids of Sacrifice* (New York: Anchor Books, 1976), p. 128.

119. Storing, "Address by A Plebeian," 6:131.

120. Ibid.

121. Ibid.

122. Storing, "Letters of Agrippa," 4:74.

123. Storing, "Essays by Candidus," 4:125.

124. Storing, "Essay by Alfred," 3:142.

125. Storing, "Speeches of Patrick Henry in the Virginia State Ratifying Convention," 5:220.

126. Storing, "Speech of William Findley in the Pennsylvania Assembly," 3:8.

127. Storing, "Essay of an Old Whig," 3:30.

128. Storing, "Letters from the Federal Farmer," 2:226.

129. Storing, "Letters of Centinel," 2:143.

130. Storing, "Essay of an Old Whig," 3:21.

131. Storing, "Essays by the Impartial Examiner," 5:188. Emphasis added.

132. Storing, "Address by a Plebeian," 6:140.

133. Houston Baker, Jr., *Modernism and the Harlem Renaissance* (Chicago: University of Chicago Press, 1987), ch. 1.

134. See Leo Strauss, *The City and Man* (Chicago: University of Chicago Press, 1964), and *Persecution and the Art of Writing* (Chicago: University of Chicago Press, [1952] 1988).

135. Storing, "Essays by the Impartial Examiner," 5:186.

136. Storing, "Letters of Centinel," 2:155.

137. Ibid., 2:158.

138. Storing, "Reply to Medium by a Citizen," 6:45–46.

139. Storing, "Samuel Chase: Notes of Speeches Delivered to the Maryland Ratifying Convention," 5:81.

140. Storing, "Letters of Centinel," 2:155.

141. Storing, "Mercy Warren," 6:240–241.

142. Storing, "Letters of Centinel," 2:154–155.

143. Storing, "Patrick Henry," 5:237.

144. Storing, "Address by Sydney," 6:108.

145. Storing, "Luther Martin," 2:26.

146. Storing, "Letters of Centinel," 2:164.

147. Storing, "Letters of Cato," 2:107.

148. Ibid., 2:105.

149. Storing, "Address by Denatus," 5:261.

150. Storing, "Letters of Centinel," 2:137–138; and "The Yeomanry of Massachusetts," 4:224.

151. Storing, "Essay by a Georgian," 5:129–130.

152. Storing, "Letters of Centinel," 2:186.

153. See Storing, "Samuel Chase: Notes of Speeches Delivered to the Maryland Ratifying Convention," 5:79–91, and "Address of a Minority of the Maryland Ratifying Convention," 5:92–100, as well as "A Letter from a Gentleman in a Neighboring State, to a Gentleman in this City," 4:7–14.

154. Storing, "Letters of Agrippa," 4:107.

155. See Michael J. Sandel, *Liberalism and the Limits of Justice* (Cambridge: Cambridge University Press, 1982); and John Rawls, *A Theory of Justice* (Cambridge, Mass.: Harvard University Press, 1971).

156. This distinction can be made plain by looking at organized labor, which prides itself on solidarity, which is the product of a shared interest where I worry about you because what happens to you may happen to me; thus "We are all in this together" is the rallying cry. On the other hand, fraternity, as embodied in a "family" anchored by love, is better understood through the trope of mutual regard, affection, or caring rather than interest; thus the rallying cry might be "What do you need?"

157. Storing, "Letters of Cato," 2:112.

158. Wolin, *The Presence of the Past,* p. 86.

159. Storing, "Notes of Speeches Given by George Clinton Before the New York State Ratifying Convention," 6:188.

160. Storing, "Patrick Henry," 5:231–232.

161. Berger, *Pyramids of Sacrifice,* pp. 129–130.

162. Storing, "Essay by Cornelius," 4:141–142.

163. Storing, "Letters from the Federal Farmer," 2:345.

164. Storing, "The Government of Nature Delineated; or, An Exact Picture of the Federal Constitution by Aristocrotis," 3:202.

165. Storing, "Patrick Henry," 5:235.

166. Storing, "Essays by a Farmer," 5:62.

167. Wolin, *The Presence of the Past,* p. 87. Emphasis added.

168. Storing, "Essays by a Farmer," 5:65.

169. Storing, "Luther Martin," 2:46. Emphasis in the original.

170. Storing, "Letters of Agrippa," 4:94.

171. Storing, "Letters of Cato," 2:110. Emphasis in the original.

172. Storing, "Essays by a Farmer," 5:31.

173. Storing, "Essay of an Old Whig," 3:35.

174. Brutus, Jr., claims that "in Boston, the printers have refused to print against this plan, and have been countenanced in it. In Connecticut, papers have been handed about for people to sign, to support it, and the names of those who declined signing it, have been taken down in what was called, a black list, to intimidate them, into compliance" (Storing, "Essay by Brutus, Jr.," 6:40).

175. Storing, "Essays by a Farmer," 5:36. Emphasis in the original.

176. Storing, "Letters of Agrippa," 4:94.

177. Ibid.

178. Storing, "James Monroe: Some Observations on the Constitution," 5:286.

179. Ibid.

180. Storing, "Letters of Cato," 2:112. It should be acknowledged that Cato was perhaps a bit more extreme in his line of argument on this particular theme than his Anti-Federalist brethren; he went so far as to suggest that "the extent of many of the states in the Union, is at this time, almost too great for the superintendence of a republican form of government, and must one day or other, evolve into more vigorous ones, or by separation be reduced into smaller" (2:111).

181. Storing, "Letters from the Federal Farmer," 2:249.

182. Ibid., 2:320.

183. Ibid., 2:249.

184. Storing, "Essay of a Democratic Federalist," 3:60.

185. Ibid., 3:61.

186. Storing, "Essays of Brutus," 2:396–397.

187. See chapter 1 this volume.

188. Storing, "George Mason's Objections to the Constitution of Government Formed by the Convention," 2:11.

189. Storing, "Address by Cato Uticensis," 5:124.

190. Storing, "Letters of Centinel," 2:192.

191. Storing, "Essay by Alfred," 3:143.

192. Storing, "A Friend of the Republic: Anti-Federalist No. 2," 4:244.

193. Storing, "A Countryman from Dutchess County," 6:64–65.

194. Storing, "Essays by a Farmer," 4:207.

195. Storing, "Letters of Agrippa," 4:71.

196. Hannah Arendt, *On Revolution* (New York: Penguin, 1965), p. 130.

197. Storing, "Letters from the Federal Farmer," 2:291.

198. Storing, "Speeches by Melancton Smith," 6:165.

199. Storing, "Essay of an Old Whig," 3:44.

CONCLUSION: FRUITFUL HERESY

1. Claude G. Bowers, *Jefferson and Hamilton* (Boston: Houghton Mifflin, [1925] 1966), p. 511.

2. Thomas Jefferson, *Notes on the State of Virginia,* in *The Portable Thomas Jefferson,* edited by Merrill D. Peterson (New York: Penguin, 1988), p. 217.

3. Thomas Jefferson, "First Inaugural Address," in ibid., p. 293.

4. Thomas Jefferson, "Second Inaugural Address," in ibid., p. 318.

5. See Joyce Appleby, "What Is Still American in the Political Philosophy of Thomas Jefferson," in her *Liberalism and Republicanism in the Historical Imagination* (Cambridge, Mass.: Harvard University Press, 1992).

6. This is the argument made by David P. Szatmary in his book *Shays' Rebellion* (Amherst: University of Massachusetts Press, 1980), and I think it is the right one. His well-supported claim—"As they [the Shaysites] began to perceive the government as tyrannical, some rebels became more conscious of their group identity. Opposing a ruthless, commercially oriented government, they became more and more aware of the need for agrarian solidarity to protect their common way of life" (p. 96)—goes quite far in establishing the rebellion as a resistance movement against the rapidly, and sometimes violently, encroaching Hamiltonian world.

7. See Drew McCoy, *The Elusive Republic* (Chapel Hill: University of North Carolina Press, 1980); and Lance Banning, *The Jeffersonian Persuasion* (Ithaca, N.Y.: Cornell University Press, 1978).

8. Alexander Hamilton, *Report on Manufactures* (1791), in *Political Thought in America,* edited by Michael B. Levy (Chicago: Dorsey Press, 1988), p. 107. Emphasis added.

9. Thomas Jefferson, "Letter to John Bannister, Jr.," in ibid., p. 68.

10. Thomas Jefferson, "Letter to James Madison," in ibid., pp. 69–70.

11. Jefferson, *Notes on the State of Virginia,* p. 217.

12. Thomas Jefferson, "Letter to John Trumbull (1789)," in *The Portable Thomas Jefferson,* pp. 434–435.

13. Alexis de Tocqueville, *Democracy in America,* translated by George Lawrence, edited by J. P. Mayer (New York: Harper & Row, [1835] 1988), ch. 5.

14. This is an occasional Anti-Federalist reference to the Constitution.

15. "Speeches of Rawlins Lowndes in the South Carolina Legislature," in Herbert J. Storing ed., *The Complete Anti-Federalist* (Chicago: University of Chicago Press, 1981), 5:157.

16. C. Wright Mills, *The Power Elite* (Oxford: Oxford University Press, 1956), p. 3.

17. Robert Nisbet, *The Quest for Community* (San Francisco: ICS Press, [1953] 1990), p. 3.

18. Horatio Alger, *Ragged Dick and Mark, the Match Boy* (New York: Collier Books, 1962), pp. 214–215.

19. Ibid., pp. 215–216.

20. Hannah Arendt, *The Human Condition* (Chicago: University of Chicago Press, 1958), p. 58.

21. Philip Abbott, *Seeking Many Inventions* (Knoxville: University of Tennessee Press, 1987), p. 175.

22. Although the *Port Huron Statement* was the product of SDS, its principal author was Tom Hayden. The copy that I am working from is excerpted in Levy, *Political Thought in America,* p. 463.

23. Ibid.

24. Ibid.

25. Ibid., p. 466.

26. Kirkpatrick Sale, *Human Scale* (New York: Coward, McCann & Geoghegan, 1980), pp. 55–61.

27. Ibid., p. 521.

Bibliography

Abbott, Philip. *Seeking Many Inventions: The Idea of Community in America.* Knoxville: University of Tennessee Press, 1987.

———. *The Exemplary Presidency: Franklin D. Roosevelt and the American Political Tradition.* Amherst: University of Massachusetts Press, 1990.

Ackerman, Bruce. *We the People: Foundations.* Cambridge, Mass.: Harvard University Press, 1992.

Adair, Douglass. "Fame and the Founding Fathers" and "The Tenth Federalist Revisited." In *Fame and the Founding Fathers: Essays by Douglass Adair.* Edited by Trevor Colbourne. New York: W. W. Norton, 1974.

Adams, Willi Paul. "Republicanism in Political Rhetoric Before 1776." *Political Science Quarterly* 85, no. 3 (1970): 397–421.

———. *The First American Constitutions: Republican Ideology and the Making of the States' Constitutions in the Revolutionary Era.* Chapel Hill: University of North Carolina Press, 1980.

Aeschylus. *The Orestes Plays of Aeschylus.* Translated by Paul Roche. New York: Mentor, 1962.

Alger, Horatio. *Ragged Dick and Mark, the Match Boy.* New York: Collier Books, 1962.

Allen, J. W. *The History of Political Thought in the Sixteenth Century.* New York: L. MacVeagh, The Dial Press, Inc., 1928.

Ames, Fisher. "Dangers of American Liberty." In *Works of Fisher Ames,* vol. 2. Edited by Seth Ames. New York: Burt Franklin, 1971.

Appleby, Joyce. *Liberalism and Republicanism in the Historical Imagination.* Cambridge, Mass.: Harvard University Press, 1992.

Arendt, Hannah. *The Human Condition.* Chicago: University of Chicago Press, 1958.

———. *On Revolution.* New York: Penguin, 1965.

———. *On Violence.* New York: Harcourt Brace Jovanovich, 1969.

Armstrong, E. "The Political Theory of the Huguenots." *English Historical Review* 4 (January 1889): 13–40.

Ashcraft, Richard. "Revolutionary Politics and *Locke's Two Treatises of Government:* Radicalism and Lockean Political Theory." *Political Theory* 8, no. 4 (November 1980): 429–485.

———. *Revolutionary Politics and Locke's Two Treatises of Government.* Princeton: Princeton University Press, 1986.

Augustine, St. *Concerning the City of God Against the Pagans.* Trans. Henry Bettenson. Harmondsworth: Penguin, 1984.

Bailyn, Bernard. *Pamphlets of the American Revolution,* 2 vols. Cambridge, Mass.: Harvard University Press, 1965.

———. *The Ideological Origins of the American Revolution.* (Cambridge, Mass.: Harvard University Press, 1967.

Baker, Houston, Jr. *Modernism and the Harlem Renaissance*. Chicago: University of Chicago Press, 1987.

Bancroft, George. *History of the Formation of the Constitution of the United States of America*. New York: D. Appelton and Company, 1882.

Banning, Lance. "Republican Ideology and the Triumph of the Constitution, 1789 to 1793." *William and Mary Quarterly* 3d ser., 31 (1974): 167–188.

———. *The Jeffersonian Persuasion: Evolution of a Party Ideology*. Ithaca, N.Y.: Cornell University Press, 1978.

Barber, Benjamin. *Strong Democracy: Participatory Politics for a New Age*. Berkeley: University of California Press, 1984.

———. *The Conquest of Politics: Liberal Philosophy in Democratic Times*. Princeton: Princeton University Press, 1988.

Barker, Ernest. "The Authorship of the *Vinidiciae Contra Tyrannos*." *Cambridge Historical Journal* 3, no. 2 (1930): 164–181.

———. *Church, State and Study*. London: Methuen, 1930.

Beard, Charles A. *An Economic Interpretation of the Constitution of the United States*. New York: Free Press, [1913] 1986.

Becker, Carl. *The Declaration of Independence*. New York: Harcourt, Brace, 1922.

Bellah, Robert, Richard Madsen, William Sullivan, Ann Swindler, and Steven Tipton. *Habits of the Heart: Individualism and Commitment in American Life*. New York: Harper & Row, 1984.

Benda, Julien. *The Treason of the Intellectuals*. New York: W. W. Norton, [1928] 1956.

Berger, Peter L. *Pyramids of Sacrifice*. New York: Anchor Books, 1976.

Berger, Peter, and Thomas Luckmann. *The Social Construction of Reality*. New York: Doubleday, 1966.

Berns, Walter. *Taking the Constitution Seriously*. New York: Simon & Schuster, 1987.

Birnbaum, Philip, ed. *Encyclopedia of Jewish Concepts*. New York: Hebrew Publishing Company, 1991.

Boorstin, Daniel. *The Genius of American Politics*. Chicago: University of Chicago Press, 1953.

———. "Our Unspoken National Faith: Why Americans Need No Ideology." *Commentary* 15, no. 4 (April 1953): 327–337.

Bowers, Claude G. *Jefferson and Hamilton*. Boston: Houghton Mifflin, [1925] 1966.

Brinton, Crane. *The Anatomy of Revolution*. New York: Vintage, 1938.

Brown, Robert E. *Middle-Class Democracy and the Revolution in Massachusetts*. Ithaca, N.Y.: Cornell University Press, 1955.

———. *Charles Beard and the Constitution*. Princeton: Princeton University Press, 1956.

Bruell, Christopher. "A Return to Classical Political Philosophy and the Understanding of the American Founding." *Review of Politics* 53, no. 1 (Winter 1991): 173–186.

Brutus, Stephen Junius. *A Defense of Liberty Against Tyrants*. Translated by Julian Franklin. New York: Pegasus, [1579] 1969.

Burke, Kenneth. *The Philosophy of Literary Form: Studies in Symbolic Action*. Berkeley: University of California Press, 1974.

Calvin, John. *The Institutes of the Christian Religion*. Chicago: Henry Regency Company, [1536] 1949.

DePauw, Linda Grant. *The Eleventh Pillar: New York State and the Federal Constitution*. Ithaca, N.Y.: Cornell University Press, 1966.

Diamond, Martin. "Democracy and *The Federalist:* A Reconsideration of the Framers' Intent." *American Political Science Review* 53, no. 1 (March 1959): 52–68.

Diggins, John P. *The Lost Soul of American Politics: Virtue, Self-Interest, and the Foundations of Liberalism.* Chicago: University of Chicago Press, 1984.

———. "Consciousness and Ideology in American History: The Burden of Daniel J. Boorstin." *American Historical Review* 76 (1971): 99–118.

———. "Comrades and Citizens: New Mythologies in American Historiography." *American Historical Review* 90 (June 1985): 614–649.

Dolan, Fredrick M. "Anti-Federalist Hermenutics; or, the American Critique of Reason." Unpublished paper delivered at American Political Science Association's annual meeting. Washington, D.C., 1991.

Douglass, E. P. *Rebels and Democrats: The Struggle for Equal Rights and Majority Rule During the Revolution.* Chapel Hill: University of North Carolina Press, 1955.

Duncan, Christopher M. "Tyrants and Witches in the American Cold War as Seen by Arthur Miller." *Michigan Journal of Political Science* no. 14 (1991–1992): 1–17.

Dunn, John. *The Political Thought of John Locke.* Cambridge: Cambridge University Press, 1969.

Durant, Will, and Ariel Durant. *The Age of Reformation.* New York: Simon & Schuster, 1957.

Durkheim, Emile. *Suicide.* Glencoe, Ill.: Free Press, [1897] 1951.

Dutcher, George M. "The Rise of Republican Government in the United States." *Political Science Quarterly* 55, no. 2 (1940): 199–216.

Ebenstein, William, ed. *Great Political Thinkers: Plato to the Present,* 4th ed. New York: Holt, Rinehart and Winston, 1969.

Edwards, David. *The American Political Experience.* Englewood Cliffs, N.J.: Prentice Hall, 1988.

Elkins, Stanley, and Eric McKitrick. "The Founding Fathers: Young Men of the Revolution." *Political Science Quarterly* 76, no. 2 (1961): 181–216.

Elton, G. R. *The Body of the Whole Realm: Parliament and Representation in Medieval and Tudor England.* Charlottesville: University Press of Virginia, 1969.

Epstein, David F. *The Political Theory of the Federalist.* Chicago: University of Chicago Press, 1984.

Erikson, Erik. *Young Man Luther.* New York: W. W. Norton, 1958.

Euben, J. Peter. "The Battle of Salamis and the Origins of Political Theory." *Political Theory* 14, no. 3 (August 1986): 359–390.

Fallon, Richard H., Jr. "What Is Republicanism and Is It Worth Reviving?" *Harvard Law Review* 102 (1989): 1695–1735.

Farrand, Max, ed. *The Records of the Constitutional Convention 1787.* 4 vols. New York: W. W. Norton, [1911] 1974.

Fiske, John. *The Critical Period of American History, 1783–1789.* Boston: Houghton Mifflin, [1888] 1901.

Ganter, Herbert Lawrence. "Jefferson's *Pursuit of Happiness* and Some Forgotten Men." *William and Mary Quarterly* 2nd ser., 16, no. 3 (1936): 422–434; no. 4 (1936): 558–585.

Geertz, Clifford. *Interpretation of Cultures.* New York: Basic Books, 1973.

Grazia, Sebastian de. *The Political Community: A Study of Anomie.* Chicago: University of Chicago Press, 1948.

Greene, Jack P. *The Quest for Power: The Lower Houses of Assembly in the Southern Royal Colonies, 1689–1776*. Chapel Hill: University of North Carolina Press, 1963.

Hall, David. *The Antinomian Controversy 1636–1638*. Middletown, Conn.: Wesleyan University Press, 1968.

Hamowy, Ronald. "Jefferson and the Scottish Enlightenment: A Critique of Garry Wills's *Inventing America: Jefferson's Declaration of Independence*." *William and Mary Quarterly* 3d ser., 36, no. 4 (1979): 503–523.

Hanson, Russell L. *The Democratic Imagination in America: Conversations with Our Past*. Princeton: Princeton University Press, 1985.

Harlow, Barbara. *Resistance Literature*. New York: Methuen, 1980.

Hartz, Louis. *The Liberal Tradition in America*. New York: Harcourt Brace Jovanovich, [1955] 1983.

Herzog, Don. "Some Questions for Republicans." *Political Theory* 14, no. 3 (August 1986): 473–494.

Hobbes, Thomas. *Leviathan*. New York: Liberal Arts Press, 1958.

Hoffert, Robert W. *A Politics of Tension: The Articles of Confederation and American Political Ideas*. Boulder: University of Colorado Press, 1992.

Hofstadter, Richard. *The American Political Tradition and the Men Who Made It*. New York: Vintage Books, [1948] 1974.

———. *The Age of Reform*. New York: Vintage Books, 1955.

———. *The Progressive Historians: Turner, Beard, Parrington*. New York: Knopf, 1968.

Horwitz, Morton J. "History and Theory." *Yale Law Journal* 96 (1987): 1825–1835.

———. "Republicanism and Liberalism in American Constitutional Thought." *William and Mary Law Review* 29 (1987): 57–74.

Huntington, Samuel. *Political Order in Changing Societies*. New Haven: Yale University Press, 1968.

Hurston, James H. "Country, Court, and Constitution: Antifederalism and the Historians." *William and Mary Quarterly* 3d ser., 38 (July 1981): 337–368.

Hyneman, Charles S., and Donald S. Lutz, eds. *American Political Writing During the Founding Era, 1760–1805*, 2 vols. Indianapolis: Liberty Press, 1983.

Jacobitti, Suzanne D. "Individualism and Political Community: Arendt and Tocqueville on the Current Debate in Liberalism." *Polity* 23, no. 4 (1991): 585–604.

Janda, Kenneth, Jeffrey Berry, and Jerry Goldman. *The Challenge of Democracy*. Boston: Houghton Mifflin, 1991.

Jefferson, Thomas. *The Portable Thomas Jefferson*. Ed. Merrill D. Peterson. New York: Penguin, 1988.

Jensen, Merrill. *The Articles of Confederation*. Madison: University of Wisconsin Press, 1940.

———. "The Idea of a National Government During the American Revolution." *Political Science Quarterly* 58, no. 3 (1943): 356–379.

———. *The New Nation: A History of the United States During the Confederation, 1781–1789*. New York: Alfred A. Knopf, 1950.

John of Salisbury. *Policraticus: The Statesmen's Handbook*. Ed. Murray F. Markland. New York: Unger, 1979.

Kammen, Michael. *Deputyes and Libertyes: The Origins of Representative Government in Colonial America*. New York: Alfred A. Knopf, 1969.

Keefe, William, Henry J. Abraham, William Flanigan, Charles O. Jones, Morris S. Ogul, and John W. Spanier. *American Democracy*. New York: Harper & Row, 1990.

Kenyon, Cecelia M. "Men of Little Faith: The Anti-Federalists on the Nature of Representative Government." *William and Mary Quarterly* 3rd ser., 12 (January 1955): 3–43.

———. "Republicanism and Radicalism in the American Revolution: An Old Fashion Interpretation." *William and Mary Quarterly* 3rd ser., 19 (1962): 153–182.

Kessler, Sanford. "Tocqueville's Puritans: Christianity and the American Founding." *Journal of Politics* 54, no. 3 (August 1992): 776–792.

Kohn, Richard H. *Eagle and Sword: The Beginnings of the Military Establishment in America.* New York: Free Press, 1975.

Kramnick, Issac. "Republican Revisionism Revisited." *American Historical Review* 87, no. 3 (1982): 629–664.

Kramnick, Isaac, ed. *The Federalist Papers* by Madison, Hamilton, and Jay. New York: Penguin Books, [1788] 1988.

Kuhn, Thomas. *The Structure of Scientific Revolutions.* Chicago: University of Chicago Press, 1962.

Kundera, Milan. *The Unbearable Lightness of Being.* New York: Harper & Row, 1984.

Ladd, Everret Carll. *The American Polity.* New York: W. W. Norton, 1987.

Lasch, Christopher. *The True and Only Heaven: Progress and Its Critics.* New York: W. W. Norton, 1991.

Lerner, Ralph. *The Thinking Revolutionary.* Ithaca, N.Y.: Cornell University Press, 1987.

Levy, Michael B. ed. *Political Thought in America,* 2nd ed. Chicago: Dorsey Press, 1988.

Lewis, Ewart. "The Contribution of Medieval Thought to the American Political Tradition." *American Political Science Review* 50, no. 2 (December 1956): 462–474.

Lienesch, Michael. "In Defence of the Anti-Federalists." *History of Political Thought* 4 (February 1983): 65–87.

———. *New Order of the Ages: Time, the Constitution, and the Making of Modern American Political Thought.* Princeton: Princeton University Press, 1988.

Locke, John. *The Second Treatise of Government.* Indianapolis: Bobbs-Merrill, [1690] 1952.

Lutz, Donald S. *Popular Consent and Popular Control.* Baton Rouge: Louisiana State University Press, 1980.

———. "The Relative Influence of European Writers on Late Eighteenth-Century American Political Thought." *American Political Science Review* 78, no. 1 (1984): 189–197.

———. *The Origins of American Constitutionalism.* Baton Rouge: Louisiana State University Press, 1988.

Machiavelli, Niccolo. *The Prince.* Translated by George Bull. New York: Penguin, 1982.

MacDonald, Forrest. *We the People: The Economic Origins of the Constitution.* Chicago: University of Chicago Press, 1958.

———. *E Pluribus Unum: The Formation of the American Republic 1776–1790.* Indianapolis: Liberty Press, 1965.

———. *Novus Ordo Seclorum: The Intellectual Origins of the Constitution.* Lawrence: University Press of Kansas, 1985.

Macphearson, C. B. *The Political Theory of Possessive Individualism: Hobbes to Locke.* Oxford: Oxford University Press, 1962.

MacWilliams, Wilson Carey. *The Idea of Fraternity in America.* Berkeley: University of California Press, 1973.

Madison, James, Alexander Hamilton, and John Jay. *The Federalist Papers.* Ed. Isaac Kramnick. New York: Penguin Books, [1788] 1988.

Maier, Pauline. "John Wilkes and American Disillusionment with Britain." *William and*

Mary Quarterly 3d ser., 20 (July 1963): 373–395.

———. *Resistance to Revolution*. New York: Vintage, 1974.

Main, Jackson Turner. *The Antifederalists: Critics of the Constitution 1781–1788*. New York: W. W. Norton, 1974.

———. *The Upper House in Revolutionary America, 1763–1788*. Madison: University of Wisconsin Press, 1967.

———. *The Sovereign States, 1775–1783*. Madison: University of Wisconsin Press, 1973.

Mansbridge, Jane J. *Beyond Adversary Democracy*. Chicago: Chicago University Press, 1983.

Matson, Cathy D., and Peter S. Onuf. *A Union of Interests: Political and Economic thought in Revolutionary America*. Lawrence: University Press of Kansas, 1990.

McCoy, Drew. *The Elusive Republic: Political Economy in Jeffersonian America*. Chapel Hill: University of North Carolina Press, 1980.

McLaughlin, Andrew. *The Confederation and the Constitution 1783–1789*. New York: Harper, 1905.

———. *The Foundations of American Constitutionalism*. New York: New York University Press, 1932.

McNeill, J. T. *The History and Character of Calvinism*. New York: Oxford University Press, 1954.

Meilaender, Gilbert. "A View from Somewhere: The Political Thought of Michael Walzer." *Religious Studies Review* 16, no.3 (July 1990): 197–201.

Merriam, Charles E. *A History of American Political Theories*. New York: Macmillan, 1903.

Michelman, Frank I. "Forward: Traces of Self-Government." *Harvard Law Review* 100, no. 4 (1986): 4–77.

———. "Law's Republic." *Yale Law Journal* 97, no. 8 (July 1988): 1493–1537.

Miller, Joshua. *The Rise and Fall of Democracy in Early America, 1630–1789*. University Park: Pennsylvania State University Press, 1991.

Miller, Perry. "The Marrow of Puritan Divinity." *Publications of the Massachusetts Historical Society* 32 (1937): 247–300.

Mills, C. Wright. *The Power Elite*. Oxford: Oxford University Press, 1956.

Montesquieu, "The Spirit of the Laws." [1748]. In *Great Political Thinkers: Plato to the Present*, 4th ed. Ed. William Ebenstein. New York: Holt, Rinehart & Winston, 1969.

Morgan, Edmund S. "The Case Against Anne Hutchinson." *New England Quarterly* 10, no. 4 (1937): 635–649.

———. *The Birth of the Republic 1763–89*. Chicago: University of Chicago Press, 1956.

———. *The Puritan Dilemma*. New York: Little Brown, 1958.

———. *Visible Saints*. New York: New York University Press, 1963.

———. *Puritan Political Ideas: 1588–1784*. Indianapolis: Bobbs-Merrill, 1965.

———. "The Puritan Ethic in the American Revolution." *William and Mary Quarterly* 3d ser., 24 (January 1967): 3–43.

———. *Inventing the People: The Rise of Popular Sovereignty in England and America*. New York: W. W. Norton, 1988.

Nevins, Allan. *The American States During and After the Revolution, 1775–1789*. New York: Macmillan, 1924.

Nisbet, Robert. *The Quest for Community: A Study in the Ethics of Order and Freedom*. San Francisco: ICS Press, [1953] 1990.

Oakeshott, Michael. "Rationalism in Politics." In his *Rationalism in Politics and Other Essays*.

Indianapolis: Liberty Press, 1991.

Onuf, Peter S. *The Origin of the Federal Republic: Jurisdictional Controversies in the United States, 1775–1787*. Philadelphia: University of Pennsylvania Press, 1983.

———. *Statehood and Union: A History of the Northwest Ordinance*. Bloomington: Indiana University Press, 1987.

Paine, Thomas. *The Thomas Paine Reader*. Edited by Michael Foot and Isaac Kramnick. New York: Penguin, 1987.

Pangle, Thomas L. *The Spirit of Modern Republicanism*. Chicago: University of Chicago Press, 1988.

Parrington, Vernon Louis. *Main Currents in American Thought*, vol. 1. New York: Harcourt, Brace, 1930.

Peterson, Merrill D., ed. *The Portable Thomas Jefferson*. New York: Penguin, 1988.

Pettit, Norman. *The Heart Prepared*. New Haven: Yale University Press, 1966.

Pitkin, Hannah Fenichel. *The Concept of Representation*. Berkeley: University of California Press, 1967.

———. "Justice: On Relating Private and Public." *Political Theory* 9, no. 3 (August 1981): 327–352.

Plato. *The Republic*. Trans. Allan Bloom. New York: Basic Books, 1968.

Pocock, J. G. A. "Machiavelli, Harrington, and English Political Ideologies in the Eighteenth Century." *William and Mary Quarterly* 3d ser., 22 (October 1965): 549–583.

———. "Languages and Their Implications: The Transformation of the Study of Political Thought." In his *Politics, Language and Time: Essays on Political Thought and History*. New York: Atheneum, 1971.

———. "Virtue and Commerce in the Eighteenth Century." *Journal of Interdisciplinary History* 3 (1972): 119–134.

———. *The Machiavellian Moment*. Princeton: Princeton University Press, 1975.

———. "Virtues, Rights, and Manners: A Model for Historians of Political Thought." *Political Theory* 9, no. 3 (August 1981): 353–368.

———. *Virtue, Commerce, and History: Essays on Political Thought and History. Chiefly in the Eighteenth Century*. Cambridge: Cambridge University Press, 1985.

———. "Between Gog and Magog: The Republican Thesis and the *Ideologia Americana*." *Journal of the History of Ideas* 48, no. 2 (1987): 325–346.

Pole, J. R. *Political Representation in England and the Origins of the American Republic*. London: Macmillan, 1966.

———. *The Seventeenth Century: The Sources of Legislative Power*. Charlottesville: University Press of Virginia, 1969.

Randall, John Herman, Jr. *The Making of the Modern Mind*. New York: Columbia University Press, [1926] 1976.

Richardson, Fredrick L. "Early American Political Authority, 1773–1778." Ph.D. dissertation, Brandeis University, 1973.

Robbins, Caroline. *The Eighteenth-Century Commonwealthman: Studies in the Transmission, Development, and Circumstances of English Liberal Thought from the Restoration of Charles II Until the War with the Thirteen Colonies*. Cambridge, Mass.: Harvard University Press, 1959.

Roche, John P. "The Founding Fathers: A Reform Caucus in Action." *American Political Science Review* 55, no. 4 (December 1961): 799–816.

Rodgers, Daniel T. "Republicanism: The Career of a Concept." *Journal of American History*

79, no. 1 (June 1992): 11–38.

Rossiter, Clinton. *1787: The Grand Convention*. New York: Macmillan 1966.

Rousseau, Jean-Jacques. *The Social Contract*. Translated by Maurice Cranston. New York: Penguin, 1983.

Rutland, Robert. *The Ordeal of the Constitution: The Anti-Federalists and the Ratification Struggle of 1787–1788*. Norman: University of Oklahoma Press, 1966.

Sale, Kirkpatrick. *Human Scale*. New York: Coward, McCann & Geoghegan, 1980.

Sandoz, Ellis. *A Government of Laws: Political Theory, Religion, and the American Founding*. Baton Rouge: Louisiana State University Press, 1990.

Sartre, Jean-Paul. *Being and Nothingness*. Trans. Hazel Barnes. New York: Washington Square Press, 1956.

Schaar, John. "Liberty/Authority/Community in the Political Thought of John Winthrop." *Political Theory* 19, no. 4 (November 1991): 493–518.

Schlesinger, Arthur M. "The Lost Meaning of 'The Pursuit of Happiness.' " *William and Mary Quarterly* 3d ser., 21 (July 1964): 325–327.

Shalhope, Robert E. "Republicanism and Early American Historiography." *William and Mary Quarterly* 3d ser., 39 (April 1982): 334–356.

Sherry, Suzanna. "Civic Virtue and the Feminine Voice in Constitutional Adjudication." *Virginia Law Review* 72 (1986): 543–616.

Smith, Edward C., ed. *The Constitution of the United States: Case Summaries*, 11th ed. New York: Barnes & Noble, 1974.

Smith, J. Allen. *The Spirit of American Government*. New York: Macmillan 1907.

Smith, Page. *The Constitution: A Documentary and Narrative History*. New York: Quill Paperbacks, 1980.

Steiner, George. *In Bluebeard's Castle: Some Notes Towards the Redefinition of Culture*. New Haven: Yale University Press, 1970.

Storing, Herbert J. *What the Anti-Federalists Were for*. Chicago: University of Chicago Press, 1981.

———, ed. *The Complete Anti-Federalists*, 7 vols. Chicago: University of Chicago Press, 1981.

Strauss, Leo. *Natural Right and History*. Chicago: University of Chicago Press, 1950.

———. *Persecution and the Art of Writing*. Chicago: University of Chicago Press, 1952.

———. *The City and Man*. Chicago: University of Chicago Press, 1964.

———. *Liberalism, Ancient and Modern*. Ithaca, N.Y.: Cornell University Press, 1968.

Sunstein, Cass R. "Beyond the Republican Revival." *Yale Law Journal* 97 (1988): 1539–1590.

Szatmary, David P. *Shays' Rebellion: The Making of an Agrarian Insurrection*. Amherst: University of Massachusetts Press, 1980.

Thomas Aquinas, St. *Summa Theologica*. Trans. Fathers of the English Dominican Province. New York: Benziger Bros., Inc., 1947.

Tinder, Glenn. *The Political Meaning of Christianity*. Baton Rouge: Louisiana State University Press, 1989.

Tocqueville, Alexis de. *Democracy in America*. Translated by George Lawrence. Edited by J. P. Mayer. New York: Harper & Row, [1835] 1988.

Tönnies, Ferdinand. *Community and Society*. New York: Harper & Row, [1887] 1963.

Trevor-Roper, Hugh R. *The Gentry, 1540–1640*. London: Cambridge University Press, 1953.

Unger, Roberto Mangabeira. *Knowledge and Politics*. New York: Free Press, 1984.

―――. *Politics*. Cambridge: Cambridge University Press, 1987.

Urofsky, Melvin I., ed. *Documents of American Constitutional and Legal History*. New York: Alfred A. Knopf, 1989.

Villa, Dana R. "Beyond Good and Evil: Arendt, Nietzsche, and the Aestheticization of Political Action." *Political Theory* 20, no. 2 (May 1992): 274–308.

Walzer, Michael. *The Revolution of the Saints: A Study in the Origins of Radical Politics*. New York: Atheneum, 1968.

―――. "Philosophy and Democracy." *Political Theory* 9, no. 3 (August 1981): 379–399.

―――. *The Company of Critics*. New York: Basic Books, 1988.

―――. "A Particularism of My Own." *Religious Studies Review* 16, no. 3 (July 1990): 193–195.

Webbing, Robert. *The American Revolution and the Politics of Liberty*. Baton Rouge: Louisiana State University Press, 1988.

Weber, Max. *The Protestant Ethic and the Spirit of Capitalism*. New York: Scribners, [1905] 1958.

Welch, Susan, John Gruhl, Michael Steinman, and John Comer. *American Government*. St. Paul, Minn.: West, 1988.

West, Thomas. "Leo Strauss and the American Founding." *Review of Politics* 53, no. 1 (Winter 1991): 157–172.

Wills, Garry. *Inventing America: Jefferson's Declaration of Independence*. New York: Doubleday, 1978.

Wolin, Sheldon. *The Presence of the Past: Essays on the State and Constitution*. Baltimore: Johns Hopkins University Press, 1990.

Wood, Gordon. "Rhetoric and Reality in the American Revolution." *William and Mary Quarterly* 3d ser., 23 (1966): 119–134.

―――. *The Creation of the American Republic, 1776–1787*. New York: W. W. Norton, [1969] 1972.

―――. *The Radicalism of the American Revolution*. New York: Alfred A. Knopf, 1992.

Wright, Benjamin Fletcher. *Consensus and Continuity 1776–1787*. New York: W. W. Norton, 1958.

Zuckerman, Michael. "The Social Context of Democracy in Massachusetts." *William and Mary Quarterly* 3d ser., 25, no. 4 (1968): 523–544.

―――. *Peaceable Kingdoms: New England Towns in the Eighteenth Century*. New York: Alfred A. Knopf, 1970.

Index